Steven Richmond earned his doctorate in Russian history from The University of Chicago in 1996. He taught history in Istanbul, Turkey for more than ten years. He was formerly a visiting scholar at The School of Oriental and African Studies, The University of London, an associate of The Center For Middle Eastern Studies, The University of Chicago, and a research fellow of The Netherlands Institute in Turkey.

'Superb. A witty, well-researched and fluent account of the British Empire's most famous and influential diplomat – told with the zest and panache of a thriller. Times, diplomacy and reputations have changed, but Stratford Canning, Victorian Britain's imperious envoy to the Ottoman Empire, changed the course of history. Steven Richmond has given us a brilliant portrait of this ambitious but frustrated statesman, lonely, hard-working and often maligned – the only diplomat honoured with a statue in Westminster Abbey. This timely book, appearing when Turkey is again a significant regional power, will appeal not only to students of history and diplomacy but to all those wanting to know more about Britain's imperial heyday. This compelling insight into the politics and strategy of the time paints a vivid picture of daily life, thought and intrigue in that most mysterious of cities, Constantinople.'

Michael Binyon, *The Times*

'This is a wonderful book. Steven Richmond's biography of Stratford Canning is the definitive study of the long-time British ambassador at Constantinople, whom Tennyson eulogized as "the Voice of England in the East". The book is meticulously researched and given additional depth by Richmond's background in Russian studies and his years of teaching and research in Istanbul. This is that rare scholarly work of history which, like those of Sir Steven Runciman, reads like a novel. It is beautifully written, with a superb sense of place and persona, bringing Canning and others to life in the capital of the Ottoman Empire when it was, as Richmond describes, "the diplomatic city *par excellence*".'

John Freely, author of *A Travel Guide To Homer: On the Trail of Odysseus Through Turkey and the Mediterranean*

'Steven Richmond tells the remarkable story of Stratford Canning, a man sent to Istanbul almost by accident but who became, often reluctantly, a central figure in the "Eastern Question". Richmond levels an impartial eye on his subject, noting Canning's virtues and vices. This well-researched and well-written study picks a sure-footed path through the voluminous correspondence of the Eastern Question. The author masterfully analyses what he aptly terms "The Stratford Legend" and narrates a valuable case study of nineteenth-century British diplomacy in the East.'

Benjamin C. Fortna, Professor of the History of the Middle East, The School of Oriental and African Studies, The University of London

Stratford and Eliza Canning and their daughters Louisa, Catherine and Mary, in the ballroom of the British Embassy at Constantinople, 15 December 1854.

THE VOICE
OF ENGLAND
IN THE EAST

Stratford Canning and Diplomacy
with the Ottoman Empire

STEVEN RICHMOND

I.B. TAURIS

LONDON · NEW YORK

New paperback edition published in 2017 by
I.B.Tauris & Co. Ltd
London • New York
www.ibtauris.com

First published in hardback in 2014 by I.B.Tauris & Co. Ltd

ISBN: 978 1 78453 707 4
eISBN: 978 0 85773 387 0
ePDF: 978 0 85772 365 9

A full CIP record for this book is available from the British Library
A full CIP record is available from the Library of Congress

Library of Congress Catalog Card Number: available

Typeset in Garamond Three by OKS Prepress Services, Chennai, India

CONTENTS

ACKNOWLEDGMENTS

I wish to acknowledge my indebtedness to Walter Leaf for his book, *Troy. A Study in Homeric Geography* (1912), especially for its expatiation on 'the significance of impressions gained by personal contact with the scenes of history.'[1]

I am very grateful to those who helped me in many ways which were vital to this work:

In Istanbul – Ekrem Ekıncı, John and Dolores Freely, Fokke Gerritsen, Melvin Kenne, Onno Kervers, F. Cenan Kocareşid, Susan Nemazee and Peter Westmacott, Cüneyd Okay, Emin Saatçı, Ferdinand Schirza, Ian Sherwood, Victoria Short, Mary Ann and Benjamin Whitten.

In London – Mark Bertram, Danielle Doran, Helena Drysdale, Kathryn Ward Dyer, Caroline and Andrew Finkel, Benjamin C. Fortna, Elizabeth, Priscilla and Giles Hunt, Briony Llewellyn, Bobbie Brookes Nation, Charles Newton, Michael Riley, Thomas Short, Susan Spindler and Peter Brown, Lois and David Sykes, Betty Whittall and Paul McKernan. At I.B.Tauris & Co. Ltd. – Lester Crook, Tomasz Hoskins and the academic reader of my text.

In the United States of America – Wayne Altree, Carel Bertram and Fred Donner, Patricia McKelvey and Eugene Putala.

This book is dedicated to my parents.

MAPS

Pages 19–21
'The Ottoman Empire in 1801'
from William Miller, *The Ottoman Empire, 1801–1913*.
Cambridge: Cambridge University Press, 1913.

The Bosphorus
from J. G. Bartholomew, ed. *Handy Reference Atlas of the World*.
Seventh Edition. London: John Walker Co. Ltd., 1904.

Constantinople, Galata, Pera, Scutari
A detail from *The Dardanelles and the Troad. The Bosphorus and Constantinople*, map by Stanford's Geog. Establishment. [Early 1920s].

ILLUSTRATIONS

INTRODUCTION

'THE STRATFORD LEGEND'

1

Stratford Canning's journey to the Ottoman Empire is a story of his time, a representation of the increased mixing of distant peoples which emerged over the first half of the nineteenth century. The advent of steam travel in the 1820s and 1830s and of the telegraph in the 1850s radically affected communication in both voyage and post. These and other innovations transformed many fields of human relations, and Canning's long career spanned fundamental changes in the practice of diplomacy[1] and the mechanics of empire. But his journey to the Ottoman Empire is also a timeless story, a tale of a young and narrow individual sent far from home against his will 'to live in a very wide world.'[2]

For 50 years Stratford Canning kept returning to Constantinople[3] despite the hardships of the post and his deep desire to settle at home. His first diplomatic mission to the Ottoman capital began in 1808–09 at the height of the Napoleonic Wars, and his last was undertaken in autumn 1858, over two years after the conclusion of hostilities in the Crimean War. He was fascinated by the life and beauty of the city, as is vividly demonstrated in the paintings of characters and scenes that he commissioned from a local artist in 1809–10.[4] But Canning was drawn to Constantinople primarily because it was the diplomatic city *par excellence*. Here at the geographical mixing point of lands, waters and peoples, and the political focal point of European international relations, diplomacy had real meaning and was played out for the highest stakes. While ambassador at Bern, Switzerland between his first two missions to Constantinople, he lamented, 'I have nothing on earth to do ... I become daily more expert in the lordly arts of twaddledom, politeness and gaiety.'[5] A return to the Ottoman capital for a new posting there meant that 'I was now on the scene of the action'.[6]

This study of Stratford Canning and diplomacy with the Ottoman Empire is designed to convey both what and '*how* things happened — what diplomacy was like at that time, how things occurred, what the atmosphere was like, and what the people were like,' as George F. Kennan, the diplomat-scholar, described the ambition of his own books.[7] It is also a consideration of empire, of imperial interaction and imperial thinking, at the dawn of the industrial era. And it is intended to portray the old capital of empires, Constantinople, to evoke, in the words of Gibbon, 'the genius of the place'.[8]

2

When Sultan Abdülmecit issued significant reforms concerning religious tolerance on 21 March 1844, Stratford Canning was extolled in British newspapers as 'the Reformer of Turkey' and even credited with 'the most remarkable diplomatic achievement in the annals of Turkey'.[9] And as recently as 2010, in a history of the Crimean War published in the United Kingdom and the United States, Canning was identified as 'directly guiding the reform programme of the young Sultan Abdülmecid and his main reformist minister Mustafa Reshid Pasha.'[10]

But Stratford Canning certainly did not reform the Ottoman Empire. No foreign representative could ever do anything like this for the state to which he was accredited. The reform movement of the Ottoman Empire was home-grown and comprehensive. It was indigenous to Ottoman history. It was conceived and enacted by Ottoman statesmen. And it began to take course before Stratford was even born. His career happened by chance to coincide with the rise of this movement and 'Stratford Canning supported the reform party with characteristic energy and vigour,' according to his protégé and long-time associate, Austen Henry Layard, the excavator of Nineveh.[11]

Canning's support for Ottoman domestic reform, as well as for Ottoman international peace, was purely a calculation of British foreign policy relating to the so-called Eastern Question.[12] This policy was intended to promote the stabilisation of the Ottoman Empire in the hope of creating a strategic balance between it and the Russian Empire which would prevent war between the two powers. 'War, once begun, would spread through Europe...' as George Canning, then British foreign secretary, older first-cousin and mentor to Stratford, wrote in his instructions for Stratford's mission to Constantinople which began in October 1825.[13]

The other goal of this policy was to check Russian expansion in order to maintain the British imperial route to India, which ran through Ottoman Anatolia and Egypt. This was the main cause of Stratford's career and perhaps of his life, and he was still espousing it at age 90 in the year 1877: 'We are dependent on the Porte for our most direct and speediest communication with India. In proportion as Her Majesty's territories in that country become more identified with the Government at home, it is desirable that the established means of intercourse between both should be, as much as possible, rapid and sure.'[14]

The actual achievement of Stratford Canning in his diplomacy with the Ottoman Empire was to negotiate realistically and resourcefully and to communicate with conviction. For A. J. P. Taylor he was 'an outstanding British diplomat' and 'the man who presented the issues clearly and without pretence.'[15] The accurate title for Stratford Canning is not 'the Reformer of Turkey' but rather the conclusion of the epitaph (composed by Alfred Tennyson) that still adorns his statue in Westminster Abbey: 'the Voice of England in the East'.

3

Stratford Canning's image as an imperial peacemaker underwent a sudden transformation during the bloody course of the Crimean War.

Especially after the death of Lord Raglan in the Crimea on 28 June 1855, and the Russian capture of the British fortress at Kars in eastern Anatolia on 23 November of the same year, Stratford was widely blamed for the war, both its unexpected outbreak and its tragic course; and he came to be portrayed as nothing short of an imperial warmonger, thus satisfying the desire of the weary British public and many politicians to have a scapegoat for the whole tragedy.

Canning was in some ways a natural candidate for this scapegoat role. There was an imperious aspect to his character and appearance which easily lent itself to a reputation for bellicosity.[16] He had long been involved with the Ottoman Empire. He was a prominent figure in the final diplomatic episodes before the outbreak of the Crimean War. And in general during serious breakdowns of international relations, the first targets of public opinion are often the process and providers of diplomacy.

The warmonger image of Stratford Canning has been generally accepted by historians, with a few prominent exceptions, notably Harold Temperley. 'That Stratford de Redcliffe was the human agency which caused the Crimean War has long been a popular belief,' declared Temperley in 1933.[17] 'It has often been asserted that he wanted war between Turkey and Russia and ultimately got it,' Temperley added in 1936, referring to this idea as 'The Stratford legend'.[18]

'The Stratford legend' was partly due to a customary disdain for diplomats among a certain part of the British public and press. This sentiment was seized upon and inflated during and after the Crimean War but existed earlier.[19] Contempt for Stratford himself as a seeming paragon of diplomatic privilege was evident in a Manchester newspaper on 6 June 1836, in a fictional vignette between 'John – A genuine Manchester man'; 'Sandy, one who has been amongst prints and fustians all his life-time, and yet how immeasurably he outstrips Stratford Canning in his knowledge of the real interests, and his conceptions of the real dignity of the nation'; and Jonathan, an egalitarian-minded American who was apparently meant to represent New World resentment of European aristocratism and intrigue, when he declared: 'Stratford Canning is of the diplomatic tribe, the smallest fry of which receives more from your nation than we pay to our President. Such men have an interest in promoting wars, just as spies have an interest in promoting sedition.'[20]

The great public disdain for the profession of diplomacy during and after the Crimean War was expressed starkly by the satirical journal *Punch* on 24 April 1858, in its 'A Specimen of Mr. Punch's Dictionary of Diplomatic Definitions'. This included:

AMBASSADOR. Should be written *Em*bassador, *quasi*, '*en bas-odeur*,' – from the French, *en bas*, 'below' – one who is below – either the demands of his office, or the dignity of the nation he represents. The essence of the embassadorial mission, etymologically as well as practically, is therefore *sub*mission.

DIPLOMACY. From the Greek δίπλος, meaning double; the science of duplicity.

DIPLOMATIC RELATIONS. The very poorest relations, to judge by recently published correspondence, that ever disgraced the family of nations.[21]

Stratford did retain respect among the public and press during and immediately after the Crimean War. On 2 January 1858 one British newspaper predicted that 'Future historians will dwell upon the career of Lord Stratford, as offering one of the most salient features of our times.'[22] But since then most historians have dismissed him one way or another according to the premises of 'The Stratford legend'.

4

The legend was also due to the uninspired national assessment of Stratford's career that took place upon his death at the age of 93 on 14 August 1880. His heyday and achievements had fallen far into the past and were obscured by British public outrage against Ottoman policies in Bulgaria in 1878.[23] Another factor was 'the fashion in these days to disparage diplomacy .... Diplomacy is supposed by many to lead to crooked ways and even to dishonesty,' as the *Glasgow Herald* noted in its obituary of Stratford.[24] *The Times* obituary declared him to have been a 'diplomatic autocrat at Constantinople'.[25]

A few weeks after his death, a pension of £500 per annum 'with the benefit of survivorship' was granted by the Queen from the Civil List, on the initiative of Gladstone as prime minister, to Stratford's widow and three unmarried daughters.[26] The radical *Reynolds's Newspaper* declared the grant an act of 'Aristocratic Pauperism' and accused Stratford of having been the 'prototype' of a special set of ambassadors who were both 'imperious' and bellicose: 'Whilst ambassador at the Porte, his hasty, harsh, overbearing manners and deportment kept him perpetually in hot water both there and in other countries. He had a personal quarrel with the late Emperor Nicholas of Russia. It was this which led to the war with that country, and brought about the enormous loss of men and money attendant thereupon.' This suggestion, that Stratford had a personal rivalry with Tsar Nicholas, which was the cause of the Crimean War, is a particularly ridiculous aspect of 'The Stratford legend'.[27]

'Lord Stratford de Redcliffe,' the newspaper continued, 'was the prototype of Sir Bartle Frere,[28] both being obstinate to pigheadedness, pertinacious, precipitate, arrogant, and imperious. The former hurried us into the Crimean War with the same headstrong recklessness as the latter did into hostilities with the Zulus. Now, we ask why and wherefore are the tremendously burthened taxpayers of England to support in ease and comfort for the rest of their lives the family of this deceased nobleman? We believe he did not die in actual poverty, but in comfortable circumstances.'[29]

Stratford's finances were in fact always a concern. He was born a product of the professional class and lost his father when he was six months old. His mother, Mehitabel, maintained the family trading house with some success at first, but a relative was later required to help pay for Stratford's education. Early in his career he managed to earn a lifetime retainer from the Foreign Office, but this was suspended for the years he served in Parliament, which provided no salary. As Gladstone later defended the pension for Stratford's survivors, speaking to the House of Commons on 23 March 1888: 'He had never been a wealthy man. All his life he had devoted himself to the Public Service, and the services which he rendered in Constantinople were undoubtedly of the highest order ... Lord Stratford, as I have said, was not a wealthy man, and I believe it is a well-known fact – there is no disgrace in it – that his private means and economies disappeared in consequence of the repudiation by the Turkish Empire of its debts.'[30] At death Stratford's net wealth equalled £62 3s 2d (sixty-two pounds, three shillings and twopence).[31]

'The Stratford legend' is also a product of the nature and trends of historical consideration. Jules Cambon observed in his 1926 study of diplomatic practice that 'In general, diplomats are not, as military men are, the spoilt children of historians. The latter hardly mention their names, and the secrecy of negotiations, which was so often disputed by their contemporaries, is dispensed to them generously by the silence of posterity.'[32] And Bernadotte E. Schmitt noted that, 'Even with full documentation and reliable memoirs or biographies, it is seldom easy to write satisfactory diplomatic history.'[33]

A. J. P. Taylor suggested in his 1956 essay, 'The Rise and Fall of Diplomatic History', that the subject was in decline, with students moving away from analysis of diplomatic records 'for the study of public opinion'. He attributed this phenomenon to the opening of 'what is called the age of the masses' and to the suspicion of diplomacy that traditionally occurs during and after the outbreak of wars. 'Wars are the eclipse of diplomacy, and therefore of diplomatic history ... we continue to live in a war atmosphere in the immediate present – first the Second World War against Germany, then the more insidious "Cold War", which seems equally impervious to diplomacy.' This all led, according to Taylor, to 'The Depreciation of diplomacy',[34] and it included a depreciation of Stratford's career.

5

The real Stratford Canning was by nature intense, stern and sometimes overbearing. Throughout his life he exhibited 'boundless industry',[35] and even his appearance suggested severity. At age 17 he was struck by a 'sharp illness' which 'left traces in my constitution', as he later noted, and this may have affected the development of his personality.[36] A few years later his own mother expressed concern about his 'impetuosity' and implored him to 'moderate' it.[37] But he was not without a sensitive side, and as he outgrew his narrowness and parochialism, he came to appreciate and even defend people and ways foreign to him. He was of course highly self-confident and greatly ambitious; and yet for decades he was unsure about his career path and it was only at age 55 that he fully accepted diplomacy as his profession (after having left it for almost ten years in a misplaced attempt to become a parliamentary statesman). He was well-educated, fond of letters and expression, versed in the use and meaning of texts, and a prominent force behind the creation of the influential *Quarterly Review* (1809–1967).[38] His qualities were recorded in many first-hand accounts by acquaintances and colleagues. A. H. Layard detailed his first encounter with Stratford Canning, which occurred in July 1842:

> Sir Stratford received me immediately. I was greatly struck by his appearance. His hair was already white. His tall and spare form was not altogether erect, as he had the habit of stooping. There was, perhaps, a somewhat too evident assumption of dignity and reserve in his manner, which was intended to impress people with the utmost respect for the Queen's Ambassador, and if the occasion required it, with awe. His earnest grey eyes seemed to penetrate into one's very thoughts. His thin, compressed lips denoted a violent and passionate temper. His complexion was so transparent that the least emotion, whether of pleasure or anger, was at once shown by its varying tints. A broad and massive overhanging brow gave him the air of profound wisdom and sagacity. He was altogether a very formidable-looking personage, and he made upon me the impression which he no doubt intended to produce. His manner towards me was, however, kind and considerate .... I received the utmost kindness from Sir Stratford and Lady Canning – a kindness of which I was most sensible and for which I have ever

been the more grateful, as it was shown to one who was a stranger, and who had, at that time, no claims whatever to it.[39]

Another valuable portrait of Stratford but from 15 years later, after the conclusion of the Crimean War, was provided by the great Edward Lear, father of Nonsense Literature. He had stayed with the Cannings at the British embassy residence in Therapia on the Bosphorus for two weeks in August 1848 while recovering from malaria, which he had contracted on travels in Greece. Years later, on 15 December 1857 at Corfu, Lear again encountered Stratford and he noted his impressions in a letter to a friend:

> He is a remarkable old gentleman, & I was surprised to see him so unbroken & with his eagle eye still so clear ... nothing can be more regal and sostenuto than his manners, and one can only believe in his temper by observation of his brow and eye .... Just as he went off in the steamer there was an Earthquake, big enough to send people out of their houses & the bells ringing, but whether the coincidental concussion was caused by, or for, Lord S. de Redcliffe, I leave you as a more educated man than myself to determine.[40]

And from the same period there is the portrait of Stratford Canning by Edmund Hornby, who had been sent by the Foreign Office to Constantinople during the Crimean War in order to administer British and French interests concerning the Ottoman debt. Hornby wrote of Stratford in his *Autobiography* that:

> No doubt he had a temper which was really too easily roused and over which he had but little control, but a more noble and affectionate nature no man, nay, no woman, ever possessed. He was *gentilhomme* from the crown of his white head to the soles of his feet .... He had a fine head, distinguished features, white hair, and a good clear complexion. He was a good horseman and was extremely fond of horses .... To meet him going to the Porte was a sight worth seeing – two mounted Cavasses in

front, himself, then the secretaries, then two grooms, and
finally two other Cavasses – all splendidly mounted, the people
all bowing and showing him the profoundest respect.[41]

One of Stratford's embassy assistants during the Crimean War, who
subsequently served as his personal secretary from 1858 to 1865, was
Edmund Calvert. In a letter dated 26 October 1881, a year after
Stratford's death, Calvert wrote:

> Dear fine old Lord Stratford! What a character! So terrible to
> his great + strong enemies, and yet no less singularly kind
> where he chose to bestow kindness! In looking over some old
> papers not long ago I came upon a letter from the great
> departed … I cannot express how deeply I was touched on
> again reading over words so full of genuine good will and
> thoughtfulness about small matters which few persons would
> have given themselves the trouble of touching upon at all, and
> I was the more sensible of this kind considerateness from its
> contrast to treatment the very which I had just experienced
> from other high quarters.[42]

The last introductory word here among those who knew Stratford
Canning well belongs to his old family acquaintance. Charles Ellis
served George Canning in the 1820s as an Undersecretary of State for
Foreign Affairs, and he knew Stratford from even before that time.
Ellis's father had been one of George Canning's closest friends and
political allies: they were two of the founders of the Tory satirical
journal *The Anti-Jacobin* (1797–98), and the elder Ellis served as
George's second at his duel with Castlereagh on 21 September 1809
on Putney Heath. On 31 January 1858, the younger Ellis wrote to
Lord Clarendon concerning Stratford:

> He [Stratford] is an odd fish and perhaps no one living knows so
> much of his character as yours aff[ectionate]lly. For in old times
> I was the constant peacemaker between him and his lamented
> cousin [George] and was often put forward to stand the brunt of

his first explosions, but He is an honourable and good man and much more open to reason than is generally supposed.[43]

All of these personal portraits of Stratford refer to his temper but also suggest that this was mitigated by his softer quality. Layard's and Lear's accounts both remarked on his brow, his eye[44] and 'manner'. In the latter, Layard sensed something assumed but Lear (who was observing Stratford at a later stage of life and after the great trial of the Crimean War) identified something superlative. Perhaps both observations were valid. It would have been reasonable for Stratford to cultivate a persona of 'dignity and reserve' as a part of his diplomatic *modus operandi* at the great seat of empires, where for many centuries supreme importance has been placed on the customs of ceremony and appearance. And after all public officials, and perhaps especially foreign representatives, are effective sometimes more for what they appear to be than for what they are. But it seems that Stratford's 'very formidable-looking personage' and 'regal and sostenuto' manner were in large part also natural to him.

These qualities were captured also in artistic depictions of Stratford, especially in George Richmond's chalk portrait of 1853[45] and in George Frederic Watts's oil portrait of 1856–57,[46] both of which repose in the National Portrait Gallery UK and the latter being still on display in Room 23 (along with a portrait of Canning's polar opposite in the British Empire, the orientalist and explorer, Richard Burton – Canning was as strait-laced as Burton was unbound). The Gallery's caption of Watts's portrait refers to Canning's 'exercising great influence over the Sultan and his advisors in the diplomatic events leading up to the Crimean War'.[47] This idea, that he held special power at the Ottoman capital, remains the most persistent part of his legend.

6

The real career of Stratford Canning at Constantinople is a study in diplomatic communication. His interaction with the Ottoman government was conducted almost entirely through dragomans, professional interpreters who were drawn from Ottoman Levantine families. The relationship between an ambassador and his dragoman was always complex, especially because it involved sharing an embassy's sensitive papers and tasks with a subject of the host government. Stratford was at first too immature (arriving at Constantinople at age 22) and too provincial to understand the abilities and sophistication of the dragomans, but he soon came to appreciate and respect them. Nevertheless, the notion of 'Stratford's longstanding dislike of the embassy dragomans,' as was asserted in an academic article from 1979,[48] has been another component of 'The Stratford legend'.

In 1896 Stratford's vast personal archive – consisting of drafts and copies of official dispatches, notes to and from embassy colleagues, and correspondence with family and friends – was reposited by his surviving children, Louisa and Mary Canning, at the Public Record Office at Chancery Lane, London (today comprising collection FO 352 of The National Archives United Kingdom). The event was deemed worthy of reporting in *The Times* of 4 April 1896, and this even included an analysis of the archive's documents: 'The collection is unique both in its wide range and in its comprehensive character .... It is not, however, merely the range in point of time or geographical distance that gives these papers their unique importance. They also excel probably all similar collections in their exhaustive comprehension of all classes of diplomatic information.' As Stratford's personal archive included a detailed correspondence on the leading international questions of the day, it comprised, according to *The Times*, 'really a sort of history of European politics in epistolary form.' The archive also provided special perspectives on foreign circumstances: 'For the internal history of the countries to which he was accredited, and, of course, especially in Turkey, a prodigious series of Consular reports, interpreters' minutes of interviews, and other local information will some day prove of inestimable value.'[49] Out of these different forms of communication emerges a fascinating literature of diplomacy in which characters strive to express themselves across cultural and physical distance while they simultaneously attempt to maintain, as Harold Nicolson formulated in his 1939 study of diplomatic method, 'that guarded under-statement which enables diplomatists and ministers to say sharp things to each other without becoming provocative or impolite.'[50]

The Times report on the archive also noted, 'The truth is that Lord Stratford de Redcliffe preserved almost every written thing, and his collection has consequently attained such proportions that his biographer estimated the total number of documents at a round million.'[51] This assessment related only to Stratford's personal archive and did not include the holdings of public archives, including the massive Foreign Office collection for correspondence with the Ottoman Empire (today designated as FO 78, also located at The National Archives UK). *The Times* observed upon his death in August 1880 that, 'To the last he was a prolific writer.'[52]

Stratford's tremendous written output was one of his means for establishing the text or terms of diplomatic issues. But probably more than anything it represented his fondness for composition as well as the intense aspect of his personality. It was also due to the literary practice of the day in which he was trained. 'The style of Lord Stratford, formed early in the century, is very different from the lighter and less pedantic style which writers of the present day affect; its complete and rolling sentences we should perhaps irreverently consider somewhat long-winded,' as was observed in 1889.[53] Stratford's style was perceived to be thus already in his own day, and on occasion it unnecessarily burdened his counterparts. It was probably a significant motivation in the Russians' refusal to accredit him as ambassador to their court in 1832 because of their experiences with him at Petersburg in 1825.[54] It also sometimes overtaxed his own compatriots, and one may sympathise with Queen Victoria and Prince Albert for that day in August 1843 at Windsor Castle when they sat down to tackle Stratford's dispatches, as witnessed by Charlotte Canning, a lady of the bedchamber who happened to be the wife of Stratford's cousin, Charles Canning: 'The Queen & Prince set to work to read the contents of 3 red boxes, a large packet of Stratford's of whose voluminous writings Her Majesty complained, saying he has always so much to say it is sometimes quite alarming.'[55]

Stratford's massive production of historical material and his demanding compositional style have exasperated many students of his career and probably comprise another factor that has contributed to the persistence of 'The Stratford legend'. Yet another challenge in studying his career is to examine primary materials composed in Ottoman Turkish. The following work includes discovery and analysis of such documents which were translated into English by Canning's dragomans and repose at The National Archives UK. Ottoman primary documents from Istanbul archives, which were discovered and analysed by the Turkish researchers Y. Hakan Erdem (2005, 2011), F. Ismail (1979) and Turgut Subaşı (2002), are also cited here.[56]

7

Stratford himself undertook an examination of his personal archive. After retiring from diplomacy in late 1858, he worked for years on a substantial memoir that consisted of an explication of the archive's materials plus a commentary on his career. Completing this in 1874, he provided the archive and memoir to his chosen biographer, the orientalist Stanley Lane-Poole. This memoir and many private letters from the archive were subsequently lost at some point and have never been found. Therefore the sole source for them is the Lane-Poole biography.

Lane-Poole's two-volume work was published in 1888, eight years after Stratford's death. Lane-Poole employed the memoir thoughtfully but followed its conclusions closely and incorporated 'copious extracts' from it, as one contemporary reviewer noted.[57] Another found that Stratford's memoir had influenced Lane-Poole's biography so much that 'A rather large part of the work is autobiographical'.[58] And one reviewer declared Lane-Poole to be not the author but 'rather the editor' of the biography.[59] Among later historians, Roderick Davison called Lane-Poole's biography 'Somewhat eulogistic',[60] V. J. Puryear dismissed it harshly as 'The standard apology',[61] and R. W. Seton-Watson found it to be a 'classic Victorian biography'.[62]

Lane-Poole noted in his introduction that 'The proof sheets of the work have been submitted both to Lord Stratford's immediate representatives, and to the Secretary of State for Foreign Affairs.'[63] The equivalent of such a work today would likely be labelled 'authorised' or 'official'.

Lane-Poole's biography was infused with a fundamental Occidental stereotype about 'Turkish character'[64] and 'the Turkish mind',[65] including cryptic statements such as: 'The Oriental takes you as you would be taken and to acquire his respect you must *impose* yourself upon him; and it is impossible even now (and how much more forty years ago) to compel the Turkish mind to action without the aid of such outward machinery.'[66] One prominent component of this stereotype was the belief that Stratford intellectually and professionally towered over his hosts at Constantinople. In Lane-Poole's words, Stratford held 'high-handed authority'[67] and 'transcendent authority over the Turks';[68] 'it needed all of Canning's influence to soothe the irritation of the Porte';[69] 'under the protecting influence which now emanated from the British Palace [embassy], the Turkish ministers revealed the full details';[70] when located at Constantinople he was 'the guide of the faltering Turks',[71] but when he was not then 'Lord Stratford's absence freed the Turkish ministers for the moment from the dominating influence of his will.'[72]

There is not one piece of historical evidence that Stratford wielded authority over the Ottomans, that he inspired fear or calm in them, that he intimidated or dominated them in any way. As Harold Temperley declared in his thorough examination of Stratford's role in the outbreak of the Crimean War, published in *The English Historical Review* in two parts in 1933 and 1934: 'Stratford did not enjoy complete authority at Constantinople, in spite of testimony of so many to the fact. The descriptions of him as "the real Sultan" or the "Padishah", though amusing enough, are, in fact, misleading.' And concerning the Ottomans, Temperley found that 'Their policy was their own...'[73] It was indeed.

Ottoman statesmen did in fact have significant respect for Stratford Canning. At the beginning of his career, during a moment of complicated diplomacy at a pivotal point of the Napoleonic Wars in the spring of 1812, Sultan Mahmut II pronounced him the sole diplomat at his court whom he found 'reliable'.[74] And at the end of

Stratford's career, during the Crimean War in the 1850s, the great Ottoman statesman Mustafa Reşit Paşa said of him that 'He is often overbearing' but also 'has more pluck in his little finger than the whole Divan put together.'[75] The Ottomans had significant respect also, as will be seen in the story that follows, for the methods of Stratford's diplomacy, for his austere manner and appearance, for the power of the empire which he represented, and eventually for his long and substantial tenure at their capital (although they naturally also grew tired of him for this). But that was all: significant respect, no more and no less. Despite Lane-Poole's claims, Stratford never held over the Ottomans 'high-handed authority', 'transcendent authority' (whatever that means), 'immense influence', 'influence to soothe', 'protecting influence' or 'dominating influence'. Furthermore, Stratford himself disregarded such claims in his own day, referring to them in 1858 as 'braying panegyrics'.[76] His recognition of the limits of his influence was actually one of his strengths in dealing with the Ottomans. Even when he sometimes saw his role with them in a somewhat missionary light, he still maintained a realistic sense of what was diplomatically possible. For just as the Ottomans held significant respect for him, he held the same for them for their own qualities and for the power of their vast empire.

Lane-Poole wrote the biography under the influence of Alexander Kinglake's account of the Crimean War, *Invasion of the Crimea*, the first volumes of which were published in 1863.[77] This was long hailed in Britain as a masterpiece of history and the definitive word on the Crimean War; and Kinglake was one of the notables who attended the unveiling of Stratford Canning's statue in Westminster Abbey on 23 May 1884.[78] Whereas Lane-Poole deified Stratford as benevolently leading the Ottomans, Kinglake demonised him as maliciously dominating them and pushing them into the Crimean War. 'Him they feared, him they trusted, him they obeyed' and 'Lord Stratford had power over the minds of Turkish Statesmen ... To his will they bent,' Kinglake wrote.[79] But deification and demonisation are the same operation of extremism and melodramaticism, and the works of Lane-Poole and Kinglake were equivalent in professing the fiction that Stratford reigned supreme at Constantinople.

In Kinglake's history, according to *The Encyclopedia Britannica* of 1911, Stratford 'appears as a kind of magician who is always mentioned as the "great Elchi" and who influences the fate of nations by mystic spells cast on pallid sultans.'[80] Kinglake did indeed assert in his work that the Ottoman leaders referred to Stratford as 'the great Ambassador' in the sense of signifying his superiority. But this assertion by Kinglake was pure fabrication on his part, a misinterpretation of the title that the Ottomans employed for all ambassadors, *Büyük Elçi*. The title most probably originated as a Turkish calque on the European rank of Minister or Ambassador (*elçi*) Extraordinary (*büyük*), and it certainly had nothing to do with perceptions about anyone's individual greatness. The designation of *Büyük Elçi* for all ambassadors was maintained in the Turkish Republic and is still in use today.

Lane-Poole clearly understood Kinglake's misusage of 'Great Elchi' and he specifically remarked on it that 'Every Turkish scholar knows that the title is founded on a misconception. It is only in England that the words bear the special signification which Mr. Kinglake has made immortal. In Turkey every full ambassador is styled *Buyuk Elchi* or "Great Envoy," to distinguish him from the mere *Elchi*, which is the term applied to an ordinary minister plenipotentiary. The ambassadors of France and Russia were as much Great Elchis at Constantinople as Canning himself.'[81]

Nevertheless, Lane-Poole willfully adopted Kinglake's term and likewise exploited it. Over and over in his biography, 128 times, Lane-Poole referred to Stratford Canning as either 'the Great Elchi' or 'the Elchi'.[82] In English it has the sound of an ogre's or wizard's title; and Lane-Poole's incantation of it was a method for conjuring Kinglake's image of Canning as an imperial supernatural at Constantinople.

The term and image have themselves proven remarkably powerful and long-lasting. 'Elchi' entered English vocabulary and still remains a part of it today, according to *The Oxford English Dictionary*.[83] And the 'Great Elchi' image of Stratford Canning has been invoked in many studies[84] and is still prevalent today. A history of the Crimean War, published in the United Kingdom in 2004, includes the assertion: 'Known to the Turks as "the Great Elchi", Redcliffe was an experienced diplomat and a man with enormous influence within the Porte.'[85] From the same year, the entry for Stratford Canning in *The Oxford Dictionary of National Biography* includes the statement that he 'was to dominate the politics of Constantinople for a generation as the "Great Ambassador"...'[86] The entry for him in a volume of *The History of Parliament* series, published in 2009, contains the claim: 'From the immense influence he wielded over the sultan, and the impetus he gave to internal reforms in Turkey, he made his reputation, and gained the nickname of "The Great Elchi" [ambassador].'[87] And a history of the Crimean War published in the United Kingdom and the United States in 2010 includes the claim: 'The "Great Elchi", or Great Ambassador, as he was known in Constantinople, had a direct influence on the policies of the Turkish government.'[88]

But, again, Stratford did not possess any special power or any special nickname at Constantinople. His actual influence with the Ottomans was based on his skills in diplomacy and on the convergence of strategic interests which existed at that time between the Ottoman and British empires. Sometimes this led to achievement on his part, but at other times it resulted in futility, with the Ottomans being unmoved.

More than any other works, Kinglake's history and Lane-Poole's biography have been responsible for the persistence of 'The Stratford legend' and its notion of his dominance over the Ottomans. The legend, however, came into existence before the appearance of these two works, arising both as a political idea and as a cultural or religious belief. As the American Protestant missionaries of Constantinople put it in their farewell address to Stratford on 12 October 1858: 'we love to consider Your Lordship's influence as one of the important providential means, by which God has been pleased to carry on his work, aside from direct Missionary instrumentalities.'[89] The legend therefore holds political, sociological and psychological significance when it is viewed as a symbol. But more meaningful than the legend is the genuine story of Stratford Canning and his journey to a distant people, a fabled metropolis and the making of peace and war.

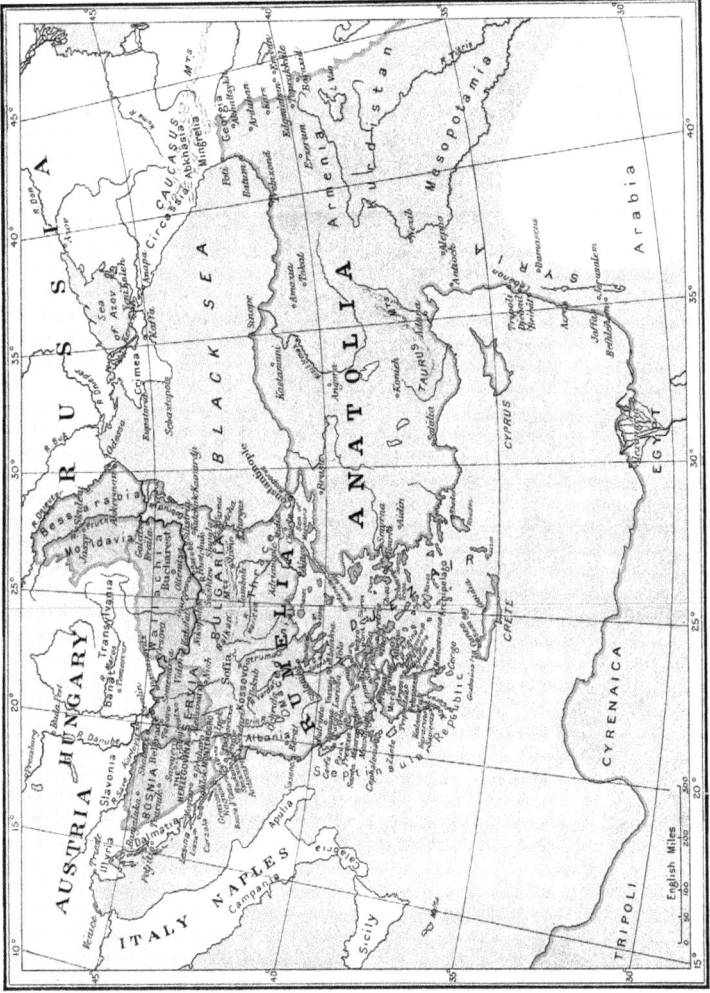

'The Ottoman Empire in 1811'.

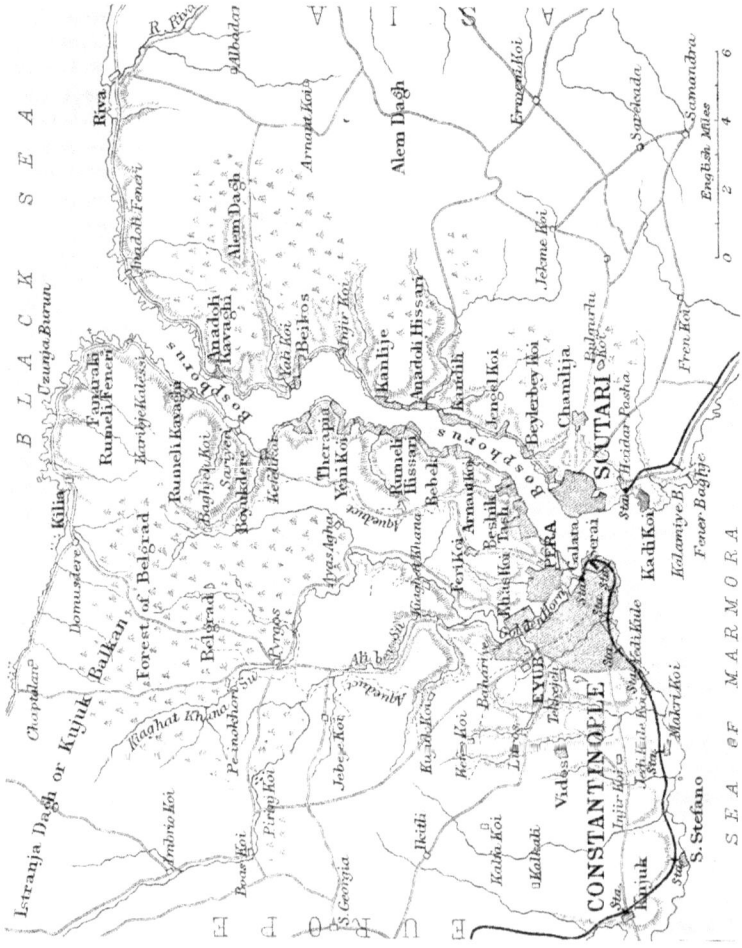

The Bosphorus.

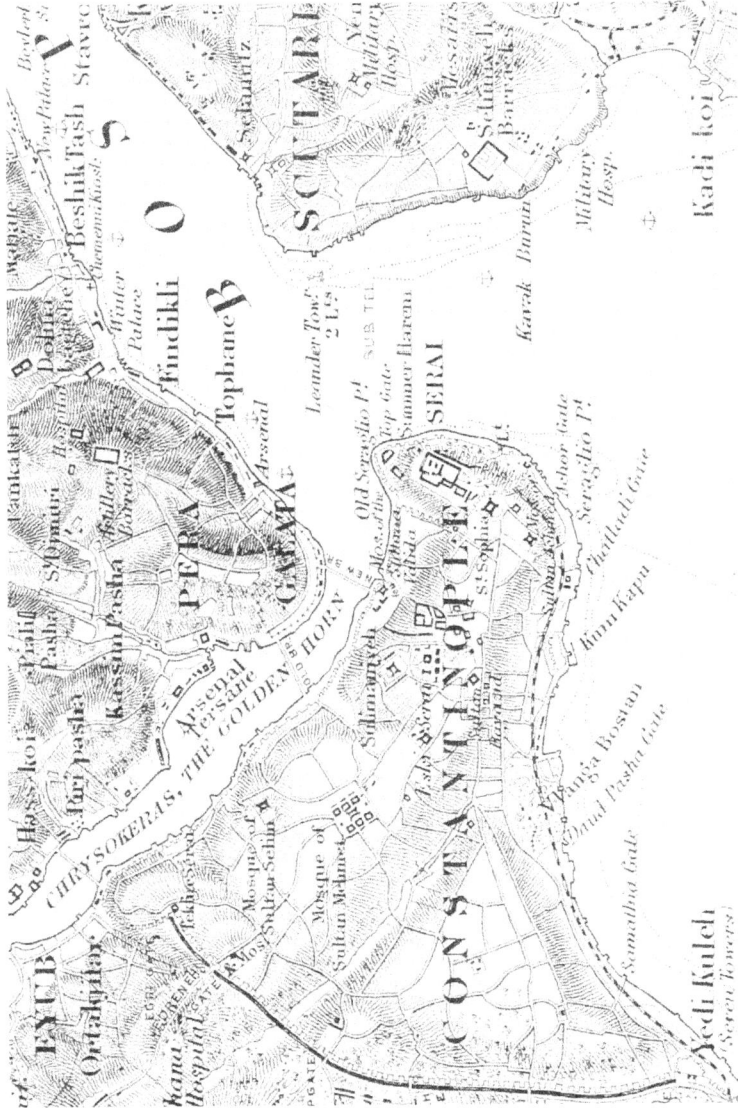

Constantinople, Galata, Pera, Scutari.

PART I

BRITISH-OTTOMAN PEACE, 1808–10

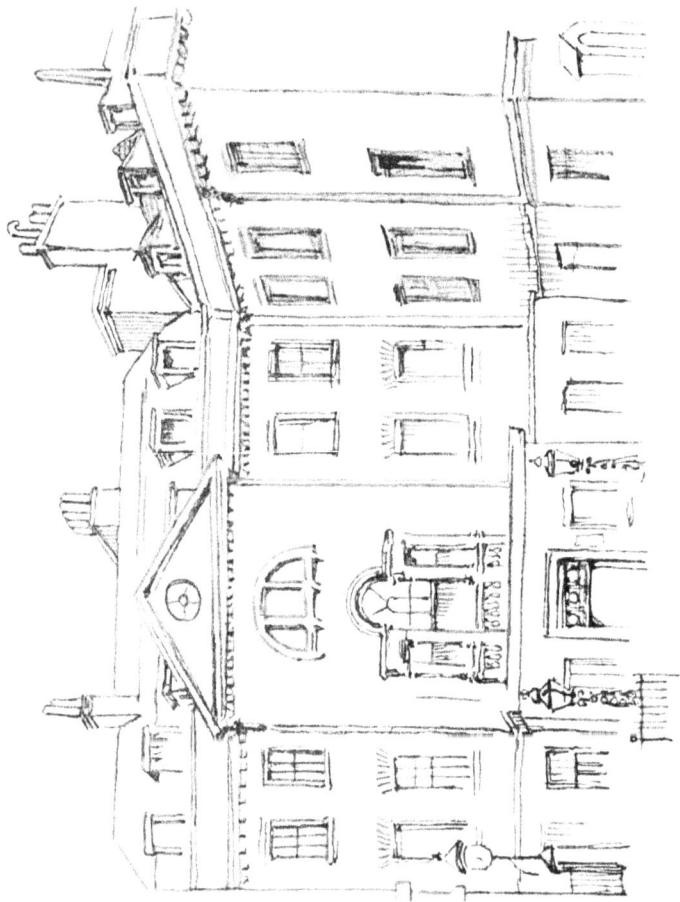

Old Foreign Office, Downing Street, London. Employed from 1793 or 1799 until 27 August 1861. Demolished by May 1862.

CHAPTER 1

APPRENTICESHIP IN DIPLOMACY

1

The land route was impossible, blocked by the empire of Napoleon. The sea route stretched more than 3,000 miles from Portsmouth and Spithead, through Gibraltar and across the Mediterranean to the Dardanelles, the Bosphorus and Constantinople. The young man expected to be away for just a few months and then return to his studies at Cambridge. He was not at all happy about undertaking the voyage. 'I almost envy you for being in England at such a moment as this...' he wrote home to a friend. 'I never before felt so deeply the misery of my insignificance.'[1] The 22-year-old was convinced he was being sent into obscurity. He had no idea that he was headed directly into the centre of European diplomacy, now and for half a century.

Stratford Canning had been drafted for a diplomatic mission to the Ottoman capital by his older first cousin. George Canning had become foreign secretary in March 1807 and had advocated engaging the Ottoman Empire as far back as 1798 when Napoleon invaded Egypt. The Turk should not be shunned just 'because he wears a long beard and a long gown,' George Canning had argued.[2] Now in June 1808 George was sending young Stratford as an assistant on a critical mission to reestablish diplomatic relations with the Ottoman Empire.

In February 1807 the British had dispatched a large squadron under the command of Vice-Admiral John Duckworth to attack the Dardanelles. As with the Gallipoli expedition of 1915, the mission was extremely complicated and hastily planned. Duckworth's squadron managed to breach the Dardanelles and to take up position at the Ottoman capital. Even though this was an unprecedented naval feat, the goals of the mission still remained unfeasible and the squadron was in effect caught at Constantinople. After a few weeks of skirmishes and negotiations, they made a dramatic and costly retreat back through the Dardanelles, which had in the interval been reinforced by the Ottomans with French assistance. Diplomatically the expedition was a complete failure, only weakening Britain's international position and breaking her diplomatic relations with the Ottoman Empire for the first and only time before World War I. It also seriously destabilised the political situation at Constantinople: the sight of foreign warships in the Bosphorus was a great shock to the Ottomans and sparked fierce uprisings by the elite palace guards, the Janissaries, lasting two years and destroying several Ottoman sultans and statesmen.

Shortly after the British expedition to the Dardanelles, the Grenville government broke up and George Canning became foreign secretary in the new cabinet. Within a few weeks he sent a diplomatic mission to the Ottomans for the purpose of reestablishing relations with them.[3] His instructions to the envoy, Sir Arthur Paget, dated 16 May 1807, were to make peace with the Ottoman government, to promote peace between the Ottomans and Russians, and to counteract French interests in the region.[4]

This mission, however, amounted to nothing as the Ottomans were preoccupied with palace revolutions at Constantinople, a war with the Russians in the Danubian Principalities that began in 1806, suspicions about British designs, and diplomatic tensions with the French. Stalling for time, the Ottomans would not open negotiations with the British and kept them at bay and Paget was never even able to alight from his ship. After three months of delays at the Dardanelles, he finally headed home.[5] 'Nothing can be compared to the hatred and contempt borne by the Turks toward the Russians,'

Paget had written to George Canning.[6] His immediate predecessor at Constantinople, Charles Arbuthnot, reached a similar conclusion: 'the Russians will always continue to be the abhorred enemies of the Turks.'[7]

When the French and Russians suddenly allied in July 1807 according to the Treaty of Tilsit,[8] the British found themselves in the impossible situation of being in a state of war simultaneously with the French, Russians and Ottomans. And the Ottomans now found themselves in a state of war with the British and Russians and facing a real possibility of war with the French.

A few months after Paget's departure, the Ottoman government sent word to the British that they wished to reestablish relations. In a letter dated 13 February 1808, they expressed a desire for peace and seemed to imply that Paget had quit the Dardanelles impatiently.[9] This communication reached George Canning in London only in late April 1808. A few weeks later he organised a diplomatic mission to the Ottoman Empire to negotiate peace and reestablish diplomatic relations. He offered its lead to Robert Adair, an experienced diplomat who had recently concluded a term as ambassador in Vienna.[10]

George included his cousin Stratford, who was younger by 16 years, on the mission as an assistant to Adair. Part of his purpose in doing so may have been 'to keep a constant eye' on Adair, as Stratford himself understood.[11] He was also under the impression that the mission would last only a few months.[12] At this point George did not tell Stratford that he had made a deal with Adair whereby the ambassador could leave Constantinople upon negotiating a peace with the Ottomans.

2

George was like a father to Stratford. Both had lost their own fathers as infants. 'Raised by his own Merits' reads the epitaph on George's statue in Westminster Abbey. In fact he was rescued from real poverty by his uncle and aunt, Stratford's parents. They steered him toward Eton, where he blossomed, founding a student journal, *The Microcosm*, which was so witty that it was read by the King and Queen. At Christ Church, Oxford he took a prize for Latin verse. Torn between a feel for the dramatic and a sense of the practical, George had difficulty choosing a career. He wrote to a friend at Oxford that he thought he had 'to aim at the House of Commons, as the only path to the only desirable thing in this world, the gratification of ambition; while at the same time every tie of common sense, of fortune, of duty, draws me to the study of a profession.'[13]

George chose 'ambition' over 'common sense', becoming the disciple of Pitt and entering Parliament by age 23. His rise and career were brilliant. 'Canning is a genius, almost a universal one; an orator, a poet, and a statesman,' Byron himself said in 1823.[14] And in his long verse of the same year, *The Age of Bronze*, canto XIII, Byron lauded Canning as 'Our last, our best, our only orator'.[15] But George suffered in real ways from the unsettled life of a politician. Cabinet intrigue drove him into a duel with his colleague, Castlereagh, on 21 September 1809. On the eve of this George wrote to his wife that he hoped his son would not become a politician because 'He would feel, & fret, & lament, & hate, & despise, as much as his father.'[16] George seems to have wished the same for his surrogate son, Stratford, and thus had he planned out for him a practical existence.

George shaped Stratford's education, career and whole life. He secured a place for the nine-year-old 'Stratty' in the lower school of Eton on the suggestion of Harry Canning, the boy's oldest brother. 'I do think the plan a very good one,' George recorded in his letter-journal on 15 February 1795, 'for if he turns out a clever boy, as he promises to do, it opens to him a field for a very distinguished exercise of his talents, in the course of his education there; and if he should be fortunate enough to go to King's Coll., Cambridge (as from his age he has a fair chance of doing) there is the further prospect of an establishment for life, sufficient if not for his whole support – at least whereon to build his fortune.'[17] George also provided funding for the boy's education either out of his own pocket or from a relative.[18]

Stratford would fulfill George's plan well, becoming captain at Eton and securing his school's place at King's College, Cambridge in 1806. In March 1807 George became foreign secretary. He took

Stratford into his home to live and hired him as a précis writer at the Foreign Office. The position, which Stratford managed by shuttling back and forth between London and Cambridge, '... consisted principally in making summaries of the official correspondence carried on between the secretary of state and the diplomatic agents employed under his direction abroad,' as Stratford noted in his memoir. 'I had also to assist occasionally in writing out fair the drafts of instructions from the same source.'

The work gave Stratford an excellent training in diplomatic communication and procedure. It also exposed him to the characters and colour of diplomacy. 'Having a room in his house and a place at his table whenever he dined at home,' Stratford wrote of George, 'I saw him in the free play of his genius and in the full enjoyment of his success . . . . At dinner I sat at the foot of the table opposite to him, and my curiosity was not a little excited when I looked around the company and wondered which of the guests was the Austrian ambassador, or which the representative of some other Great Power.'[19] George's course for Stratford also included field work: he sent him as an assistant on a critical diplomatic mission to Copenhagen in autumn 1807, before the dramatic British seizure of the Danish fleet.

George thus provided Stratford with a comprehensive apprentice-ship in diplomacy in the days when no formal instruction of it existed. This deficiency was likely one of the things that Stratford had in mind when he noted in retirement, 'the diplomatic service, when I went into it, was no profession at all.'[20] British ambassadors learnt on the job what diplomacy was and how to carry it out after having established themselves in completely different fields. But Stratford learnt the practice of diplomacy and developed a feel for its meaning – first under George at the head of the Foreign Office and then under Robert Adair on the mission at Constantinople – all in his formative years and during the height of the Napoleonic Wars. This unique diplomatic education was the foundation for his extraordinary diplomatic skills and career. An obituary published upon his death in August 1880 noted that he had been 'trained to diplomacy from his youth. . .'[21]

But at age 21 Stratford was not interested in having a career in diplomacy or probably in any profession. He was too young to appreciate the practical value of the opportunity and training that George had provided him, and he was still dreaming of becoming a statesman in Parliament like his cousin and benefactor. So when George decided to attach him to Adair's mission to Constantinople in the summer of 1808, it was about the last thing Stratford wanted to do. He went on the mission out of devotion to George. The bond between them was essential: Stratford's father had been the surrogate father to George, and George in turn had become the same to Stratford.

3

George Canning and Robert Adair, the mission leader, were from different ends of the political spectrum in London and they were not friends. Adair was a close associate of Charles Fox, the Whig leader, who while foreign secretary, had sent him as ambassador to Vienna in 1806.[22] Adair was widely known as a drinker and, as the Earl of Malmesbury formulated rather harshly, 'such a dupe to women, that no secret was safe with him.'[23] The unfortunate tendency was described more kindly by Adair's grand-nephew and close friend, the Earl of Albemarle: 'Throughout life my kinsman was an enthusiastic admirer of the fair sex, which he generally "loved not wisely but too well".' Adair's appearance and demeanor were somewhat sorry and invited teasing even among relatives. 'His name calls up the image of a tall, thin man,' the Earl of Albemarle noted, 'with a sallow complexion and a melancholy cast of features, who was known in the family as the "knight of the woeful countenance".' Adair had specialised in writing 'probationary odes' for satirical Whig publications, including the Rolliad, and was 'a great buff and blue squib maker'.[24]

All of these factors combined to project Robert Adair as a permanent lightning-rod for Tory satire. George Canning himself was the chief protagonist and it would be noted in Adair's obituary in 1855 that, 'For several years Canning had made Adair the butt of his piercing wit.'[25] Adair was skewered relentlessly in Canning's wild

satirical journal, *The Anti-Jacobin* (1797–98), including most
famously 'BOBBA-DARA-ADUL-PHOOLA'[26] (a lyricisation of
'Bob Adair is a dull fellow').

Despite these shortcomings, Adair was endowed with unusual
diplomatic experience and skills, and he was a pleasant character and
genuine raconteur. All these assets were appreciated by George
Canning. Adair himself knew that 'I had no right to count upon his
partiality towards one so openly opposed as I was to the Government
of which he made a part. But Mr. Canning had many generous
qualities .... He saw that, with all my defects, I had served England
faithfully and zealously, and all party differences were forgotten the
moment he saw me.'[27] Another factor may have been the connection
through Fox, who before his death in 1806 had been the mentor to
Adair and also a close friend of the Canning family.[28]

Adair was eager to take on the critical peace mission to the
Ottoman Empire. But he did not desire to reside at Constantinople,
which among European diplomats was still considered very much a
hardship posting. This was doubtless due in large part to the fact that
the Ottomans had never renounced their ancient practice of
imprisoning foreign representatives upon a declaration of war
with their country. Adair therefore made a special deal with Canning.
'I accepted the mission under an express agreement that after having
made the peace,' Adair recorded, 'I should be at liberty to return
home, and resume my seat on the Opposition benches of the House
of Commons.'[29]

As with the previous mission that George Canning had sent to
the Ottoman Empire under Paget, Adair was instructed to make
peace with the Ottomans and to promote peace between them and the
Russians. The British were greatly concerned about French plans to
disrupt their route to India. 'I cannot too strongly recommend to
your attention,' George Canning wrote in his official instructions
to Adair, dated 26 June 1808, 'the necessity of endeavouring to
counter-act the Project entertained by the French Government to
procure the permission of the Porte for marching an Army through a
part of the Ottoman Territories for the purpose of penetrating to the
British Possessions in India.' Canning further instructed Adair that

he was not to proceed past Palermo until he had contacted the
Ottomans and they had reconfirmed their desire to negotiate the
peace, as well as named a plenipotentiary and place for the purpose.[30]
These latter provisions were no doubt inspired by the frustrations
Paget had experienced in the previous year.

4

The sea journey to Constantinople was long and slow but not without
some drama and even pleasures. The embassy departed from Spithead
on 29 June 1808 aboard the frigate *Hyperion*. On the way to Gibraltar,
while crossing Lagos Bay on 9 July, they were boarded by an officer of
the Portuguese Volunteers who 'intreated Captain Broody to give
him a supply of Arms and Ammunitions,' as Stratford wrote in a kind
of mission log that he kept during the sea voyage. 'He pointed to a
pink ribband which he wore round his right arm as the badge of
Insurrection + said that he was commissioned by the Governor of
Lagos. We learnt from him that every person who did not join the
patriotick party, was put to death. The captain of the *Hyperion* at first
refused his request, but at Mr. Adair's recommendation he granted
him a small supply.'[31]

They arrived at Gibraltar on 16 July 1808 and after a stay there
reached Palermo, Sicily on the night of 3 August. Here a long delay
was incurred while Adair attempted to secure Ottoman reconfirmation of the mission. This gave Stratford an opportunity to explore the
island. Like his cousin he had studied the classics and Sicily ignited
his imagination. He went exploring with the British consul and
managed to locate the ancient temple of Segesta, 'which is one of the
most perfect buildings that time has spared,' as he wrote to his sister,
Bess. They 'had the satisfaction of dining in this consecrated spot,
and did not forget to make a libation of claret to the divinity of the
place. Tell George to fancy what a quiz I must have been, standing as
I was in mute satisfaction, with a *Virgil* in one hand and a bottle of
claret in the other.'[32]

A new delay occurred now but this was due to British problems,
not Ottoman. Adair had sent the interpreter of the mission, Thomas

Barthold, forward from Sicily to Malta to consult with the British governor there, Sir Alexander Ball, about proceeding to the Dardanelles to secure the Ottoman reconfirmation. 'A few days after this,' as Stratford recorded in his log of the mission, 'Mr. Adair received instructions from England to send home Mr. Barthold, as information had been received of his being unfit to be trusted. Mr. Adair immediately recalled him from Malta, at the same time desiring him to be looked to. Sir Alexander Ball had already been on his guard, + seemed to entertain the same suspicions of his character. Two or three days before we left Palermo, Mr. Adair sent him to England with false Dispatches.'[33] The Foreign Office had apparently only now either learnt or appreciated that back in 1799 Barthold had been fired by the Levant Company as a dragoman of the British embassy in Constantinople because he had gone absent without leave for over one year.[34] Since then he had somehow been reinstated to the Foreign Office and served on the unsuccessful Paget peace mission of 1807.[35]

At Palermo the embassy was joined by a new assistant. David Morier was born in Smyrna in 1784, son of a prominent English factor there. Morier had been raised in England and knew no Turkish but he had returned to the Levant to serve for three years in Greece as the assistant to his older brother's mission at Janina (Ioannina) to the rebel Ottoman governor, Ali Paşa. He had then been an assistant on the unsuccessful Paget mission to the Dardanelles, after which he had served in Egypt and then went to Malta to await new instructions from the Foreign Office.

David Morier and Stratford Canning were about the same age and of similar backgrounds. Stratford had been raised at Eton and Morier had studied for two years at Harrow. They were also both upright and serious but they were of very different temperaments. While Morier was completely easy-going and likeable to all, Stratford was prone to over-seriousness and flashes of temper. Despite their differences they immediately became friends. A month after Morier joined the embassy he wrote to his mother of Stratford that 'he is the most amiable, well educated young man with the highest religious and moral feelings you could find ... He is only 21, but with all the liveliness of that age he has a good sense which would do honor to a man of 40. He is full of Greek and Latin but makes no parade of it, and he has such a sense of humour and fun that he makes a delightful companion.'[36] The friendship would be vital to Stratford during this first mission to Constantinople, enabling him to survive his homesickness. Morier was, as Canning later recalled, 'my constant associate, my never-failing resource...'[37] They would remain friends for 65 years.

The Barthold incident had delayed the mission more than a month at Palermo. Adair boldly decided that he could wait no longer for reconfirmation from the Ottomans and that he would immediately press on to the Dardanelles. Stratford immaturely implored Adair not to deviate from his instructions but the ambassador was resolute. 'He said,' Stratford wrote to George, 'that he should adhere to the spirit not the mere letter of them – that he was perfectly acquainted with the views + sentiments of Government upon the subject – + that, in short, he had made up his mind as to the matter.'[38] Adair himself wrote to George Canning that he was proceeding onward to the Dardanelles because of 'the vast importance of the moment,' including 'to get the mediation for the Russian Peace with Turkey out of the hands of France...'[39]

5

Adair's embassy sailed away from Sicily on 5 September 1808 and arrived at Malta two days later. The island colony was awash with British subjects who had been forced to leave the Ottoman Empire after Duckworth's breaching of the Dardanelles and a state of war being declared with Britain in February 1807. Adair and Stratford were pressed for useful commercial and diplomatic information and lobbied for assistance by 'the crowd of officious Consuls + ignorant Merchants, who attacked him, + even me, at all hours + in all places during our short stay at Malta...' as Stratford recorded. The exodus of merchants from Smyrna had stopped production of many vital goods there and necessitated their importation from Malta where prices inflated and 'many adventurers [speculators] were making large fortunes by it,' Stratford observed. 'So much indeed that one of the most respectable members of the Levant Company told me that a continuance of the war was decidedly favourable to the interests of the merchants. After this, how could any credit be given to the reports of persons thus detached from their country as much by interest as by distance?'[40] Stratford's first encounter here with Levantines was unfortunate. But even before the mission he already suffered, it seems, from a condescending attitude toward Levantines which was at that time not rare among European elites.

Adair himself did not enjoy the experience at Malta and decided to leave after only three days. On 10 September 1808 the embassy set out for the Aegean archipelago and the Dardanelles on the *Sea Horse*, escorted by the British brig, *Saracean*. On 23 September they reached Cape Doro, close enough to the Dardanelles to send word to the Ottoman castles there. Slowly the embassy was allowed to approach, first to the island of Tenedos, and then up to Cape Janissary.[41] They had finally arrived at the Dardanelles but in terms of time their journey to Constantinople was less than half completed.

CHAPTER 2

THE TREATY OF THE DARDANELLES

1

Adair felt that he was diplomatically prevented from going ashore until he had ascertained that an Ottoman plenipotentiary had been appointed for the peace negotiations and had arrived for that purpose. He therefore instructed David Morier to conduct the first meeting with the Paşa of the Dardanelles, Mehmet Hakki. The meeting was arranged for 27 September 1808 and the Paşa requested that Morier be conveyed to the Inner European Castle of the Dardanelles late at night and 'he begged him to go in disguise, in order to elude the notice of the French Emissaries,' as Stratford recorded in his log of the mission. 'Mr. Morier at first objected to this; but, upon being pressed with great earnestness he consented to it.'[1]

For this purpose two Ottoman officials came on board to dress up Morier and 'after enveloping me in a ponderous scarlet beniche were employed nearly a quarter of an hour rolling up about twenty yards of muslin which was to serve as my head piece,' as Morier wrote home a few days later. Something was needed in order to provide a base for the turban but Morier did not happen to possess anything of the sort. Therefore 'one of the officiating Turks very kindly accommodated me with his own *fesch* [fez] all reeking with the effluvia of his own scalp (happily bald) which nothing on earth would ever have induced me to put on my head but the urgent necessity of the occasion and the most ardent zeal for the public service. I had the precaution, however, to turn this same skull cap the wrong side out.'[2] It was not the ultimate sacrifice for country, but it was, in its own way, a profound demonstration of devotion to duty. Morier thus went ashore and at half past one in the morning he was 'introduced to the Pasha with great secrecy...' He learnt only that negotiations were impossible as an Ottoman plenipotentiary had not yet been appointed and instructions were still being awaited from Constantinople. He returned to the ship by dawn.

Two days later, on 29 September, the embassy made a conciliatory move. It sent a written note to the Paşa declaring that Britain had unilaterally decided 'to refrain from every act of hostility against the Turkish trade'. This perhaps suggests that the British had previously threatened to enact a blockade of the Ottoman coasts, or that they had already enacted this.[3] The embassy also requested 'that Mr. Pisani, head Dragoman of the English Mission, might be sent for without delay.'[4] The British sorely lacked an interpreter of Turkish because of the earlier dismissal of Barthold.

Bartholomeo Pisani had been a British dragoman for over 30 years. His Levantine family, of Venetian Cretan heritage, had served the British as dragomans in Constantinople since the early 1700s.[5] For the past 21 months Bartholomeo Pisani had been living in exile, first in Bursa and then possibly in the western Anatolian city of Kütahya, having been banished there by the Ottoman government in response to the British breaching of the Dardanelles.[6] Dragomans serving a belligerent power sometimes were arrested by the Ottomans, being either sent out of the capital or even imprisoned along with the ambassador they served at *Yedi Kule* (the Ottoman fortress of Seven Towers, the site of the once-resplendent *Porta Aurea* or The Golden Gate portal of Byzantine emperors, located at the southern end of the fifth-century Theodosian Walls of Constantinople). When the Ottomans and Russians had gone to war back in August 1787, Bartholomeo Pisani's older brother, Nicolo Pisani, chief dragoman of the Russian embassy, had been imprisoned at *Yedi Kule* along with the Russian minister, Iakov Bulgakov.[7]

2

After waiting more than a week Adair sent Stratford ashore, on 11 October 1808, to meet the Paşa and give him a letter intended for the Reis Efendi, the Ottoman foreign minister, Sehid Mehemmed Sayd Galib. Stratford's meeting with the Paşa produced some promising information. The Paşa 'informed me,' Stratford recorded in his mission log, 'that a Courier who had left [Constantinople] four days before had just brought an answer from the Porte…' This was translated aloud into French by the Paşa's secretary with Stratford writing it down. It announced that the Ottoman government had appointed Mercoufagi Vaahid Efendi as the official plenipotentiary for the negotiations and that he had set out for the Dardanelles a few days earlier. The message also related that the Porte had consented to the embassy's request to be joined by Dragoman Pisani.[8] The Paşa also agreed to transmit Adair's letter to the Reis Efendi. In the letter Adair reminded the Reis Efendi that France and Russia had agreed at Tilsit to partition the European territories of the Ottoman Empire in the Balkan regions of Wallachia and Moldovia. 'The government of the Sublime Porte is too wise therefore,' Adair wrote, 'not to profit by this favourable opportunity of making peace with his Majesty.'[9]

Despite the good news for the British embassy, several more weeks of limbo followed as the plenipotentiary did not arrive. Adair, Stratford and the British embassy waited. It was all a repeat of Paget's mission the previous year: stuck on-board ship at the Dardanelles, delay upon delay. 'During the whole of this time,' Stratford wrote in his log, 'we were living on board the Sea Horse exposed to every sort of inconvenience + privation, that distance from shore, continual bad weather, + confinement, + severe cold can bestow. The Gales of wind were so frequent + so violent that to go ashore was really a service of danger.'[10]

The conditions and delays were souring young Stratford's first impressions of the Ottomans. He wrote home on 19 October 1808 that 'they are, almost to a man, proud, ignorant, sly, jealous, and cruel … cringing to his superiors, quarrelling with his equals, preying upon his dependents, and indiscriminately cheating them all. There are doubtless some exceptions, and I shall do my best to find some of them when we get to Constantinople.'[11]

On 27 October a request arrived from one of the Ottoman castles for the ship's surgeon to be sent to tend to one of the Ottoman governors. The surgeon was instructed to convey a message expressing Adair's 'sorrows at the strange delay of the Turkish Government,' and to request that he 'might be sent back immediately, as he did not know at what moment, in case of further delay, he should be obliged to go away,' as Stratford recorded. 'The Surgeon was also instructed, if any attempt should be made to pump him [for information], to throw out a hint of the probability of an English fleet making its appearance before long at the Dardanelles, as the peace with Spain left so much of our Navy unemployed.'[12]

Two days later, on 29 October, the British embassy received a letter from the Reis Efendi. This firmly stated that the Ottoman government wished to conclude peace with England. The Reis Efendi assured that 'no acts of enmity have ever passed between the Sublime Porte and the Court of England ... although the improper and causeless conduct of the former ambassador, resident at Constantinople, under an idea of acting in concert with Russia, has produced an appearance of coolness.' The reference was to Arbuthnot's collaboration with Duckworth to breach the Dardanelles and to threaten the capital in February 1807. The Ottomans were still understandably upset about this attack. But the Reis Efendi's letter also confirmed the information that the Paşa of the Dardanelles had given to Stratford: that Vaahid Efendi had been appointed as the Ottoman plenipotentiary to negotiate with Adair and that he had already left Constantinople for the Dardanelles.[13]

Three days later, 'on November the 2nd in the evening Mr. Adair received a Letter from Vaahid Efendi, announcing his arrival at the Inner Asiatick Castle .... We learned also that Mr. Pisani, the Dragoman, was come,' Stratford recorded in his log. Pisani joined the embassy the next day.[14] His arrival provided the British embassy with a desperately needed interpreter of discussions, documents and developments. The arrival of the Ottoman plenipotentiary plus the release of Pisani in November 1808 were indications by the Ottomans that they were politically closer to making peace.

3

Delay however continued. Several more weeks passed without any other indications that negotiation would begin. Stratford was growing increasingly impatient. 'Without being on the spot it is almost impossible to conceive the many difficulties peculiar to this country which impede the progress of Business,' he wrote to George on 18 November 1808. 'The habitual and systematic slowness of the Turks, who have the utmost aversion to everything that bears the least appearance of dispatch. So much so that they have a common Proverb among them signifying that – Business is hastened with delay. Secondly their love of artifice + its never failing companions jealousy + suspicion....' Not only the Ottoman government but also the Levantine interpreters came in for Stratford's wrath. 'As the Turks hold the European languages in contempt, + the Europeans do not think it worthwhile to learn Turkish, no communication can take place between the two Countries but by means of Interpreters, who are brought up in a state of poverty, which makes them equally submissive to their masters + open to the temptations of bribery....'

Stratford complained in his letter to George about 'the mischiefs likely to arise from the want of sense of honesty in the interpreters. Even Mr. Pisani, who has been, as you know, for many years the established Dragoman of the English Mission, seems disposed, in spite of the most ardent professions of zeal, is probably connected with some of the Levant merchants who openly avow that the present state of hostilities between England + Turkey is more favourable to them than the Restoration of Peace.'[15]

In this, Stratford was being completely unfair. In fact there had never been any evidence or even suggestion of Pisani's being too closely associated with merchants or being unprofessional or disloyal in any way. Quite the contrary: his official record with the embassy going back over 30 years was a steady stream of praise and gratitude from his superiors. Moreover, he had just paid for his loyalty by spending a year and a half in exile.

Two more empty weeks passed. Stratford lamented to George on 1 December 1808: 'I had hoped by this time to have written to you from Constantinople, but hitherto every day produced some unexpected delay, and time which in other countries brings the most intricate Business to an end, seems in this only to put new obstacles in the way of its Execution. . . .' He also continued with his rant against Pisani. 'In my last letter I told you how much the progress of Business was impeded by the unfortunate necessity of using Interpreters. Mr. Pisani was then ill + unwilling to do anything; he had since recovered his health + is now so over diligent that he plagues Mr. Adair out of his life . . . . It does not appear that Pisani is in any way dishonest; but the poor man is in his dotage.'[16]

Only a few years removed from Eton, Stratford was still too narrow and immature to appreciate the venerable Pisani's abilities, suffering, efforts and character. Stratford in general could not yet comprehend the dragomans. But as he gained experience and grew during the eventful and important mission, at the height of the Napoleonic Wars with the fate of the whole continent in the balance, Stratford would come to value and respect his interpreter colleagues. Everything Stratford accomplished over the next three and a half years at Constantinople was due to the efforts of Bartholomeo Pisani. In fact, everything he accomplished during his many missions to Constantinople throughout the next 49 and a half years was done with the help of dragomans, many of them the descendant relatives of Bartholomeo Pisani.[17]

While there can be no excuse for Stratford's prejudice, his impatience can be partly explained by the exasperating delays of the mission. Adair was also pessimistic and reaching his limit. 'I am afraid,' he reported to George Canning, 'that we are still too far asunder to enable me to give hopes of an amicable conclusion.'[18] On 17 December 1808 he sent a message to the Ottoman plenipotentiary, Vaahid Efendi, which included the pointed question: 'Does your Excellency think that, supposing the treaty I offer you to be rejected, Great Britain will interpose in any form or shape whatever to prevent Russia from occupying and uniting to her own dominions any part of the territories of the Sublime Porte which she may judge convenient for the security of her frontiers?'[19] But the Ottomans remained unmoved.

'Every day new obstacles seemed to rise up in the way of Peace,' Stratford recorded in his mission log. 'Conference succeeded to Conference without success, + all the possible means of delay were put into action by the Turkish Plenipotentiary. Monstrous claims were advanced, withdrawn, + again brought forward – the most trifling + customary forms of diplomacy became subjects of cavil + tedious discussion .... Even the intervals between the times of meeting were lengthened out upon various pretences, + questions referred to Constantinople, in order, it seemed, to retard the progress of business.'[20]

The Ottomans did have some understandable reasons for delay. They were still struggling with court revolutions in Constantinople, as well as with their war against the Russians that had begun in 1806. Britain's naval invasion of their capital had occurred only the previous year and many Ottoman statesmen remained suspicious of the country. And the Ottoman delay was likely also strategic, probably due to their calculation that stalling at the Dardanelles would improve their negotiating position. But in delaying they were also at risk of losing the British embassy and the prospects for British support against France.

Finally Adair reached his limit or decided that real action was needed. On 30 December he dramatically went ashore to meet Vaahid Efendi and directly said he would break off negotiations and sail home if the treaty were not accepted immediately. Vaahid Efendi's response was reported by Adair to George Canning as follows: 'If the peace should not be signed... he said he was a lost man, and that he must take refuge in England.'[21] Agreement was soon achieved, and Stratford described the dramatic moment in vivid detail: 'At length, on the 1st of January, when patience was exhausted, when all hopes of Peace were gone, when the sails were set, the Dragomans dismissed,

+ everything prepared for our instant departure, + even the French Consul rowing out in his boat to enjoy an imaginary triumph, Vaahid Efendi gave way.'[22]

4

The articles of the 'Treaty of the Dardanelles' (as the peace agreement came to be known), signed on 5 January 1809, provide a portrait of the major questions of European diplomacy of the day as well as of the practical relations between the British and the Ottomans. The key strategic aspects of the treaty were contained in five secret articles. Among these, the first three detailed conditional British military support to the Ottomans against the French. 'Should France, unjustly, declare war against the Sublime Porte, or should she manifest any threats towards her...', read the first secret article, 'His Majesty, the Honored King of England, engages to exert all his attention + inclination in affording the Sublime Porte assistance...' Specific naval and military aspects of this pledged support were spelled out in the first three secret articles. The fourth provided that if Britain were to make peace with Russia before the Ottoman Empire did so, Britain would use its good offices to secure a peace between the other two countries, 'honourable + Beneficial to the Sublime Porte, + with Independence to, + Complete Integrity of the Ottoman Dominions.'[23] These four secret articles were British concessions to the Ottomans' difficult strategic position.

Another strategic concern of the Ottomans was embodied in Article XI of the patent treaty: an affirmation of 'the ancient regulation of the Ottoman Empire'.[24] This was the prohibition against any foreign ships of war passing the Turkish Straits, the Dardanelles and Bosphorus. By this article the Ottomans gained effective British support for repealing the Russians' right to pass the Straits that they had gained in previous treaties. And this was the first time that the Ottomans secured official recognition of their 'ancient regulation' by a Western power.[25] Also by Article XI, the Ottomans had directly gained a British pledge that they would not repeat the breach of the Straits that they had committed less than two years earlier.

The 'Straits Question' – control of the Turkish Straits, and the rights of foreign powers to pass them – was an old concern of European diplomacy. Back in 1686 the point had been made rather vividly when 'the Turks told the French ambassador,' according to the historian A. C. Wood, 'that the Sultan would sooner open the doors of his harem to strangers than permit entry to the Euxine [the Black Sea].'[26] And the analogy was repeated in the year 1700 when the Russians were informed by the Turks, as Wood also discovered, that: 'The Sultan considers the Black Sea as his own house to which strangers cannot penetrate; it is a virgin shut up in the harem, hidden from the view of strangers, and he would rather have war than permit other nations to navigate on this internal sea.'[27] Now in the early nineteenth century, the Straits question was to become and remain, through the Crimean War and then World War I, one of the most important diplomatic and strategic problems of Europe.

The longest and perhaps most interesting part of the patent treaty was Article IX. This related to the issuing of the 'berat', the Ottoman licence for Western embassies to provide Levantine Ottoman subjects with diplomatic status in order to function as dragomans or consuls. In the Article, the number of British dragomans was limited 'as they shall stand in need of'; and the British affirmed that they 'shall not grant the "Barat" of Dragoman in favour of individuals who do not execute that duty ... [and] the "Barat" shall not be granted to any person of the class of tradesmen or bankers, nor to any shopkeeper or manufacturer in the public markets, or to one who is engaged in any matters of this description...'[28]

The Ottomans had long been very concerned about the corrupt sale of *berats* by Western ambassadors. 'These *berats* were distributed by the European diplomatic missions, in abusive extension of their rights under the capitulations,' as described in the 1960 edition of *The Encyclopedia of Islam*. 'Originally intended for locally recruited consular officers and agents, they were sold or granted to growing numbers of local merchants, who were thus able to acquire a privileged and protected status.'[29] As this status included exemption from significant parts of Ottoman law and taxation, many Ottoman Levantine merchants were eager to obtain *berats* and ambassadors could turn a major profit from selling them. In order to procure a *berat* licence from the Ottoman government, a Western embassy was required to pay a chancery fee, and this often had to be renewed with payment upon the ascension of a new sultan. But these payments would be more than covered by the hefty bribe that a merchant would pay an ambassador. In this and other ways, ambassadors would substantially supplement their salaries, and the post became famous throughout Europe for its unofficial possibilities for generating private capital.

As the number of *berats* proliferated among Ottoman merchants into the hundreds and thousands, the Ottoman tax rolls were significantly reduced and their sovereignty over their own citizens challenged.[30] Ottoman attempts to curtail the corruption in *berats* were therefore asserted forcefully in the 1770s under Sultan Selim III.[31]

Another type of secret diplomatic payment, but this one going from the British government to the Ottoman, was addressed in a fifth secret article of the treaty. This was written out and signed separately from the other four secret articles. This fifth secret article provided that, '... His Majesty, the Honoured King of England, in confirmation of his friendship, will readily undertake to give the exalted Ottoman Court, by way of assistance, Three Hundred Thousand Pounds Sterling, or Ten Thousand Two Hundred Purses of Turkish Money, in Two Installments, in the course of about Six Months from the Day of the Exchange of the Ratifications of the Treaties of Peace...'[32]

Adair drew up and signed this article separately from the other four secret articles in order to provide his government with the possibility of later getting out of the payment while preserving the rest of the treaty. 'The Separate Article concerning an Aid of £300,000 is so perfectly optional,' as Adair explained, with a degree of self-satisfaction, in his dispatch to George Canning on 6 January 1809, 'and I have spoken out so fairly to the Turkish Plenipotentiary on it, that His Majesty's Government can be put to no difficulty in refusing its Ratification.'[33]

Unfortunately this separate, fifth secret article was not drafted as 'perfectly' as Adair believed. The other four secret articles specifically spelled out that British military support to the Ottomans was contingent upon their being 'unjustly' attacked or threatened by France. But the fifth secret article pledged British financial aid to the Ottomans completely unconditionally. This was not at all the intention of the British government, and George Canning was forced to send Adair a somewhat tough dispatch. He directly criticised Adair's 'omission' and explained that the government was in fact willing to provide 'pecuniary succours' to the Ottomans only 'to assist the Porte in the event of a war commenced against the Porte by France, and in that event alone. It is therefore His Majesty's pleasure that you should not present the ratification of this Article for exchange, unless that event shall have actually occurred.'[34]

Despite Adair's 'omission' concerning the fifth secret article of the treaty, George Canning still found it proper to relate to Adair official 'approbation of the firmness, temper, and perseverance which you have manifested under all the difficulties and delays which attended the progress of the Treaty, and of the terms upon which it has been finally concluded.'[35] While this was a somewhat standard formulation that ministers abroad were usually afforded at the conclusion of a treaty or a mission, George Canning's message to Adair likely meant to reflect his real approval. For the Treaty of the Dardanelles was a great achievement by Adair at an urgent time. And perhaps George had been influenced by a warm letter Stratford had sent him on 7 January 1809: 'I wish I could find terms to describe Mr. Adair's Conduct, as it seems to me to deserve,' Stratford wrote. 'I have been a witness of his unremitting Exertions from first to last + the many difficulties with which he had to contend, permit me to say that you owe a great deal to him. It was by his management at his own risk that the Negotiation was set on foot; + nothing but the greatest degree of diligence, temper and Perseverance could ever have brought [this] to a successful issue.'[36] Stratford had already learnt much from Adair about diplomacy and had yet more to learn.

5

Stratford still had much to learn also about himself. The Ottoman officials had some logical reasons for delay, including the political upheavals at Constantinople and the ongoing war with the Russians in the Principalities. And delay was, after all, a staple of diplomacy. But the young Stratford sorely lacked feeling for ways and perspectives foreign to him. He simply dismissed the Ottomans in his mind and in his letters to home.

Even though the peace had been concluded, delays managed to continue and '... going up to Constantinople gave rise to as much discussion + trouble of every sort, as the Treaty itself,' as Stratford noted in his log.[37] A special decree from the Ottoman government in the capital was required before the British ship could be allowed to pass up the strait. For this purpose, Adair sent Morier by land to Constantinople on 7 January 1809. He arrived on 11 January 1809,[38] after which another two weeks were required to secure this permission.

Late one evening during the embassy's wait at the Dardanelles, Stratford was pacing the deck of the ship with Adair, 'when he suddenly turned round to me and said,' as Stratford recalled many years later, 'that after the exchange of ratifications, he was to be the King's ambassador at Constantinople, but that, instead of remaining there, he was to go on to Vienna ... He then inquired whether I should like to have the appointment of secretary to the Turkish Embassy, which, on his departure, might lead to my having for a time the direction of its affairs as minister plenipotentiary.' This was a shock to Stratford. He had never wanted to go on this mission, and the conclusion of the peace treaty had raised his hopes that he may return home soon and resume his studies at Cambridge.

He thanked Adair and politely refused, declaring that 'the proposed opening in diplomacy, if realized in my favour, would only take me away from a line which I preferred.'[39] It seems he had no inkling that the offer would be proposed again by Adair and strongly supported by George Canning. Waiting at the entrance to the Dardanelles and the Bosphorus, those great crossroads of places and times, Stratford Canning unknowingly stood at the threshold of international and historical renown, but also to years of personal hardship.

On 25 January 1809 the British embassy was finally authorised to pass the castles of the Dardanelles and sail up the strait. The next day the ships reached Constantinople,[40] seven months after having left home. Stratford had arrived at a career of diplomacy and would never return to his studies at Cambridge.

CHAPTER 3

STRANDED AT CONSTANTINOPLE

1

Even today few sights are more memorable than the first vision of Istanbul. It has always been this way. 'Certainly – no city is so wonderfully beautiful when you approach it – it was far beyond my idea,' Edward Lear described his arrival there by ship on 1 August 1848, after which he stayed with the Cannings on the Bosphorus for six weeks. 'I think the perpetual change as the steamer moves on, of ruined walls, immense domes – brilliantly white minarets – all mixed with such magnificent cypress, pine & plane foliage is truly wonderful.'[1]

Stratford was similarly struck when he first sailed into the city on 26 January 1809. About his arrival and first impressions there, he wrote home a few weeks later: 'The grandeur of the city as we approached it, the variety of dresses, and the tones of so many different languages, that each person seemed to have some twenty or thirty of those tongues and voices which Homer and Virgil talk about – all roused my curiosity....' He was so fascinated with the 'manners of the inhabitants, their way of living, the shops, the markets, the mosques and dismal burying grounds...'[2] that he commissioned a local Greek artist to paint a large series of the varied scenes plus studies of government officials attired in their robes and headdresses. These pictures, drawn in 1809 and 1810, Stratford kept his whole life. Fifteen years after his death, in 1895, the collection was purchased from his survivors by the South Kensington Museum, the predecessor of the Victoria and Albert Museum, where the works still repose. The identity of the painter has always remained unknown. 'The Greek artist's pictures,' as described by their curator, Charles Newton, 'which show eighty-six single figure costume subjects, ranging from the Sultan and his officers down to a knife-grinder, and thirty-nine images of manners, customs, architecture and topography, are important because they are a last glimpse of a Turkey barely influenced by Western ways; little did Canning know that he was recording the end of true Oriental splendour unalloyed with the drab West.'

The fascinating works include a large and detailed interior of Hagia Sophia mosque, when it was still rarely visited by non-Muslims; a depiction of the *Rufai* or howling dervishes, including one who seems to have lost his balance; a wrestling match probably in the pit at Suleymaniye, 'in the presence of veiled ladies,' from Newton's description; 'a splendid picture of Sultan Mahmud leaving the palace in procession on his way to Friday prayers, surrounded by the plumed head-dresses of the Soulaks, his body-guard, and some of his chief officers.'[3] Another painting is the most realistic depiction ever made of the rampageous Janissary scrum for salaries in the *Divan meydanı* or second courtyard of Topkapi Saray, which includes the original designs and colours of the porch inside *Bâb-üs Selâm*, the Gate of Salutation; and there is a fine work of the Sultan on his throne in the *Arz Odası* or throne room, located in the *Enderun* or the third courtyard of Topkapi Saray. There is a depiction of the delivery of the Sultan's dishes and soup (including a very imperious spoon); and there are finely detailed studies of many public servants and artisans that offer a rare depiction of their trades and garments. There are paintings of mosques, fountains, markets, a coffee-house; unprecedented studies of Ottoman sabres, of local architecture and of the city's monuments, including those extant on the Byzantine Hippodrome. A panorama of the northern Bosphorus and the opening to the Black Sea, including the diplomatic village of Büyükdere on the European coast and *Yuşa Tepe* or Giant's Hill on the Asian, is very beautiful. The works also include a panorama of *Yedi Kule*, the fortress of the Seven Towers, where ambassadors were held in arrest during a declaration of war; a panorama of the Bosphorus at Tophane, the cannon foundry, where ambassadors often disembarked and ascended the hill up to their embassies in Pera, the diplomatic quarter of the city; and the only known nineteenth–century painting of Rue de Pera, the embassy row, with an Ottoman delegation approaching the entrance of what is probably the French embassy. And one work depicts the Kaymakam meeting with a European official who is most likely Stratford Canning.[4]

In the foreground of several of the paintings three figures recur: one gentleman in European dress, another in Armenian, and a third in Ottoman uniform. These appear to represent Stratford himself, an interpreter or guide, and a Janissary guard, as they made their way around the city.[5] All the paintings by the Greek artist are remarkably realistic, colourful, detailed and precise, exhibiting what could be called a photographic quality. Stratford had made for himself a set of watercolour snapshots of the city, with himself included in some, by which later in life and back home he could remember his days there.

Charles Newton is certainly correct in observing that the pictures demonstrate how, 'Canning was obviously deeply impressed by the scenes of everyday life around him; the exotic ceremonial and gorgeous silk must have contrasted with his memory of the gloomy days of his youth in Hackney and the relative sobriety of the playing fields of Eton.' The pictures are also significant, as Newton explains, in being a unique and vivid record of Ottoman life on the eve of the country being irrevocably affected by the importation of Western institutions such as 'English steam engines, French fashions and German militarism' and also costumes that were 'often hideously incongruous, like the "Stambouline" or European frock coat which looked very odd on the Sultan's officials, particularly the Eunuchs.'[6]

2

Stratford had arrived at the capital of the Ottoman Empire at a pivotal moment in the whole course of its history, when its existence as a sovereign independent state was under threat, and as it struggled to settle on a course of comprehensive reform in order to meet this challenge.

Since reaching the gates of Vienna in 1699 (not for the first time), the Ottoman Empire had lost to the Russians all of the Caucasus and the whole northern shore of the Black Sea, including the Sea of Azov and the strategically vital mouth of the Don river at Taganrog, the Cuban region, the Crimea and westward to the Dniestr river. While the territory of the Ottoman Empire remained vast at the time of Stratford's arrival – stretching the length of northern Africa, across the entire Near-East up to the Persian Empire, throughout all of the Arabian peninsula, and deep into Europe including Greece, Bulgaria, Albania, Kosovo and Serbia up to Austrian Dalmatia – several of these regions had begun to assert claims for autonomy, likely inspired by the idea of the nation as expressed in the French Revolution.

The Ottomans had already launched themselves on the path of reform after a disastrous war with the Russians and their having to accept the burdensome Treaty of *Küçük Kaynarca* in 1774. This occurred at the same time as the Europeans' partitions of the state of Poland, a fate that the Ottoman leaders realistically feared for their own country. They began military and social reforms at this time but the program was resisted fiercely by many of the entrenched old orders of society, such as the *Derebeys* or lords of the landed gentry, and the Janissaries, the military lords, elite palace guards, shock troops and keepers of the old regime.

Stratford's arrival at Constantinople in January 1809 occurred while the fierce politics of Ottoman reform were still being played out. Two years earlier a Janissary uprising had swept away the first leader of Ottoman reform, Sultan Selim III, as well as many of his ministers and even his immediate successor. The new Sultan, Mahmud II, who had come to rule in 1808 and only a few months before Stratford's arrival, was attempting to continue reform while accommodating the dangerous Janissaries.

Stratford's first major task at the city was to research and compose a very thorough report on the court revolutions and the Ottoman political struggles over reform. This was titled, 'Account of the three last Insurrections at Constantinople, and of the present State of the Turkish Empire', and was submitted by Stratford to Adair on 25 March 1809. The report was based on his interviews with Ottoman ministers, dragomans and other Ottoman Levantine subjects who were friends of the embassy, as well as with British factors and other foreigners resident at Constantinople. This report is perhaps the first serious study of Ottoman reform ever undertaken by a Westerner at Constantinople. Stratford was fascinated by the political and cultural issues of Ottoman reform and by the whole historical drama of how the Empire was confronting the challenge of entering the modern era of industrialisation and communication.

Stratford's report began with an overview of the recent events. The Ottoman Empire had seen three palace revolutions from 1807 to 1808, finally resulting in the ascendancy of Sultan Mahmut II. Stratford correctly identified the upheaval as a manifestation of Ottoman political struggles that had begun during the reign of Sultan Selim III in the 1770s, over whether to adopt Western military institutions and other fundamental changes. 'The Encouragement which he gave to the Introduction of European Arts first awakened the suspicions of the Janissaries, who, bigoted in favor of their national customs, distrust every appearance of innovation, and in the pride of their ignorance, disdain improvements, if purchased by the confession of inferiority.'

Stratford had a high opinion of the new Sultan Mahmut II. 'The present Sultan has already given marks of firmness + good sense, sufficient to afford ground of reasonable hopes.' He had made peace with Great Britain, showed signs of resisting France, and willfully faced his domestic opponents. 'He has spoken openly to the Janissaries, + declared to them his readiness to redress their grievances, but at the same time his determination to be obeyed.'

Next, Stratford identified the need for Ottoman modernisation. While it was universally believed in the West that the Ottoman state and society had severely deteriorated over the previous century, Canning explained that the Ottoman Empire was not 'by any means in so desperate a state as strangers have supposed. The great sources of national Independence remain unimpaired, + want only a proper application to be made equal to the Exegencies of the Times. The Turks have not yet lost that high spirit of pride, + personal bravery + religious fanaticism, which formerly led them to conquest.'[7] Stratford affirmed that the Ottoman Empire was still strong and even stable but in ways which led to stagnation and had prevented the country from matching the rapid technological progress of the other European powers. Ottoman reformers had advocated breaking the grip of various traditional orders of society which had for centuries held exclusive military, social and economic power. But these orders, such as the *Derebeys* and the Janissaries, had fiercely resisted the changes.

This political struggle was still very little known to Westerners. Canning was sufficiently sophisticated to comprehend, as is clear from his report, that he had arrived at the capital of the Ottoman Empire at a pivotal moment in its long history. His report also shows that he was obviously fascinated by these politics and by the grand issue of how the Ottoman Empire would or would not open itself up to foreign institutions. Stratford was observing an important act in the great historical drama of how civilisations mix with each other. This process – which occurs at first usually via the exchange of technology but later also through the interaction of ideas – was termed 'the main drive wheel of history' by William H. McNeill.[8] Stratford understood that he was witnessing history at Constantinople.

The report was well researched and quite balanced, demonstrating Stratford's respect for Ottoman strengths and capabilities as well as his recognition of their needs. The report is in stark opposition to Stratford's emotional letters home, which were full of animosity toward his hosts. He was in a difficult situation: young and inexperienced, far from home and very out of touch with his family and friends, in a posting that was in many ways a hardship to him. He possessed some of the predominating Western attitudes toward the Ottomans, which saw them as uncivilised and hopeless. But Stratford was also able in the more healthy parts of his young mind to transcend his own difficulties and ignorance in order to perceive the abilities of the Ottomans and to be curious about them as human beings. 'Very false notions are entertained in England of the Turkish nation,' he wrote to George on 27 April 1809, a few weeks after submitting his report. 'You know much better than I do the mighty resources and native wealth which this enormous empire possesses.'[9] Stratford saw the Ottomans as real people with real possibilities. He was himself highly inspired by what J. B. Bury termed the Enlightenment 'idea of progress',[10] and, unusually for his time, he was able to apply this concept to the Ottoman Empire. Here were some of the intellectual bases of Canning's later programme of supporting the Ottoman reform movement, and in general for his deep involvement with the country over the coming half-century. Of course, his prime interest in the Ottoman Empire was always based upon his task and goal of securing Britain's route to and exploitation of India.

3

Two weeks after Stratford submitted his report, an armistice between the Ottomans and Russians collapsed and on 5 April 1809 they resumed warring in the Danubian Principalities.[11] Adair confirmed this and informed George Canning on 18 April, adding that since the 'renewal of the war on the Danube, I have received various and most urgent applications from the Ottoman Government for pecuniary assistance from his Majesty.'[12] The renewal of hostilities prompted the appointment of a new Grand Vizir, Jusuf Paşa, who assumed office on 24 April.[13] The resumption of war between the Ottomans and Russians was a catastrophe for the British, for this would weaken both powers and thus play directly into the hands of the French. After the reestablishment of relations between the British and Ottomans, the prime goal for the mission to Constantinople had been to promote peace between the Ottomans and Russians. But now that goal seemed gone and without it Stratford began to lose his enthusiasm for Constantinople and to pine for home.

He now abandoned hopes for Mahmut's reforms and dismissed the whole process, really the whole government. 'I myself am a daily witness of the personal qualities of the inhabitants, qualities which if properly directed are capable of sustaining them against a world of enemies,' he wrote to George on 27 April 1809. 'But the government is radically bad .... Destruction will not come upon this empire either *from the north or from the south*; it is rotten at the heart; the seat of corruption is in the government itself.'[14]

At some point around this time, Stratford received a shock which must have made him feel even worse. Robert Adair was still eager to leave Constantinople but no one in London could be found to replace him. Back in January 1809, when they were waiting to pass the Dardanelles, Adair had offered Stratford leadership of the embassy, but the young man had politely refused. Now Adair made a new offer to Stratford that must have had the prior approval of George Canning: to become an official secretary and then chief of mission of the British embassy to the Sublime Porte, with the rank of minister plenipotentiary,[15] with Adair leaving at the first opportunity to become British ambassador at Vienna. This was all quite unheard of for a 23-year-old. By previously agreeing to this deal, George had been able to placate Adair as well as to give Stratford a solid foundation in an important and stable profession.

Stratford could not agree or disagree. He urgently desired to return to England and his studies at Cambridge, and he had no wish for a career in the Foreign Office. But he understood that George wanted him to take the practical offer. He became the official secretary to the embassy in May 1809, but with a hope of being soon replaced. The prospect of staying on in Constantinople made Stratford increasingly discouraged. He could only hope for a replacement to come for Adair or himself, but until then he was effectively trapped in Constantinople.

David Morier was also feeling unhappy and bored in his position. He proposed to Adair that he go off to the theatre of fighting between the Ottomans and the Russians, in the Danubian Principalities, and fight on the side of the Ottomans. Adair refused Morier's romantic request but obliged instead by sending him to Persia to assist in the British mission there. Morier went off in the autumn of 1809 for ten months.

Discouragement multiplied for Stratford. On 12 June 1809 he wrote a long, pessimistic letter to his sister, Bess. It exuded loneliness, almost desperation:

> You seem to have very little expectation of my returning home within the year, yet I assure you nothing is further from my thoughts than staying here so long. The ratifications of the Treaty must come in a few days, and with them I expect leave to return. In truth I am very tired of staying abroad, and my absence has already been much longer than I bargained for. The novelty of a place, however amusing at first, cannot long recompense one for the want of society and the absence of friends. Constantinople is not a fit place for gentleman to live in, and did not political circumstances make it at this moment more interesting than usual it would be quite intolerable. However, the hope of getting away in a month will keep up my spirits, and I shall try to employ the rest of my time in leaving nothing unseen that can deserve my attention.

He described a visit he had made to the diplomatic prison at the Seven Towers, 'with all the horrors of the dungeons and dark passages.' When he was shown the apartment in which the Russian ambassador had been held 20 years earlier, 'I whistled and tried to look brave: but at the same time I felt a something which quickened my step towards the door.' He also explained in the letter that 'At present the great object of my ambition is to see the slave-market, into which Europeans are very seldom admitted.'[16] The young man must have been feeling very low to have visited one place where he could be imprisoned as a foreign representative, and to have planned a visit to another place where he could be sold as a non-Muslim slave if he were not a foreign representative. 'Be sure you do not turn Musselman,' his worried mother admonished him.[17]

Stratford needed to get away from things. The next month, at the end of July 1809, he secured leave to make a tour of Anatolia. He traveled on horseback, accompanied by a Janissary and a Greek attendant. An Ottoman ferman guaranteed him free passage and introduction to local officials. At Bursa, the old Ottoman capital, he climbed to the top of Mount Olympus, whence in the distance he could see Topkapi Saray back in Constantinople. At Smyrna, 'One of the first objects that drew my attention on the road was a threshing-floor of primitive construction, reminding me of Virgil's description in the *Georgics*: (i 173ff.).' At Ephesus he climbed through the classical sites and found the Homeric rivers, the Caÿster (*Küçük Menderes*), the Caïcus (*Bakircay*), and the Meander (*Büyük Menderes*), and 'It was with an *Iliad* in my hand that I crossed the Caÿster.' Sites and texts went together for him. Stratford would always remain 'thoroughly penetrated with a love of letters,' as *The Times* would note in its obituary of him over 70 years later.[18]

During these travels Stratford paid tribute to a prominent local family of the *Derebeys*. 'There was a wild air of grandeur about them ... The master, a hale old man with a white flowing beard and a mild expressive countenance, received me in a large saloon surrounded in Turkish fashion on three sides by a broad divan .... His manners were noble, easy, and polite.' He treated Stratford to pipes, coffee and sherbet, and gave him a carpet to sleep on. 'His family's influence, together with that of the whole class, underwent a rough curtailment when Sultan Mahmud not long afterwards realized his repressive policy at the expense of so many privileged guilds and half-independent grandees.'

Stratford must have experienced relief from his excursion to Anatolia. But the journey did not overcome his sadness, which prevailed at the last site he visited before returning to Constantinople. Mount Sipylus was the scene of one of the grimmest of all the classical legends: the liquidation of the 14 children of Niobe, demonstrating the savagery and pettiness of the gods. The Greeks, Stratford later noted in his memoir, believed the frequent rains at the foot of the mountain represented 'the tears of the unhappy mother'.[19]

David Morier had gone to Persia at the end of August 1809. Stratford was without his good friend and by November he was despondent. 'How pleasant and short is the reign of the imagination!', he wrote home now. 'A few months have passed away – my curiosity is satisfied – the novelty is gone. I have seen all that is to be seen, and wish only to see it no more. I should not regret the cessation of these amusements if there were any society in which we could take refuge ... But we are completely insulated, and living only in a state of honourable banishment. With the exception of the few English who are here, and of the Austrian, Spanish and Swedish missions – all very meager – the Christian population of this city is an *omnium gatherum* from all the dunghills of Europe.'[20]

'My heart was not there,' Stratford understood and wrote in retirement many years later. 'I had no predilection for diplomacy. My tastes, my hopes, my prospects were at home, in my native land, in its gigantic metropolis, the seat of enlightened legislation, of civilizing power, and of honourable contention for the greatest results of thought and the noblest prizes of ambition.'[21] He was desperate to get home, to resume his studies and to aim for a career in Parliament. Morier starkly summed up Canning's situation in a letter from Persia on 7 November 1809: 'My dear fellow, who the devil will consent to take your place at Constantinople? So there you must stick till the Lord have mercy on you.'[22]

4

The next week Stratford learnt from a French newspaper the bad news from home which had been purposely kept from him. On 21 September 1809 George Canning had fought a duel with his colleague, Castlereagh, over a Cabinet intrigue. According to the account, George was only mildly wounded in the leg but the scandal had forced him to resign as foreign secretary. 'I trust in God that it is not true – but if it be, I shall indeed be very unhappy,' Stratford wrote to George on 14 November 1809. 'If you can but write me a word of comfort, in either case, you will make me grateful.'[23]

The news was devastating for Stratford and must have exacerbated his loneliness at Constantinople, especially as he lacked confirmation of the details of the duel. He must have feared having lost his mentor and surrogate father as well as a connection at the top of government. And he must have contemplated throwing everything up, quitting the Foreign Office, and running back to London.

Stratford eventually received a letter from his friend and regular correspondent, Joseph Planta, a précis writer at the Foreign Office and later the undersecretary there. Planta confirmed that George Canning was not seriously injured but that he was indeed out of office. 'With respect to your situation, he will write to you himself; he repeatedly presses all your relations and friends to beg you not to be *romantic*; he wishes you to stay quietly where you are, however disagreeable it may at present be to you, and to wait and hope for the best, in the quiet discharge of the duties of your embassy.'[24]

George made the decisive intervention with a fatherly letter he then sent to Stratford on 9 October 1809: 'I may or may not have it in my power at some future time to take you by the hand again. If not, you have a profession in which you may be useful to your country and do credit to your friends and to yourself, and you must not lightly abandon it.'[25] Stratford followed the advice of his beloved cousin and mentor, staying in his position at Constantinople and not quitting the Foreign Office, for which he later consoled himself philosophically in a letter to his sister, Bess: 'In this world we are often called upon to obey without knowing why, and to give up the exercise of our own reason to the advice of others.'[26]

Even though Stratford acquiesced in George's wishes, he could not resist an aggrieved tone in his response. 'I will not dwell upon the disadvantage of being so long a period thrown out of all society and cut off from my friends of my own age. . .', Stratford wrote to George. He also affirmed his right to opt out later. 'I will stay here quietly till Mr. Adair goes; after his departure, which will probably be about the end of February, I will take an early opportunity of writing for permission to return to England simply on the score of health.'[27] In fact he did not even wait for Adair's departure, which was delayed until July 1810.[28] On 6 February 1810 Adair communicated to the Foreign Office Stratford's formal request to be released from duty for health reasons.[29]

Stratford's request was not an empty one. E. D. Clarke, a British traveller who visited Constantinople 1800–02, observed there:

> inevitable consequences of ill health among Englishmen … There was hardly one of our countrymen, then resident in the *capital*, who did not experience occasional attacks of intermittent fever …. *Constantinople* is by no means a healthy place of residence, for persons who have not lived long enough there, to become inured to the vicissitudes of its climate. The sudden changes of temperature, owing to the draught of wind through the straits, either of the *Black Sea*, or of the *Sea of Marmora*, render such persons liable to the most fatal effects of obstructed perspirations; and what these effects are, few of the inhabitants of other countries can have formed any adequate ideas.[30]

Stratford's request to be released from the mission on health grounds was never granted. He was indeed stranded in Constantinople, as Morier had suggested. The future master diplomat had done everything in his power to quit the city and the Foreign Office and he had failed.

5

George Canning's successor as foreign secretary, Richard Wellesley, the Marquess Wellesley (oldest brother of the Duke of Wellington), had recently offered Constantinople to George Hamilton Gordon, the 4th Earl of Aberdeen. He rejected it as an empty post, explaining that he fully expected the Ottoman Empire to be invaded or controlled soon by either Russia or France and thus, he thought, a British minister at Constantinople would be useless. Going there 'would scarcely be compatible with the duty I owe to my family or to myself,' Aberdeen declared in a written response to Wellesley. He also found that the complicated situation of the Greeks, who were beginning to assert themselves more strongly against their Ottoman overlords, 'would deserve the employment of abilities and activity far greater than mine.'[31]

Aberdeen was at this time, according to Harold Nicolson, 'ignorant of continental conditions, and known only to his contemporaries as a traveller in the Levant, and as one of the earliest of our Philhellenes.' Very well-connected and 'a precocious young man', he received various offers of major diplomatic posts and was adept at rejecting them, including Sicily in 1807 when he was 23 years old, St. Petersburg in 1809 when he was 25 years old, and Constantinople in 1810. Finally he accepted Vienna in 1813 but 'only under great pressure' and then he handled the position poorly, according to Nicolson.[32]

Aberdeen's tendency to reject appointments, and his posting as ambassador to Vienna at a critical moment, were considered also by Rory Muir, an authority on Britain's defeat of Napoleon:

> Even when every allowance has been made for the need to send a man of rank, and for the spirit of the age, it was an extraordinary choice. Aberdeen was only twenty-nine years old, had never held public office, and his chief qualification, other than his title, was that Pitt and Dundas had been his guardians. This patronage had evidently singled him out for a brilliant career and he had already declined a number of diplomatic posts offered by Wellesley and Castlereagh. He accepted the Austrian embassy with some hesitation, soon regretted his decision, and within weeks of arriving on the Continent was seeking to return home.[33]

Aberdeen and Stratford would have many complex and strained dealings concerning Greek independence in the 1820s, the Ottoman apostasy controversy in the 1840s, and the Crimean War in the 1850s.

6

There was no news about a replacement for Adair. Stratford's difficult situation and bad mood were aggravated by a massive fire in Pera, the diplomatic quarter of Constantinople, on 21 April 1810. The main embassy building, the 'English Palace', was spared, but all of its offices were destroyed. The neighbouring homes and personal possessions of Adair, Morier and two dragomans were also lost. Adair reported it to be 'one of the most dreadful fires ever remembered at this place,' with many thousands of houses destroyed. 'I have to acknowledge with gratitude the Sultan's great attention to me.[34] He was present during the whole of this distressing day, and sent the Caimacam [Ottoman governor of the city] to the [English] Palace with orders to save it at every risque,' Adair wrote in his dispatch to the Foreign Office, dated 22 April 1810. 'But the savage behavior of the mob,' Adair added to his dispatch, 'far exceeded what I could have expected from the most unfeeling barbarians. One person was detected by my servants endeavouring to convey fire from the burning Offices to the Palace. Others were guilty of the most shocking excesses.'[35]

Stratford also seems to have been disturbed more by the conduct of the populace than the fire itself. 'While the fire was raging, no Water was to be obtained but at an exorbitant price,' as Stratford recorded in his official report of the fire, 'the assistance of the Porters – the protection of the Guards – the smallest exertions of the Publick Firemen were all to be bought at the same rate. Such was the insolence and rapacity of these People, that the expense of saving property amounted in some instances to more than would have been requisite to replace it. The Caimacam himself was obliged to purchase obedience to the Sultan's orders with handfulls of Gold.'[36]

The British embassy faced not only practical hardships but also real political danger. The Ottoman capital was just one and a half years removed from bloody court revolutions and further mass upheavals were a concern. 'We fear that the intelligence of the progress of the Russian arms will excite an insurrection at Constantinople the moment the people are acquainted with it,' as was proclaimed in the German newspapers and reprinted in the British press, 'and that then the life of Mr. Adair, who has many enemies in that city, and even in the Divan, will be in great danger.'[37] Such a prospect must have also weighed on the young Stratford.

By the end of May 1810, Adair was finally scheduled to take his formal leave of the Ottoman government, according to tradition, in

separate audiences with the Kaymakam (standing in for the Grand
Vizir, who was serving at the theatre of fighting with the Russians in
the Danubian Principalities) and the Sultan. The prospect of being
left on his own at Constantinople drove Stratford deeper into
despondency. Even though no replacement was coming, and despite
the frank assessment of David Morier, Stratford simply could not
accept that he was staying on for the indefinite future. 'I trust I shall
soon be at liberty to scramble over the distance which separates us at
this moment,' he wrote home to a school friend in what sounds like a
state of denial. He recognised, as he wrote in the letter, that he was
located in a very exciting place diplomatically, including the war
between Ottomans and Russians, the question whether Austria
would join France, the developing revolt in Greece. But all of this, he
declared, 'have failed to do away my detestation of this vile hole – or
this *infâme trou,* as Mr. Adair used to call it.'[38]

7

It must have been a pleasant diversion for Stratford when, also at this
time, Lord Byron arrived in town. After months of travels in Greece,
the poet had made his storied swim across the Hellespont on 3 May
1810. About one week later he sailed up to the Ottoman capital on
HMS Salsette which had come to take Adair home.

Byron and Stratford were unlikely associates but actually slightly
acquainted. They had played against each other in the first cricket
match of the Eton *versus* Harrow series, held at what is now Dorset
Square on 2 August 1805.[39] Here in Constantinople they took rides
together, including to the Sweet Waters of Europe, the pleasant fields
at the source of the Golden Horn, on 24 May 1810.[40] A few days later
Byron returned to examine the nearby land-walls of the city,
constructed under the Byzantine Emperor Theodosius in the fifth
century AD. Byron wrote in a letter to his mother:

> The ride by the walls of the city on the land side is beautiful,
> imagine, four miles of immense triple battlements covered with
> Ivy, surrounded with 218 towers, and on the other side of the

road Turkish burying grounds (the loveliest spots on earth) full
of enormous cypresses. I have seen the ruins of Athens, of
Ephesus, and Delphi, I have traversed a great part of Turkey,
and many other parts of Europe and some of Asia, but I never
beheld a work of Nature or Art, which yielded an impression
like the prospect on each side, from the Seven Towers to the
End of the Golden Horn.[41]

A few days earlier 'we went up the Tower of Galata,' as Byron's
travelling companion, John Cam Hobhouse, the later Lord
Broughton, recorded their excursion to the old Genoese quarter of
the city. '147 steps – hollow tower with a habitation at the top, view
of every part of this beautiful city...'[42]

Byron and Hobhouse saw Stratford often. Hobhouse recorded in
his travel journal that he thought 'Mr Canning a pleasing young man'
but with a vulgar voice. And Hobhouse wrote that Byron 'praises
him much'.[43] On 20 May 1810 Stratford showed Hobhouse the
paintings of local scenes and officials which he had commissioned
from the local Greek painter.[44] On 10 June 1810, Hobhouse 'dined at
the palace [embassy] where staid till late with Mr. C who says he has a
friend whom he loves as a brother. He did indeed talk of him with
tears in his eyes.'[45] Doubtlessly it was David Morier, off in Persia
since the previous autumn, whom Stratford was deeply missing here.
And during breakfast on 6 July 1810, Stratford shared with
Hobhouse his 'Account of the Three Last Insurrections at
Constantinople, and of the Present State of the Turkish Empire,'
which he had submitted to Adair in March 1809. This report
'I recollected as well as possible and wrote down on the end of this
book,' as Hobhouse recorded in his journal,[46] apparently impressed
with Stratford's work. These notes are still extant today.

8

Adair's farewell audience with the Kaymakam was scheduled for 28
May 1810 at Topkapi Saray, the seat of the Ottoman government.
The mysteries of Topkapi, the chambers and ceremonials of the great

inner sanctum, were still rarely seen by outsiders. Byron was invited along by Adair and was keen to participate, although he strenuously protested when he learnt that according to protocol he would have to walk at the end of the ambassadorial procession because the Ottomans did not recognise non-diplomatic, domestic rank. Byron agreed to follow behind the ambassador but he insisted that he was entitled to go before Stratford, who was still the secretary of the embassy. Adair consulted with the dean of the diplomatic corps of Constantinople, the Austrian Internuncio, who confirmed that the Ottomans would not recognise Byron's rank and that he thus had to pass behind all of the officials of the embassy, Canning included.

Undeterred, Byron showed up at the British Palace early in the morning of the day of the ceremony just as the embassy was preparing for the excursion down the hill of Galata and across the Golden Horn to Topkapi Saray. 'Lord Byron arrived in scarlet regimentals topped by a profusely feathered cocked hat,' Stratford later recorded in his memoir, 'and coming up to me asked what his place, as a peer of the realm, was to be in the procession.' It was a dramatic, last-minute attempt by Byron to secure a respectable standing. Stratford immediately referred Byron's request to Adair and a lengthy negotiation ensued, 'and the upshot of their private interview,' according to Stratford, 'was that as the Turks ignored all but officials, any amateur, although a peer, must be content to follow in the wake of the Embassy. His lordship thereupon walked away with that look of scornful indignation which so well became his fine imperious features.'[47] Hobhouse also recorded in his journal that Byron 'went away because he would not suffer Mr. Canning to walk before him.'[48] Fifty-six years later Stratford would recall Byron as 'Self-banish'd victim of a wayward mood,/Condemn'd for self to live, on self to brood.'[49]

Byron was so upset about the incident that he decided to quit the city. That evening, as Hobhouse recorded, 'I dined at the palace [British embassy] but Byron did not, indeed I found him packing up and going the day after but one to Smyrna ...'[50] Byron changed his mind and did not leave but he remained moody for several more days. Three days later, on 31 May 1810, Hobhouse made an excursion with Canning to the upper Bosphorus. There they met Adair in the village of Büyükdere at the home of a European financier with whom he was staying. Taking Adair's barge, they rowed into the opening of the Black Sea, the *Symplegades* of the ancient Greeks who knew it to open and close, such as during the voyage of Jason and the Argonauts. Here Hobhouse and Canning visited several monuments and sites and climbed the hills. When they returned to the diplomatic quarter, Pera, in the evening, as Hobhouse recorded, 'Byron asked me how I did – and then turned sulky, and so went to bed,'[51] upset that Hobhouse had not invited him along on the excursion. The next morning Hobhouse received a letter from Byron in which he announced that he was 'dissolving partnership, to which I replied in pencil as well as my surprise would suffer me to do.'[52]

The temperamental poet once again relented. He managed to recover his composure and to mend fences with Hobhouse as well as with his hosts. He eventually had his own excursion on Adair's barge to the upper Bosphorus and Black Sea and the surrounding sites and villages. And he also participated in the ambassador's second farewell audience at Topkapi Saray, held with the Sultan himself on 10 July 1810.[53] A week before this Byron wrote a contrite letter to Adair, expressing regret over the trouble he had caused the ambassador, accepting the verdict of having to pass at the end of the procession, and creatively invoking *Deuteronomy*, chapter 5, verse 21, to the effect of: 'I shall therefore make what atonement I can by cheerfully following not only your excellency "but your servant or your maid, your ox or your ass, or any thing that is yours."'[54] Byron later sent a written apology also to Stratford.[55]

Adair accepted Byron's biblical plea and invited him to attend the audience with the Sultan. Byron 'redeemed his pledge by joining the procession as a simple individual and delighting those who were nearest to him by his well-bred cheerfulness and good-humoured wit,' as Stratford described the moment in his memoir.[56] Byron was no doubt thoroughly pleased a little later during the audience itself at

Topkapi Saray when he was treated with distinction. During the ritual feeding, Byron was seated at one of the main dining tables along with Çelik Efendi, Canning, Captain Bathurst of *HMS Salsette* and Hobhouse.[57] After the meal came the ritual clothing of the embassy by the Ottomans in preparation for the actual encounter with the Sultan in the *Arz Odasi* or throne room, and here Byron was dressed in a ceremonial robe of high rank.[58]

In the visit of Byron, Stratford found some joy precisely when he needed it most, as Adair was leaving him on his own as head of mission in Constantinople. Stratford had no idea how long he would remain in the service of the Foreign Office. 'But I most sincerely hope not very long,' he wrote home, 'at least in this part of the world.'[59]

9

Two days after the audience of farewell with the Sultan, on 12 July 1810, Adair delivered to Stratford 'the cyphers and official correspondence of his Majesty's embassy at this Court; and I have at the same time committed to his care the Separate and Secret Article, hitherto unexchanged, of the Treaty of the Dardanelles,' as Adair reported to the Marquess Wellesley. On 14 July 1810 at three in the afternoon Stratford accompanied Adair down to the harbour of Constantinople.[60] The ambassador boarded *HMS Salsette*, which sailed off to Malta that evening with Byron and Hobhouse also on board.[61] Adair carried with him a farewell letter composed the day before by his young assistant. 'I feel deeply indebted to you,' Stratford had written, 'not only for the numberless kind offices which you have extended to me in common with others, but for the patience with which you have so generously reposed in me.' The theme of patience played prominently in the letter. 'Again and again, I thank you, and sincerely beg your pardon for any faults that I may have committed against you in moments of impatience and irritation.' Stratford was correct in this self-recognition. For the rest of his days he would be prone to bouts of 'impatience and irritation'. But here he was also demonstrating the precociousness that David Morier had immediately recognised in him upon their first meeting. It rings throughout Stratford's farewell to Adair:

> I have had the singular good fortune to become acquainted with you just at that period of life when the mind is most open to lasting impressions of good and evil, and I venture to hope that the remembrance of your example will never cease to influence my conduct when you are too far off to direct me by your advice.

Adair would indeed always remain an example for Stratford. The diplomatic tools that the ambassador had used so well on the mission to the Dardanelles – such as interpreting both the word and spirit of instructions from home, and hinting that relations might be broken off and that the British navy could be called to the Straits – would be utilised by Stratford throughout the remaining two years of his present mission as well as on his many future missions at Constantinople over the next 48 years. And Adair had been not only a diplomatic mentor but also a father figure to the young man. 'Will you excuse me, my dear sir,' Stratford concluded his farewell, 'when I say that my feelings towards you are those of a son towards an indulgent father? To this I can add nothing but a hope that you will never fail to believe me.'[62]

Adair replied from sea the next day with fatherly support and affection. He wrote to Stratford:

> I esteem you for the powers of your mind, and I love you for your many virtues: among the first of which I class a proud and independent spirit which I remarked in you from our earliest acquaintance. This spirit is to me so sacred, wherever I find it, that I cannot bear to check even its faults; for its faults are part of its virtues ... When these are accompanied with a warm and kind heart, which I know yours to be in an extreme degree, I say in two words that I am content with the man framed of such materials. He is good enough for me, and I am happy when I can call him my friend. Fare you well!'[63]

Robert Adair and Stratford Canning remained friends and continued to correspond for more than 40 years. The young diplomat would always maintain the warmest feeling for his teacher of diplomacy. 'No man possessed a more generous heart, a clearer head, or a kinder disposition,' wrote Stratford in retirement.[64]

In two years Stratford had gone from undergraduate at Cambridge to minister plenipotentiary at Constantinople. He had been separated from George Canning and then had gravitated to Adair but was now also deprived of him. Located at the diplomatic centre of a gathering continental conflagration – with the Ottoman and Russian empires at war, the British at war with the French, the Russians and French tenuously allied, the French approaching and all of Europe at the brink – Stratford had to fend for his country and himself completely on his own.

PART II

RUSSIAN-OTTOMAN PEACE, 1810–12

Yedi Kule, the Ottoman fortress of Seven Towers, and the site of *Porta Aurea* or the Golden Gate portal of the Byzantine emperors. Located at the southern end of the fifth-century Theodosian Walls of Constantinople. On his visit to the city in 1810, Byron wrote of the walls, 'I never beheld a work of Nature or Art, which yielded an impression like the prospect on each side...'.

CHAPTER 4

CHIEF OF MISSION

1

The new chief of mission of the British embassy at Constantinople had trained on the job as assistant and then secretary for a total of two years, was still in the middle of his university education and had not yet achieved 24 years of age. Stratford's instructions were to promote peace between the Ottoman and Russian empires, old rivals who had been fighting for most of the previous four years, who were at war for the fifth time in the last 100 years, and who would go to war four more times over the next 104 years.[1] The impossible mission had frustrated and driven away two of Stratford's predecessors within the past three years. His host, the Ottoman government, was the sole neutral power in Europe during the Napoleonic Wars and still emerging from two years of bloody court revolutions that had included the execution of two Sultans, a Grand Vizir and many other statesmen. His personal finances could not support the costs of the position, and his health could not withstand the climate. His communication with home required four months in each direction, and he was utterly homesick. Canning did not want to be in the Foreign Office and had several times asked to be relieved from the mission without success as no replacement could be found at home. He would not learn the local language, could not get many books in his own language, had with him only one friend his age and no elder on whom to depend. 'It was only by assuming a tone of self-confidence and determination,' he recalled many years later, 'that I could hope to make up for want of years, experience, and authority.'[2]

Stratford Canning also marshalled a much more practical source as he took over the complicated mission to Constantinople in July 1810. He inherited from Robert Adair an unusual line of communication with the Russian government. This went from the British minister in Constantinople to his Neapolitan colleague there, Count Ludoff, via Vienna to the Neapolitan minister at Petersburg, the Duke de Sierra Capriola, and from him to the Russian government.[3] This roundabout route provided the British and Russians with a means of communication otherwise not possible because of the state of war between them produced by the Russian–French alliance of the Treaty of Tilsit of July 1807. As France was widely expected to move against Russia sometime soon, both London and Petersburg now desired some sort of communication.

The Ottomans agreed to allow the line despite their strong concern that the British and Russians might be planning their own secret alliance. Only three years had passed since Duckworth's breaching of the Dardanelles and assault upon Constantinople in the spring of 1807, a product of British and Russian diplomatic collaboration. And back in July 1770 the Ottomans had suffered a devastating attack upon their Mediterranean fleet at Çeşme by a Russian fleet that had circled Europe via the English Channel and had on the way received repairs and supplies at British ports. 'The sudden appearance of these forces in the Mediterranean,' as M. S. Anderson described it, 'was one of the most spectacular events of the eighteenth century.'[4] So now in 1810 the Ottomans were understandably suspicions about the plans of the British and Russians. They permitted this line of communication because it served their own interests to allow the British to prod the Russians towards peace. The Ottomans required the line to be open for their examination – 'ostensible' to them, in diplomatic parlance – and they read all correspondence.

Stratford felt 'strongly persuaded' that the line was crucial and that he must keep it up and running by means of regular correspondence. This he did primarily with essays consisting of his 'reflections on the fate of affairs between Turkey + Russia,' as he explained in his report to the British foreign secretary, the Marquess Wellesley.[5] Stratford's argument in all of these communications to the Russians was that they should make peace with the Ottomans as soon as possible because Ottoman demands for terms would logically rise after a French attack against Russia.

This indirect line of communication comprised a virtual British mediation for peace. It was indeed a very modest mediation and totally peripheral. But it was still something, and Stratford cultivated it as a diplomatic tool that afforded him status with the Ottomans. His expectation that the line to the Russians would prove 'its eventual utility' was correct.

Stratford also cultivated his own line to the Ottoman government. He diligently sent them regular 'extracts' or analyses concerning the military situation in Western Europe.[6] The point of these was to demonstrate to the Ottomans that, as they could soon be attacked by France, they should recognise the British as a valuable ally and that they must make peace with the Russians now before an attack by the French would make it more costly later.

Stratford's other goal here was to disguise his weak position by prominently pronouncing his diplomatic voice to the Ottoman government. This technique of seizing the epistolary initiative, by sending lengthy and frequent communications to his host government, had been produced by the exigencies of the mission. It also evolved naturally from Stratford's fondness for composition and his textual approach to life. These proved useful to him also in his reporting function, 'the business of an ambassador to keep his government informed of events and opinion in the country where he serves ... his rôle of foreign correspondent to his sovereign', as the task was described by the British diplomatic historian, J. E. Neale.[7] Sending detailed and regular written reportage to both his host and home governments would remain a basic component of Stratford's diplomatic success throughout his career.

2

Just as Adair departed Constantinople in July 1810 and Stratford took over the mission, David Morier returned from his ten-month assignment in Persia.[8] He did so out of concern and loyalty to his friend. Stratford had started sending David requests to come back to Constantinople as soon as he had learnt from Adair that he was to be left alone in charge of the embassy. Stratford sorely needed the company of his friend to help him face the responsibilities of the difficult mission. Morier complied because he felt that 'it would be a great sin in my eyes to leave him so long as I can be useful. . .' as he explained in a letter to his mother. 'He is a young man whom I honour and whom I esteem in the highest degree.' In the spring of 1811 Morier would reject an offer to accompany a new Persian embassy to London and serve there as its assistant (apparently he had been well liked at the Persian court). He longed for home as much as Stratford did but he refused to abandon his friend. 'As long as Canning is kept here,' he explained in his letter refusing the Persian offer, 'without any other assistance than what he derives from my fingers, I cannot think of leaving him.'[9]

David Morier's loyalty was not naive. It had been tested by Stratford's temper. During the mission to Persia, David had written to Stratford in response to some sort of work problem that 'even at this distance I stand in awe of your lash. Pray spare me on this occasion. Were it not for that single defect, for it is a great one, you would be the best fellow I know.'[10] Morier further lamented Stratford's difficult character in a long letter to his mother, dated 31 August 1810:

> It is as much through a sense of duty as through character that I overlook some things which cause me more irritation than perhaps a christian should feel; but I willingly pardon him the moment the first irritation passes, and I just hope for his sake that he will never have business with someone with as much spirit and the same humours as his own.[11]

Stratford's difficult habits were primarily due to his own character. But they must have been exacerbated by the challenging circumstances. He was under a lot of pressure as a very young and inexperienced chief of mission in a post no one else would fill, in a country where foreign representatives could be imprisoned by the host government upon declaration of war. And all of this was faced by Stratford as the Russian–Ottoman regional war plodded on and the French continental war approached.

Morier recognised Stratford's difficult position and sympathised with the 'vexations arising from his responsibilities'.[12] The challenge was made worse by the fact that Constantinople, despite its being one of the great pleasure domes of the world, did not offer at that time practical possibilities for socialising that would be realistic for a young Englishman like Stratford. Proper Western society there was reduced and fractured because of the war. Almost all of the Western embassies were either closed or under French influence. A British visitor to Constantinople at this time, John Galt, observed:

> The whole varieties of the Frank society, with the exception of the half dozen gentlemen who compose our Embassy and Levant factory, may be considered under the snub and controul of the French minister. The British traveller, therefore, with respect to the Franks, finds himself an excluded being.[13]

Local Levantine young ladies did not appeal to Stratford because he looked down on them as less than refined. 'A lady according to our English notions,' he had written home to a friend in November 1809, 'is here an unknown animal. One might as well talk of a red goose.'[14]

The scruples of Canning and Morier would never have permitted them to explore deeply the abundant exotic entertainments of Pera, the Westerners' enclave and diplomatic quarter of Constantinople where the English Palace was located. Pera, present-day Beyoğlu, was advanced in its possibilities for intemperance and licentiousness. It attracted pleasuremongers from the ends of the earth, including diplomats, soldiers-of-fortune, merchants and adventurers, many of whom enjoyed the protection of ill-gotten *berats*. Morier detested 'the miserable apathy of a Pera life ... which is the very perfection of moral vegetation.'[15] He grew concerned that 'here my heart has become closed and as cold as ice . . . . Day after day goes by in which I see no one whose company I want. Canning is only 24, I only 27, yet we lead the life of two Trappist monks. I swear I would hang myself were hemp not so dear.'[16] The two monkish young men were living and working right in the middle of a perpetual Saturnalia.

Their living conditions were also challenging in that Pera was extremely congested and deficient in proper sanitation. According to E. D. Clarke, a British visitor to Constantinople in late 1800 and early 1801 and again in early 1802 (already quoted above concerning the challenging climate of the city):

> There can scarcely be found a spot upon earth more detestable then *Péra*; particularly in the most crowded part of it. We might be said to live in *cemeteries*; the only water used for drinking, passing through sepulchres to the feverish lips of the inhabitants, filled with all sorts of revolting impurities and even with living *animalculae*. The owner of the hotel where we resided, wishing to make some repairs in his dwelling, dug near the foundation, and found that his house stood upon graves, yet containing the mouldering reliques of the dead. This perhaps may account for the swarms of *rats*; not only in the buildings, but in the streets; whither they resort in such numbers at night, that a person passing through them finds these animals running against his legs. The prodigious multitude, however, of the *rats* is not owing to any want of *cats*; for the latter constitute the greater nuisance of the two. They enter through the crazy roofs, which consist only of a few thin planks, and render the smell of the bedchambers much more offensive than that of a dunghill.[17]

Aside from the boisterous and untidy nature of the neighbourhood, the young Stratford Canning and David Morier were also challenged by the state of their living quarters, the English Palace. It was located right in the middle of Pera and had become very run down during the year and a half it was closed and empty before the arrival of Adair's embassy. When they had first come to Constantinople in late January

1809 the palace was in such bad shape that it was unfit for habitation.[18] Morier found the palace functionally inadequate and called it 'a melancholy monument of the blunders of diplomatic architecturising...'[19]

The situation which the young men faced was certainly challenging. But, again, there is no denying that Stratford's irritable aspect was mostly due to his own nature and had been evident before he ever got to Constantinople. His own mother, Mehitabel, was concerned about her son's temper. 'I fancy I see you storming and raving when all this ill-news arrives,' she wrote to him about some family issue in 1809, advising him to 'moderate the impetuosity of your character; it is highly necessary to do so among foreigners and strangers. It is the only thing in your personality that I have any fear of.'[20] The development of Stratford's personality may have been affected by a 'sharp illness' which struck him when he was 17 years old. According to an obscure reference to it in his memoir, 'a skilful and amiable physician ... carried me through it, but it left traces in my constitution, and I became more studious and less spirited.'[21]

3

Stratford's prime diplomatic assignments – promoting peace between the Ottomans and Russians, counteracting French moves in the region – were complicated by an urgent problem. French pirates were taking captured British ships into Ottoman ports on the Aegean and sometimes even selling their goods there. The Ottoman government had not moved against the practice partly because of their desire not to antagonise the French. And some local officials looked the other way because they were making a profit.

Stratford could not make any progress. 'I find great difficulty with the Reis Efendi in commercial matters,' he recorded in reference to the French piracy on 3 August 1810. 'The Turks are not even anxious to keep up an appearance of justice. Money is what they want, + for that they will go to any lengths. Their fear of the French seems to be as great as ever...' The next day Stratford instructed his dragoman, Bartholomeo Pisani, to deliver a *note verbale* to the Reis Efendi, expressing disappointment over Ottoman inaction and warning that: 'Mr. Canning entreats His Excellency to consider well the consequences of wontonly trespassing upon the rights of His Majesty's subjects.' A few days later Stratford scheduled a conference for himself with the Reis Efendi 'in the hope of bringing him to reason, + of avoiding, if possible, a quarrel with the Porte.'[22]

Before this conference took place, 'Pisani told me,' as Stratford recorded on 11 August 1810, 'that the Dragomans of the Porte had desired him to ask me, though not officially, if it were possible to induce the English Factory to lend the Porte 3 or 4 thousand Purses [of Ottoman Piastres], offering some of the highest officers of the State as security.'[23] When reply was made that the English merchants were unable to raise the money, the Ottoman government then requested a loan from the British government itself while this time offering that 'the richest Servants of the State should stand security for the payment of the loan.'[24] Stratford refused. These unusual offers perhaps support his impression that the Ottoman government was waiting for financial assistance from Britain before moving against the French piracy.

The conference with the Reis Efendi took place on 20 August 1810. It lasted 'nearly from midday to Sunset' but got nowhere, devolving into haggling about details. 'When I left the room,' Stratford recorded that day, 'just as much business was done as when I went into it. Much anger on both sides, expressed on mine + disguised on theirs.'[25]

Another danger to British shipping in the Mediterranean came from pirates of the Barbary states of North Africa, a somewhat autonomous Ottoman province. On this matter also the Ottoman government would provide Stratford with no assistance or assurances. He therefore instructed Pisani on 7 September to tell the Reis Efendi that if the Ottomans did not do something about the Barbary pirates then 'he must not be surprised, otherwise, if the English Commanders take the matter into their own hands.'[26] Stratford's threat of military action in Ottoman waters and ports was severe and daring, especially as he had absolutely no authorisation from London to undertake military action, and as he was simultaneously preaching peace to the Ottomans in their war with the Russians.

4

Information on the war between the Ottomans and Russians in the Danubian Principalities was scarce. But Stratford was growing concerned that the Ottomans may in fact be on the verge of defeat, a result which would drive them into the arms of France. Stratford recorded on 28 September 1810:

> I told Pisani to say to the Reis Efendi that the more I considered the state of things, as it was known to me, at the Camp, the more uneasiness I felt. I begged him to let me know whether the Porte had taken into consideration the possibility of the Grand Vizir's army being beaten, + what resources it would then have to depend upon. He treated this lightly; firmly denied the probability of the Grand Vizir being beaten, + and then expatiated upon the number + bravery of the troops that remained.[27]

Despite the Reis Efendi's claims, Stratford observed that the Porte was descending into a dark mood concerning the war. On 2 October 1810 he recorded: 'Pisani writes me word this day: "No fresh news from the Camp, nor any other quarter." Turkish ministers in a very ill-humour.'[28] Stratford's observation was confirmed four days later in a meeting he held with the Kaymakam and the Reis Efendi, on 6 October 1810. 'I can scarcely describe to Your Lordship,' Stratford reported to Wellesley, 'the dejection into which the Ministers of the Porte have been thrown by the misconduct of the Vizir, and the misfortunes of the Army.'[29]

At this meeting the Kaymakam and Reis Efendi confronted Stratford with their suspicion that Britain and Russia had made a secret alliance against Ottoman interests. Stratford denied it but was unable to demonstrate it well with any new diplomatic information. Stratford had actually received no communications at all from

London since he had taken over the mission. 'The delay of every hour increases my embarrassment,' he explained to Wellesley in his request for instructions on 19 October 1810.[30] And in his prior dispatch to the Foreign Office on 3 October he had identified 'the total want of intelligence as well from England as from the Mediterranean.'[31] The next day he again pleaded to Wellesley: 'I am anxious to be provided with Your Lordship's Instructions respecting the language which it will be expedient for me to hold on such an occasion.' Stratford also explained that he might be forced to undertake serious measures due to 'distance from home and the rapid Succession of events ... even before I shall be honoured with Your Lordship's instructions.'[32]

Stratford suffered not only from the absence of direction but also from the inability to read aloud from or exhibit official dispatches from London in order to demonstrate to his Ottoman counterparts that he had backing from his government for his words and actions. No amount of authoritative style and prolific pronouncement could cover the obvious fact that he had been left in the dark by his home government. On the other hand, having no instructions left him somewhat at liberty to act however he saw fit.

Over and over, for a year and a half – from October 1810 to March 1812 – Stratford politely begged Wellesley for instructions about how to handle the Ottoman–Russian war and the French piracy. Wellesley never once responded to any of Stratford's diplomatic reports and requests. 'I concluded,' Stratford later recalled in his memoir, 'that the great man overlooked so insignificant a youth as myself, until it came to my knowledge that his brother at Cadiz [the Duke of Wellington] fared no better.'[33]

The Duke and his older brother, William Wellesley-Pole,[34] also regretted their oldest brother's professional delinquency. 'I understand that he hardly does any business at his Office, that nobody can procure access to him, and that his whole time is passed with Moll...' wrote Wellesley-Pole in March 1810 in reference to Wellesley's mistress, as was discovered by Rory Muir. To this the Duke responded on 6 April 1810, 'I wish that Wellesley was *castrated*; or that he would like other people attend to his business and perform too. It is lamentable to see Talents & character & advantages such as he possesses thrown away upon Whoring.'[35] Francis James Jackson, a British diplomat, observed on 22 February 1811, 'I have not yet seen Lord Wellesley. He never goes to the Office, and is visible nowhere but in his harem.'[36]

An authority on the history of British Foreign Office administration, Charles Ronald Middleton, found Wellesley to be:

...the most languid of foreign secretaries. He rarely corresponded with a diplomatic corps that at that time always numbered fewer than five. He procrastinated in preparing dispatches until Spencer Perceval, the prime minister, was forced to write him ultimatums to send them immediately. He filled the air with complaints about the ability of his colleagues to manage the war, about Perceval's qualities as head of the administration, and about the insufficient aid he felt his brother was getting for his Peninsular campaigns. He resigned in 1812 amidst scenes of mutual recrimination. John Wilson Croker, a shrewd judge of men, not unjustly called him the most brilliant incapacity in England.[37]

Wellesley's poor professional conduct as foreign secretary was addressed even by the editor of his own collected papers, L. S. Benjamin:

From the general tenor of Wellesley's letters during the period he was at the Foreign Office, it is clear that he was not contented with the policy of the Government, while for the Prime Minister [Perceval] he had a contempt that he did not trouble to disguise. Never, owing to his autocratic attitude, on very intimate terms with his colleagues, as time passed his relations with them became more and more strained, until in 1811 he rarely attended the Cabinet councils, and managed his own department without consulting anyone.[38]

The historian Philip Guedalla, whose many works include a biography of the Duke of Wellington, suggested in 1927 that

Wellesley's problems as a statesman at home were due to his previous imperial experience as British overlord in India. Guedalla wrote:

> There is something about the temporary occupation of an Oriental throne that seems to unfit its tenants for a more even gait...When a satrap is returned empty from his province, there is no sadder sight than his continued efforts .... the after-lives of viceroys have all the bitterness of fallen royalty without any of its faintly romantic quality. Of this depressing type the Marquess Wellesley is a conspicuous and familiar instance. He reached his greatest eminence in Calcutta before he was forty; and for the remainder of a long life he revolved gloomily round Dublin Castle and the Foreign Office in the hopeless endeavour to live within his reputation.[39]

Wellesley indeed seems to have suffered a collapse of some sort after his return from India to Britain in 1805. 'I am so fatigued and broken with long exertions and ungrateful returns that I believe my career is terminated...' he wrote to his oldest son, Richard.[40]

It seems most likely that Wellesley simply did not read Stratford's dispatches and that he was totally uninformed of the diplomatic situation in the whole eastern Mediterranean region. Wellesley sent a first communication to his embassy at Constantinople on 23 November 1810 and this arrived at the beginning of March 1811. Stratford's relief at finally having communication from Wellesley must have been cruelly dashed when he saw that it contained not one word of instruction concerning the war between the Ottomans and Russians or the French piracy. Instead it was a warning for Stratford to be on the lookout for an imposter last known to be on his way to Constantinople.[41]

Wellesley's next dispatch to Constantinople, sent on 11 December 1810, was also totally digressive, devoted to the exchange of diplomatic presents during the early part of Adair's mission back in 1809. Stratford was actually instructed to tell the Ottoman government that a special gift which the Sultan himself had presented to Adair could not be accepted because to do so would be 'repugnant to the established principles of propriety and public honor in this Country.'[42] This was certainly not what Stratford had had in mind when he implored Wellesley to provide direction.

Stratford was loathe to complete the assignment as he was sure that raising the undiplomatic issue with the Ottomans would, as he wrote in a private letter to Adair on 17 March 1811, 'expose the publick interests to a great + perhaps unnecessary danger.'[43] However he dutifully presented the matter to the deputy dragoman of the Porte, Panagios Mourousi,[44] in what must have been one of those discussions in which officials who normally operate across a professional divide are united in common lament for the ignorant directive of an overling. Mourousi warned that if the Sultan's gift were rejected by the British it would 'serve only to impair the interests of His Majesty's Service at this Court,' as Stratford reported to Wellesley. He added his own opinion: 'I must confess, my Lord, that these assertions made no inconsiderable impression on me .... most fatal consequences might ensue from wounding the pride of a Sovereign whose will is the law of his people.' Stratford asked permission to defer the issue 'until some opportunity more decidedly favourable than the present shall occur.'[45] A reply from Wellesley never arrived, but as the assignment remained active Stratford presented the issue again to the Porte and received a reply in August from Deputy Dragoman Mourousi. He explained that he had raised the issue personally with the Sultan who responded with displeasure in a long statement.

'After so decisive an answer I do not feel myself authorised,' Stratford explained to Wellesley, 'to press this very delicate matter any further without fresh instructions from Your Lordship.'[46] These of course never arrived, and the matter ended there. Wellesley's subsequent dispatches to Stratford never again achieved this astounding height of absurdity, but they all remained inconsequential and completely devoid of content concerning the vital diplomacy at Constantinople.[47]

Wellesley wrote to Stratford only about procedural and tangential issues and offered not a single word about the vital diplomatic issues. His ineptitude here is stunning, as is the fact that the United Kingdom had, during this crucial moment of the Napoleonic Wars, thrown into the post of Secretary of State for Foreign Affairs a man so incompetent in this capacity or spent in general. But protracted silence of a Foreign Office, in times of peace and even war, has in fact always been a problem faced by diplomats. George F. Kennan, who was himself often subjected to the unfortunate practice throughout his diplomatic career, and who studied it in his historical research, observed that 'governments have been this way for a long time in the past, throughout, in fact, the entire range of history of the nation state.'[48]

5

Stratford continued to do what he could on his own. News about the military situation in the Danubian Principalities was still scarce but he had correctly surmised now in October 1810 that things had taken a bad turn for the Ottomans. A key strategic point was the Ottoman fortress at Rusçuk, present-day Ruse, a town on the Danube and terminus for a road running through the Balkan mountains to Adrianople, Ottoman Edirne, the last European defence of the Ottomans before Constantinople. Back in July 1810 the Russians had attacked Rusçuk with almost 20,000 soldiers but were strongly repelled by the Ottomans.[49] The Russians were at the same time also driven back with major losses in their attack on the Ottoman camp at Shumla.

The Ottomans' success at these two battles was due to the fact that they 'make a fierce and sanguinary resistance when attacked behind their ramparts,' according to the contemporary British geographer, James Bell. 'On these occasions they issued their memorable bulletin: "That they had taken such a number of infidels' heads, that they would serve as a bridge by which the faithful might pass over to the other world."' But the Ottomans had then suffered a major setback during a Russian offensive in September and October 1810. 'They defended themselves with desperate valour; but were at length defeated, with the loss of 12,000 men in killed and wounded; and Rutshuck was compelled to surrender, with all the Turkish flotilla lying before it ...'[50]

On 22 October 1810 Stratford was able to confirm and report to London the Ottomans' loss of Rusçuk:

The Reis Efendi told Pisani that accounts of the Capitulation of Rudschuk had at length been received from the Grand Vizir himself. He was very much distressed by the state of the Campaign. Report, not denied by the Reis Efendi, that the Grand Vizir had sent his heavy baggage to Adrianople. The Reis Efendi complains again of the Vizir's conduct + regrets his own inability to obtain a change.[51]

The news of the fall of Ruşçuk alarmed Stratford. He believed the Ottomans were on the verge of defeat. His response was to send a dramatic message to the Reis Efendi. On 24 October he instructed Pisani to communicate verbally to the Ottoman minister:

> however painful the state of things at the Camp might be, yet shutting his eyes was no remedy; he must look the danger in the face and above all I *entreated* him to conceal nothing from me: It was for *the interest* of the Porte that I should know *all* + that too *immediately*: that it was my opinion that, if nothing else could be done with respect to the Grand Vizir, that at least precaution should be taken particularly at the Seraglio, to prevent his [the Grand Vizir's] doing anything *in a hurry. That was what I was apprehensive of.*[52]

Stratford was taking a big gamble by addressing the foreign minister of the Ottoman Empire in this way. Galib Efendi was a most experienced and competent statesman who had risen to the top of one of the largest powers in the world while surviving multiple court intrigues that had destroyed various colleagues. He certainly did not require any advice against 'shutting his eyes' or about the need to 'look danger in the face' or 'to conceal nothing', and he especially did not require such advice from a 23-year-old foreign representative who knew no Turkish. Stratford was also completely out of line professionally in advocating to the host foreign minister how he should handle his own head of government.

The fall of Ruşçuk had doubtlessly led Stratford to conclude that an emergency was at hand that called for such a drastic approach to the Reis Efendi. He was incorrect about the military situation but correct about the political. Militarily the Ottomans had been set back by the fall of Rusçuk but they were not on the verge of defeat and they would even recapture Rusçuk. In fact, they were stuck in a military stalemate with the Russians which had already lasted for several years despite the swings back and forth. But politically the Grand Vizir was indeed in trouble and would soon be removed from power.

Stratford understood the political situation at the capital much better than the military situation at the theatre of fighting. On either he really had no business proferring advice to the Reis Efendi. But this was a highly dramatic and unusual diplomatic moment with the fate of all Europe in the balance. And Stratford's gamble was to pay off later in another way: when in July 1811 the Grand Vizir was removed from office, Galib Efendi himself was transferred to the theatre of fighting to oversee both the military and diplomatic front. From there he called upon Stratford to assume an interesting role in the peace negotiations between the Ottomans and Russians. Stratford's dramatic and tough approach to Galib Efendi here in October 1810 and in all of their dealings had not offended the Ottoman leader but instead earned his respect.

Galib Efendi was an accomplished and experienced statesman at the head of his government, and Stratford was simply a dedicated young man thrown on his own resources far from home. But they shared a common view. In a 'Memorandum' of 29 November 1810, Stratford wrote to Galib Efendi that 'it should never be forgotten that Peace is the only end and object of War.' He also suggested that the Ottomans' making peace with Russia would help the situation with France because Napoleon 'will do all in his power to avoid a quarrel with the Porte when she is connected to Russia.'[53] Stratford advocated peace and Galib practiced peace, not at all because the young man influenced the experienced statesman, or because either man was a pacifist, but because peace in this international situation happened to be in the interests of each of their countries. Both statesmen were intelligent enough to recognise this reality.

Stratford's preaching here 'that Peace is the only end and object of War' was quite valid as an expression of diplomatic philosophy and as a method of diplomatic practice. Peace is indeed the only legitimate end of diplomacy and the best word of the diplomat. But did Stratford actually practice peace in his career at Constantinople? He certainly did work for peace between the Ottomans and Russians here in 1811–12. And he would do so many more times in his career, so much so that he would become renowned across Europe (until the Crimean War) for being what could be called an imperial peacemaker. Yet the prime goal of Stratford's work and of all his dealings at the Ottoman capital, now and over his many more years there, was to maintain Britain's route to India, to secure his country's massive occupation of a distant land and its many peoples.

6

Stratford was still terribly lonely in Constantinople. He marked the end of 1810 by submitting to London a fresh request to be released from his position and to come home. He claimed that the personal expenses of his mission were 'two-thirds greater than my appointments', as he wrote to Wellesley on 31 December 1810.[54] His previous unsuccessful request to come home, back in February 1810, had been based on health grounds.

Wellesley had trouble finding anyone in London to take the post at Constantinople. Back in February 1810 Aberdeen had rejected it as below his standing as well as beyond his ability. In February 1811 it was rejected by the son of Lord Burghersh, a former *aide-de-camp* of the Duke of Wellington.[55] In March 1811 the post was accepted by Robert Liston, who had already served as ambassador at Constantinople from 1794 to 1795. Stratford received word in June 1811 that Wellesley intended to send Liston out 'with the least practicable delay ... in the course of three or four weeks...'[56]

Stratford must have been elated to receive the news. Adair sent him congratulations in July 1811:

Most sincerely do I wish you joy by anticipation on your long promised release. On the whole however you will have no reason to regret your residence in that country or your absence from this. I hear your praises from all persons belonging to the Foreign Office with whom I am acquainted ... it is impossible for those, who, like myself, have been a little behind the scenes, not to see that you must have had many difficulties to struggle with, requiring a great share of prudence and fortitude to overcome.[57]

But months passed without Liston's arrival or any explanation from London. Wellesley simply never got around to making the arrangements for sending Liston out or informing Stratford of the delay. Stratford wrote to his sister, Bess, on 3 September 1811:

Where in the name of heaven is the *dear* Mr. Liston about all this time? I am continually on the look-out for him, but alas! I have not yet heard of his having left England, and till I hear *that* I shall not feel certain of getting away from this horrible hole. If by a miserable accident he should still be in England when you receive this, seize him and tie him on to one of Congreve's rockets, and point him in this direction. I know no other way of putting anything at the Foreign Office into motion. My patience is nearly worn out *again* .... I described all that was describable a long time ago ...[58]

7

Back in late 1810, at the height of his loneliness, Stratford had been unexpectedly treated to a highly entertaining visitor from home. Lady Hester Lucy Stanhope was the niece of Pitt and had served as his hostess to London society. After Pitt's death she left Britain and spent the rest of her days travelling in the Near East. In November 1810 she arrived in Constantinople and took up residence on the Bosphorus. 'Canning has behaved to me in the civilest, kindest manner...' she wrote home in December 1810.[59] Her physician and travelling companion noted that Stratford was 'not infrequent in his visits'.[60] She was naturally bohemian and Stratford was naturally the opposite but they quickly became close friends.

By the summer of 1811 Lady Hester had conceived a new contrarian adventure: to go to Paris and see Napoleon. She met several times with the French *chargé d'affaires* at Constantinople, La Tour-Maubourg, in order to secure a visa. She knew that the upright Stratford would never approve her adventure and so she had kept her plan and meetings secret from him. She had also grown weary of his puritanical aspect. In June 1811, just as Stratford had received word of the appointment of Liston as his replacement, Lady Hester wrote home:

> That good-natured methodistical Minister, Mr. Canning, is, it appears about to take his departure. He is much delighted at it; as for my part, I have no right to be either glad or sorry. I do not think him very agreeable, but I believe him very honest, but whether a man who is only honest is a fit Minister to watch over the intrigues of a very cunning people is the question.[61]

Stratford was in fact not too honest or naive to handle the challenging post. Lady Hester did not know that he had established and was operating a developed network of informants across the city, as was true for all the Western embassies there. On 24 August 1811 he learnt of her plan and clandestine meetings with La Tour-Maubourg and went directly to her house to confront her. She informed him that the French envoy had agreed to provide her with a visa. She had kept the plan and meetings secret, she told Stratford, out of affection for him and to spare him aggravation and embarrassment. Stratford asked her to apply to the British government for permission to go to France, and to wait until the arrival of Liston, before she saw the French envoy again. Lady Hester refused and Stratford threatened to take action. 'I told her ladyship that if such were her determination, neither I nor any of the persons immediately attached to his Majesty's mission here could go to her house again,' as Stratford wrote in his report on the incident. He also indicated to Lady Hester that he would inform Foreign Secretary Wellesley of her transgressions.

Despite the difficult nature of their meeting, it was held 'in perfect calmness', Stratford noted; and she told him that his official actions would not affect her personal feelings toward him.[62] He had called her out to a political duel and she had accepted.

Three days later Lady Hester fired a brilliant first shot by sending a scathing letter off to Wellesley and a copy of it to Stratford. She explained that she only wished to go to the south of France for health reasons:

> Had Mr. Adair been here, or any man of known character and liberal opinions, I should, in the first instance, have communicated this circumstance to him ... But Mr. Canning was young and inexperienced; full of zeal, but full of prejudice. I guessed, therefore, what might be the line of conduct he would pursue upon such an occasion.

Being cut off by Stratford from the British embassy officials did not at all bother her because, she wrote, 'they are all horribly dull (except Mr. Pisani, who is a man of merit and information)...' And she found Stratford himself:

> both a political and religious methodist, after having appeared to doubt my love for my country, he will next presume to teach me my duty to my God! Before I conclude I must make one petition to your Lordship not to receive Mr. Canning with dry bows or wry faces, or allow the fine ladies to toss him in a blanket. The best recompense for his services would be to appoint him Commander-in-Chief at home and Ambassador Extraordinary to the various societies for the suppression of vice and cultivation of patriotism. The latter consists in putting oneself into greater convulsions than the Dervishes at the mention of Buonaparte's name.[63]

Lady Hester's connections in London and even in the Cabinet were extremely well developed. Stratford immediately realised that her letter could cause him real professional harm by branding him as a petty bully who was wasting his time on trivialities. He wrote to George Canning and implored him to reconnoitre whether Wellesley had actually received Lady Hester's letter, and if so, to intercede as necessary. George reported that the letter had not made the rounds.[64] The letter, which still reposes in the personal archive of the Marquess Wellesley at the British Library, is marked as having been received at the Foreign Office on 18 October 1811,[65] but it seems never to have been read by Wellesley. The Foreign Secretary's disinclination to come to work or read mail had confounded Stratford diplomatically at Constantinople but here it perhaps saved his career.

Lady Hester was denied in her French plan but after the spat was over she and Stratford eventually recovered their fondness for each other. Later in 1811 she wrote to him from Bursa and thanked him for his 'kindness and attention' which 'I am perfectly sensible of and shall ever acknowledge with gratitude .... Let me hear that you look well and in good spirits. You ought to see this beautiful place, but when no longer a great man you might fall in love with some of these very beautiful Turkish women, and that would be a great sin.' And the next year she wrote to him from Damascus: 'I have laughed at you and scolded you, but I must ever wish you well, because I believe you to be an *honest man*, a rare thing in these times.'[66]

Stratford generously assisted Lady Hester many times during her later adventures throughout the Near East. And among the records of the British embassy at Constantinople at this time is a note that in February 1811 it obtained from the Ottoman arsenal, '... the enlargement from Slavery of one Giovanni Feluccia, a Sicilian Subject, at the repeated Solicitation of Mr. Canning at the Porte.'[67] Later Stratford would become renowned as the champion of many different minorities in Constantinople. But in 1811 he was generally still taciturn and rigid. His basic problem, as Lady Hester formulated in another letter about him, was 'the narrowness of this man's mind'.[68] That narrow mind was struggling to confront the 'wide world' of Constantinople.[69]

CHAPTER 5

PIRACY ON THE AEGEAN,
WAR ON THE DANUBE

1

Stratford had still received no explanation from London about the delay in sending out his replacement. Nor had he received any instruction about his urgent diplomatic problems: how to promote peace between the Ottomans and Russians before Napoleon invaded one or both of them; and how to dissuade the Ottomans from allying with the French. In October 1811 Stratford made yet another plea to London for instruction. As the foreign secretary would not respond to him, he now sent a letter marked 'private' to the undersecretary, Culling Charles Smith:

> I assure you that it will soon be impossible for me to make head against the French, or maintain the influence of this Mission on a decent footing, without some sign of life from the Foreign Office .... I most earnestly instruct that you will pass what I have written above upon Lord Wellesley's consideration. When you remember what I have repeatedly urged upon the Subject in the course of my Dispatches ... you will certainly see how much the public Service requires that some attention should be paid to my representations.

But by the time this letter was received at the Foreign Office on 7 February 1812,[1] Wellesley had already submitted his resignation.[2] Stratford was completely on his own.

French privateers had continued to seize British merchant ships, bring them into Ottoman ports, sell their goods and enjoy safe haven there from British reprisals. Stratford had made repeated demands that the Ottoman government issue decrees closing their ports to the French pirates. The Ottomans had constantly agreed to the demands without fulfilling them, not wanting to antagonise the French. For the same reason they also would not sanction, on the legal grounds that they were a neutral power in the war, British military intervention in Ottoman ports or waters, demarcated as within three miles of coast.

In February–March 1811 several piracy incidents occurred at Cyprus, and Alexandria and two at the island of Syra or Siros in the Cyclades. The Reis Efendi 'promises redress', as Stratford had recorded in a diary of negotiations, but by the middle of April no action had been taken. The Ottomans indicated that they would issue a ferman prohibiting the sale of seized British goods in Ottoman ports. But in May 1811 Reis Efendi Galib, had 'drawn back' from this concession.[3] Stratford met him and told him directly that the Ottoman government was 'incurring the risk of giving offence to the English Government … His Majesty's Government would be obliged to … provide for its own interests by the employment of those Means which Providence has placed at its disposal.'[4] Stratford was hinting that British military action was possible. But in fact he had not received any indication from London or from the fleet in the Mediterranean that military options were being considered.

In June 1811 another French piracy incident against a British ship occurred off the Aegean island of Euboea, and then in August another at Alexandria. The Reis Efendi again promised to issue a ferman but this was never produced. In July 1811 Galib Efendi was made *Kethüda*, roughly equivalent to Minister of Internal Affairs and *de facto* deputy Grand Vizir, and transferred to the scene of military action with the Russians on the Danube in order to oversee communication with the Russians and with the Sultan and to initiate

peace negotiations. A new Reis Efendi was appointed, Küçük Arif
Mehmed Efendi, but he maintained the same Ottoman line on the
French piracy. On 28 August 1811 Stratford found him 'obstinate as
ever'. Two days later the Reis Efendi 'refuses conference on Syra'.
Over the next three days 'all rejected'. One week later there was
'nothing but chicane'. On 5 October negotiations were 'decidedly
negative'. On 14 October 'I threaten,' Stratford noted, 'to take further
measures' but the Reis Efendi 'used most violent expressions'.
A Turkish national holiday brought a calm of one week, after which
Stratford sent his dragoman to the Porte to deliver 'an important
message' on the piracy but he was received with only 'difficulties and
coldness'.[5]

On 26 October 1811 another British ship was seized by French
privateers and brought into the Ottoman port of Syra and its goods
sold there. Two days later Stratford sent a demand to the Reis Efendi
for the promised ferman. On 29 October there was 'Very little
progress: Reis Efendi obstinate'. On 31 October there was again 'Very
little progress'.[6] The same day Stratford instructed Dragoman Pisani
to go to the Reis Efendi and to tell him: 'The affair of neutrality is
now come to a point − + the Porte must take its choice. It must
dare to act now or aid the necessary circumstances. Am I to suppose
that the Porte is tired of the English + wishes to get rid of us?'[7]

Stratford had actually already begun exploring British military
action against the French pirates. Back on 13 April 1811 he had
written to Admiral Sir Charles Cotton, commander of the British
fleet in the Mediterranean:

> I think it my duty, under the present Circumstances, to suggest
> the propriety of seizing this Opportunity to clear the
> Archipelago of French privateers. Your Excellency is the best
> judge how far this may be practicable, without committing His
> Majesty's Government, by a direct attack upon the Sovereignty
> of the Porte.[8]

But Admiral Cotton would not consider Stratford's suggested
military action without authorisation from London.

After the repeated incidents of piracy throughout 1811, Stratford then wrote to Captain Henry Hope, commander of the British squadron in the Greek Archipelago, on 3 November 1811:

I feel myself not only authorized, but in duty bound, to recommend to you most strongly to capture the French pirate ... wherever it may be found, and at the same time to liberate any English Vessels it may have seized ... the orders under which you act may be such as to prevent your paying attention to my Recommendation. But ... I will most readily take upon myself, as far as I can, the responsibility of the measure I recommend – a measure which, in my opinion, is no less just than expedient, and equally requisite for the honour of His Majesty's Service, + for the Interests of our trade.[9]

Captain Hope agreed with this argument of Stratford and accepted his suggestion.

Stratford had authorised and taken responsibility for military operation in Ottoman waters. The 24-year-old neophyte in diplomatic negotiation and foreign relations was taking another great gamble. He was acting without authorisation from the British government and against the wishes of the Ottoman, and he was seriously risking the wrath of both. He easily could have done nothing as he had still not received any direction from Wellesley. But Stratford by nature was not prone to inaction.

An immediate candidate for a military response presented itself over the coming weeks. Back on 29 October 1811 the English merchant ship *Alexander* and its rich cargo had been seized by French pirates as it was bound from Malta to Smyrna. The facts became known slowly and Stratford received confirmation on 18 November that the pirates had taken the ship and its cargo into the Ottoman Greek port of Napoli di Romania in Greece. He immediately contacted the Reis Efendi 'and I demanded a firman for the immediate Restitution of the Ship and Cargo. The Reis Efendi thought it proper to reject my demand as on former occasions.' On 23 November 1811, Stratford repeated his demands and proposed 'an official Conference for the final discussion of our differences.' All were rejected and 'nothing remained for me but to address an Official Note to the Porte...'[10] With no diplomatic possibilities remaining, the military option was initiated.

On 29 November Captain Hope aboard *HMS Salsette* sailed into Napoli di Romania to confront the French pirates, who had also captured and were holding there a second British merchant ship, *Active*. The pirate ship was defended by two French merchant vessels which 'appeared perfectly prepared to repel any attack which we might direct from our Boats,' as Hope reported to Stratford three days later. The British met with the Ottoman governor of the port and demanded that he seize the British ships and liberate them, but the governor refused. The British then informed the Ottoman governor of their intentions to liberate the captured ships and their strong desire not to engage Ottoman forces.

After this meeting the British opened fire on the French ships and attempted to board them. Although the guns of the Ottoman fortress in the harbor remained silent, individuals gave fire from the shore and this provided cover for the French pirate ship to float away. Two British sailors were severely injured from the fire. The French merchant vessels were too badly damaged to board. Captain Hope was therefore unable to capture the ships or their crew or repossess the stolen cargo, which had been removed to shore and disappeared. But he did liberate the British ships and he also had 'the satisfaction of knowing that no mischief had been done to the persons or property of the Subjects of the Sublime Porte.'[11]

2

The Reis Efendi was irate and called in Stratford. 'The Reis Efendi took fire at first,' as Stratford reported to Wellesley, 'and called the Attack of the *Salsette* an Outrage done to the Sovereignty of the Porte...', threatening serious repercussions.[12] Stratford shot right back at the Reis Efendi, accusing the Ottoman government of responsibility for the incident, and warning that an escalation in military engagement was possible:

... I must say that the Porte has no one to thank for it but herself, the French + her own officers. *Herself*, because She has consistently disregarded my warning – withheld justice – + encouraged the Enemy by her indifference to my complaints; *the French* because they have been the aggressors ... *her own officers*, because the Bey [governor] of Napoli di Romania ... had no right to refuse us our own property ... [and for] firing in time of Peace on His Majesty's Subjects .... As far as the Reis Efendi's threats about what he should do, if he is in earnest, I beg he write me an official Communication on the Subject, that I may prepare His Majesty's Government, + our Ships of war in the Archipelago for the necessary resistance to any such hostility.[13]

The Ottomans had apparently thought that the young and inexperienced Stratford would back down from talk of war; and that the British government was strait-jacketed by its desire to keep the Ottomans out of the French camp and in peace negotiations with the Russians. Stratford, however, had calculated that the Ottomans would relent because they could never afford to go to war with Britain while they were still at war with Russia and faced the possibility of invasion by France.

Stratford's 'act of decision', as he himself called it,[14] at Napoli di Romania was highly dangerous to him personally. With the Ottomans he ran the risk of arrest and imprisonment at the Seven Towers. And with his home government he had placed his whole career on the line. 'At all events should anything happen contrary to my expectation,' as he wrote to Wellesley, 'the responsibility rests with me, and I feel at ease in the reflection that His Majesty's Government can in a moment dispel every embarrassment by the mere disavowal of what has been done.' He affirmed that his drastic action had been based upon his conviction that 'the only way to preserve the Peace with this Country, and to prevent the necessity of ultimately exacting redress by force of Arms from the Porte herself, was the employment of a decisive Measure in some particular Case, while the Occasion was favourable and Justice clearly on our Side.'[15]

By pushing for military action, Stratford had demonstrated that he and his government were fully capable of taking severe measures and even of fully breaking off relations with the Ottomans.

Stratford's bold action at Napoli di Romania in November 1811 was based not only on calculation but also on observation. A recent incident involving one of his diplomatic colleagues at Constantinople had provided him with instruction, as Stratford recalled in his memoir:

> It so happened that about this time the Porte took violent offence at some proceeding of the Shah and his government. The Persian chargé d'affaires was taken publicly to task by the Sultan's minister. He was even threatened in so many words with decapitation. 'You may take my head, if you please,' he replied, 'but the master I serve will not be slow to avenge it.' This counter-menace carried the day. Huseyn Agha's head remained on his shoulders; the Porte sheathed her indignation, and the question in dispute passed with many others into limbo. Here was a true scale for measuring my risk. I seized the hint, and called upon the commander of our force in the Archipelago to take the law into his own hands.[16]

The young and inexperienced Stratford, abandoned by his superiors at home, had exploited one of the few resources available to him at Constantinople: examination of the conduct of his more experienced peers.

Stratford's situation with the Ottomans remained tense. On 24 December 1811 the Reis Efendi demanded an official explanation from the Foreign Office in London for the attack at Napoli di Romania. And he informed Stratford that until he received these from London he would no longer negotiate or meet with him concerning French piracy.

Stratford hit back hard the next day, instructing Pisani to go to the Reis Efendi and tell him:

I am here for the purpose of carrying on His Majesty's affairs, + I will not suffer the slightest insult to be offered to my publick character. To refuse to do business with me is equivalent to a Declaration of war. An Answer cannot come from England in less than 4 months.

It was also declared in the communication that as the French piracy would surely continue, British military ships would be on alert and take necessary steps:

The Commanders of His Majesty's Ships will never suffer this, + will provide *at all hazards* for the safety of their Countrymen. Indeed it will be my duty to write to them for that purpose. And I shall be obliged to begin by writing publick letters to all the English Merchants, saying that war is imminent, + that they must secure their property.[17]

Stratford's tough approach and threat of war – again, all undertaken without authorisation from London – had their effect. Later the same day, 25 December 1811, he received a conciliatory written response from the Reis Efendi. Stratford then instructed Pisani:

You will tell the Reis Efendi that it gives me pleasure to find his disposition so much more friendly than yesterday. He will always find mine in conformity with it. Indeed my sole object is to preserve harmony between two Courts who have so many interests in common.[18]

Over the next month more such communications, alternating in mood between hopeful and hopeless, went back and forth between Stratford and the Reis Efendi.[19] On 10 January 1812, Stratford reported to Wellesley that:

All chance of my being able to settle the disputes with the Porte about the late illegal captures in the Archipelago seem to be over. The Reis Efendi has retracted his promises; and now declares that the Porte will do nothing whatever toward giving satisfaction.[20]

But suddenly the Ottomans relented in full. On 14 February 1812 the Reis Efendi sent an official note to Stratford informing him that the Ottoman government had issued several fermans instructing Ottoman officials to prevent any privateers from entering or fitting out their ships in Ottoman ports, as well as from bringing their prizes onto Ottoman territory, including selling or storing them there. Severe punishments were prescribed for any Ottoman officials who may disregard the directives. Stratford was specifically informed that the fermans had been sent to all officials of the Empire as well as the French *chargé d'affaires*.[21]

The Ottomans had conceded to Stratford concerning the French piracy apparently because they had decided that they needed him as an ally in an urgent issue which was much more important to them: the stalled peace negotiations with the Russians.

3

Stratford was so burdened with work at Constantinople that his close friend at the Foreign Office, Joseph Planta, worried about him and imagined that he never got out of the embassy. 'Do reform your practice in this respect,' Planta had written him, 'to be sure it occurs to me that when a man cannot get out without a corporal and two janissaries before and two servants behind, there is some reason for his staying at home; but you *must* preserve your health, and to do that you *must* take some exercise.'[22]

Stratford in fact did enjoy going around the city. He made local excursions even though they could be dangerous, and he sometimes managed to go out alone without his guard. He was shot at once while riding his horse home from the Sweet Waters of Europe, a valley at the source of the Golden Horn, and he was shot at again while strolling in a valley on the Asian shore of the Bosphorus. Stratford described the second incident in his memoir:

Having dismissed the usual attendants, I sauntered on alone through the meadows without perceiving two Turkish sailors, who in holiday clothes and high spirits were enjoying the weather and the scene at some little distance from me. My attention was first called to them by a shout, and on looking round I saw them advancing briskly towards me with cocked pistols in their hands. I had not long to wait. They both fired at me; but their manner of holding the pistols, stock down and muzzle up, ensured a miss. Nothing daunted, they proceeded to load again, and, as running away was out of the question, I only did what was most prudent by going straight up to them. I just knew enough Turkish to say who I was, and to understand from their subsequent exclamation that they recognized me as a friend.[23]

4

The war on the Danube between the Ottomans and the Russians had been a stalemate from November 1806 until September 1811 when the Ottoman Grand Vizir and *Serdar-i Ekrem* or Commander-in-Chief, Ahmed Paşa, attacked the strategic island of Slobozia in the Danube. Ottoman forces became bogged down there and their headquarters at Rusçuk were left exposed. On the night of 13 October 1811 the Russians crossed the Danube, seized the Ottoman headquarters and trapped the Ottoman army on the wrong side of the river. The loss was decisive and Ahmed Paşa and his council immediately concluded that their government must move for peace. An armistice was affected on 15 October. Negotiations were opened with the Russians on 31 October at the town of Giurgiu and were later moved to Bucharest.[24] The Russian plenipotentiaries included André Italinsky, a former ambassador at the Porte. One of the main Ottoman plenipotentiaries was Galib Efendi, Stratford's former counterpart as Reis Efendi and since July 1811 the *Kethüda*. Galib was assisted by the Chief Dragoman of the Porte, Demetrius Mourousi, the older brother of Panagios Mourousi, Deputy Dragoman of the Porte and

Stratford's interlocutor since 1810, including during the empty controversy over diplomatic presents created by the most inane of Wellesley's inconsequential dispatches.

The Ottoman–Russian peace negotiations dragged on through January 1812 with no progress. Neither side would take the necessary initiative as both were gambling that the other would back down first in fear of Napoleon's coming attack. Their game of international brinkmanship was driving Stratford to despair. And it was maddening for him to be caught between a highly suspicious Foreign Office at Constantinople and a completely dormant Foreign Office at London. He later described this dilemma in his memoir:

> I was suspected of knowing that England had secretly made peace with Russia. My ignorance was construed into a purposed concealment. What could be done? The Porte was mistrustful and out of humour. I had no sign of life from home. I had nothing to offer but condolence, and stale exhortation; nevertheless, if I could not raise hope, I might allay suspicion.[25]

All he could do was the same that he had done for the past two years: to keep pressing both the Ottomans and the Russians for peace and to assure each that Britain had not reached any secret agreement with the other.

In January 1812 the peace negotiations broke down and the Russians informed the Ottomans that they were renouncing the armistice. The Ottomans became convinced that the Russians were planning a new military attack or that they had reached a new agreement with the French. At the end of January Ahmed Paşa wrote to General Kutuzov, the Russian Commander-in-Chief (hero of the coming Napoleonic battles of 1812, and previously an ambassador at Constantinople, 1792–94), and implored him to conclude the peace. The Grand Vizir simultaneously reported to the Sultan that his armies were in no way ready to resume fighting with the Russians and that making peace was imperative.[26]

5

Galib Efendi had an unusual idea for breaking the impasse with the Russians and he proposed it to the Grand Vizir: to invite Stratford to communicate directly with the Russians and implore them to soften their position.[27] Since July 1810 Stratford had dutifully kept up his line to the Russians via the Neapolitan embassies, undertaken with Ottoman permission as long as the communication was left open to them. What Galib now had in mind was to make Stratford's advocacy for peace much more immediate and forceful by allowing him to communicate directly with the Russians, again, as long as the entire correspondence was left open for Ottoman inspection.

Galib knew Stratford well from their many dealings in 1810–11. Their last direct communication had been back on 12 July 1811 when Galib was still Reis Efendi, just before he was made *Kethüda* and transferred to the Ottoman camp on the Danube. Stratford had declared to him via Pisani:

The present uncertain state of things between France and Russia cannot last much longer. It must either change into war, or reconciliation. It will be well for the Porte to consider beforehand how she is likely to be affected in either of these two cases .... Is not then the present moment more favourable for the conclusion of peace than any other which is likely to come if *it* be lost?[28]

Galib Efendi's response was reported by Pisani to Canning the same day: 'He agrees clearly with you, that *this is the proper moment* for the Porte to make her Peace with Russia by far. He, likewise, thinks, that the uncertainty of the position of things between Russia + Bonaparte cannot last long.'[29] Galib and Stratford had always been in agreement about the Ottomans' need to make immediate peace with Russia before the attack of France because this was the view of common sense.

Galib's proposal was approved by the Ottoman government and transmitted to Stratford by 6 February 1812. Stratford wrote to Wellesley:

I have to inform Your Lordship that the Porte has invited me to write to M. Italinsky or directly to the Russian Government on the Subject of the Present Negotiations. I have learnt through a Secret Channel that this measure was first recommended by Ghalib Efendi who says he has reason to think that it will be agreeable to the Russian Plenipotentiaries themselves, who would willingly take advantage of my occurrence to awaken a Spirit of Moderation in their Court, and thereby to facilitate the Reestablishment of Peace.

Only a few weeks had passed since Stratford's bold move of military action at Napoli di Romania, and his demands that the Ottomans close their ports to all French pirates had still not been met. But now he found himself in the commanding position of being recruited by the Ottomans for help. 'I have given the Reis Efendi to understand,' Stratford continued in his dispatch, 'that the execution of our Agreement respecting the French Privateers, and an unreserved communication of the Porte's intentions, must at all events precede any interference on my part.'[30]

The Ottomans consented almost immediately. On 14 February 1812 they completely satisfied all Stratford's demands concerning French piracy. He then agreed to address the Russians directly. To do so was another bold move by Stratford taken completely on his own and without confirmation from London. 'I am aware, My Lord, that this step is not authorized by my Instructions,' he wrote to Wellesley on 21 February, '+ that it is of a nature to require explanation.' He felt that he had no choice but to seize this 'chance of my being really instrumental to the conclusion of Peace'. He thought that he should agree now to the Ottomans' request because 'a refusal on my part would have served only to increase their mistrust, and to furnish them with a motive + pretext for listening to the insinuations of France.' He had decided that he had to get the Ottomans and Russians to peace before 'Buonaparte may effect his reconciliation with the Emperor Alexander + Russia.' And Stratford declared his belief that even though the bold step he was taking was not in accordance with his orders, it still satisfied 'the principles of His

Majesty's Government'.[31] Many years later in retirement, he described the moment another way: 'it was a great opportunity and I could hardly let it go by, without laying myself open to subsequent regret, and perhaps to eventual censure.'[32]

Stratford had opened his direct communication to the Russians on 19 February 1812. He wrote to their chief negotiator at Bucharest, Italinsky, as well as to the chief Ottoman negotiator, Galib Efendi, and to the Russian government.[33] He recommended to the Russians that they moderate their terms toward the Ottomans, especially in the negotiations concerning territory in the Caucasus, otherwise the Ottomans might join the French camp.[34]

Stratford's three letters were all sent under flying seal for a special Ottoman approval, as Stratford recorded in his memoir:

> All three letters were laid before the Sultan, who expressed his satisfaction by a written message translated for my information. 'I have seen,' he said, 'the translation of the papers written by the English minister, and I feel much gratified at the interest he has thus taken in favour of my royal affairs. Whatever may be the effect of these papers in the quarter they are designed for, the purport of them clearly shews the perfect friendship which England possesses for my Sublime Porte. Let the originals be sent to their destination.'[35]

The Sultan's formulaic praise of the British minister was surely a diplomatic move, meant to keep Stratford engaged in lobbying the Russians because this was useful to Ottoman interests. But the Sultan actually did have a high opinion of Stratford. When a Swedish representative came to Bucharest and then Constantinople to propose the good offices of his government for the peace negotiations as well as an Ottoman–Russian–Swedish alliance, the Sultan dismissed him and wrote to the Kaymakam, as F. Ismail discovered: 'none of the infidels, apart from the Englishman [Canning] are reliable. Each is seeking to further his own interests. This being the case, we must not be deceived by them.'[36] Stratford had earned respect at the highest councils of Ottoman power.

6

Stratford had broken through to the Ottomans but he still could not get any response out of his own superiors in London. He was still acting completely on his own authority and according to his own judgment. And he was still terribly lonely, as he had written home to a school friend on 7 January 1812:

> You can hardly conceive all that I have suffered, and am still suffering here. If I were to attempt a description of it, you would perhaps think me guilty of exaggeration .... The long delay in Mr. Liston's departure has not only kept me constantly in hot water and very much embarrassed me in my public transactions, but it has also prevented me from pressing for my release .... In short I am persuaded that six more months of misery here will go near to kill me outright...[37]

And Stratford wrote to his mother on 17 January 1812:

> I am in the middle of winter, the nights are long and I have no society. Add to this that the business I have lately had to transact with the Turkish Government has been even more disagreeable than usual .... In the meantime to increase the pleasures of Constantinople, the Plague is apprehended, has made its appearance. Do not be frightened at that tremendous name. Like most other things it is not so formidable when at hand as at a distance ... By far the worst part must be the continual apprehension of an invisible danger, the interruption of communications, and the trouble of taking precautions, and above all the degree of imprisonment to which one must submit and the probability of a longer detention here – for I do not suppose Mr. Liston will be very anxious to come out under such circumstances, even should every other cause of delay be removed. So the Lord have mercy upon me and supply me with patience![38]

Stratford got through the winter but the new season brought no pleasure and no news about his replacement. 'All the spring to be lost,' he wrote again to his mother on 18 March 1812. 'No chance of relief before the summer, and perhaps not then. What have I done to deserve this?'[39]

All Stratford could do was to keep writing to Wellesley and keep asking for direction and information. He wrote on 11 March 1812:

I must not omit to inform Your Lordship that having had occasion to see the Reis Efendi this morning, he questioned me respecting the long Silence of His Majesty's Government towards the Porte, in a manner which betrayed much anxiety and disappointment on that account – feelings which I have but too much reason to believe he only partakes in common with his Colleagues. I think it my duty to mention this Circumstance, and to entreat Your Lordship's attention to what I have repeatedly urged upon the same Subject in my former despatches.[40]

Stratford again implored Wellesley to provide assistance on 12 April 1812, which happened to be exactly three months to the day since Wellesley had submitted his resignation: '... without direct orders from England ... without fresh Instructions, and the more immediate Countenance of His Majesty's Government, it is next to impossible for this Mission to struggle successfully with the many and formidable enemies now united against it.'[41] Stratford wrote again to Wellesley on 21 April:

I am very much in want of instructions. Even the smallest communication direct from H. M. Government, if greater means cannot be employed, would be of great service. The French are making every effort of possible exertion. Courier upon Courier arrive here from Paris .... My Lord, I again beg for instructions and support, without which I can hardly hope to act with effect.[42]

And on 26 April Stratford again implored Wellesley in what turned out to be his last communication to him before finally receiving word that he had been long out of office:

> ... I beg Your Lordship to consider that I am a simple individual without any reputation or other pretensions on which to establish a personal influence over the Turkish Ministers. My credit arises solely from the support of my Government, as I am listened to only as I am supposed to speak with this voice .... I most humbly beseech Your Lordship not to refuse attention to what I have represented above, as well as on so many occasions.[43]

Stratford did not know that Wellesley had submitted his resignation as foreign secretary back on 12 January 1812.[44] This had become effective on 18 February.[45] Castlereagh was appointed to the position on 4 March 1812[46] and the United Kingdom now had a man of supreme competence at the helm of her foreign policy. He immediately organised the departure of Robert Liston, who finally left Portsmouth and Spithead for Constantinople on 8 April 1812, a whole year after his original appointment, and it would take him almost three more months to arrive at his post.[47]

7

When Robert Adair had left Constantinople back in July 1810 he provided to Stratford for his future use a piece of secret intelligence obtained from special contacts in Vienna. This was a French–Austrian draft plan for an invasion of the Ottoman Empire. Adair had himself informed the Ottomans of the plan before he departed, and Stratford had alluded to it several times, 'but I have always reserved the Communication of the papers themselves, until the danger should appear to be at hand, in order to make a stronger impression on the Turkish Government...' That moment had now arrived, Stratford felt, and he presented a copy of the plan to the Reis Efendi on 11 April 1812. 'The effect produced upon the Reis

Efendi was equal to my expectations...' as Stratford reported to Wellesley the next day.[48] The Reis Efendi called in the Austrian Internuncio for an explanation.

'It was not long before the Internuncio made a more advanced communication to the Porte,' Stratford recorded. The Austrian confirmed to the Reis Efendi his country's alliance with the French in the coming attack against Russia. And he hinted that should the Ottoman Empire join in with them, they would guarantee its integrity; and as a preliminary step toward this union, an Austrian officer should to be sent to the Grand Vizir's camp on the Danube.[49]

Stratford had learnt of this new development by 25 April. He conceived that if he could communicate this intelligence to the Russians, it may spur them to make peace with the Ottomans before they joined in league with the French and the Austrians. He also wanted to have his own personal correspondence with the Russians, one not subject to Ottoman control and examination, in order to elicit information from them about the state of the peace negotiations. He therefore decided to bypass the Ottomans and send his own secret communication directly to the Russians at their military headquarters at Sistova (present-day Svishtov) on the Danube and then with luck to Bucharest. This was yet another bold gamble by Stratford, for if the Ottomans were to learn of his secret communication to the Russians they would likely turn sharply against him, perhaps even imprison him, but at the very least isolate him diplomatically in some way. Stratford had decided that contacting the Russians in this way was worth risking his whole position and even his safety at Constantinople because it might make the necessary difference in getting the Russians and the Ottomans to peace.

'There was no great difficulty in writing a double set of despatches,' as Stratford later explained in his memoir, one for the communication with the Russians which was being conducted and monitored by the Ottomans, and another for his secret communication with the Russians:

> But how was the secret portion of them to be conveyed to the Russian head-quarters without an imminent risk of discovery and no slight peril to the bearer? Some time elapsed before I could find a messenger fit to be trusted. I found one at last in the person of a Scotch gentleman, Mr. Gordon, who had been travelling in Greece and wished to obtain a passage through the Turkish provinces in Europe to St. Petersburg.

It seems a rather strange coincidence that a British civilian, at precisely the correct moment, suddenly presented himself as desirous of travelling across a war-zone, just for personal purposes. One therefore wonders whether the mysterious Mr. Gordon (whose first name is never once provided in any documentation relating to him) was actually on some sort of secret service, although no evidence of this has been uncovered. Furthermore, the task was complicated and dangerous, as Stratford himself detailed in his memoir: 'He would have to traverse the Grand Vizir's camp on one side of the Danube and the Russian head-quarters on the other. He was to ingratiate himself with the Ottoman authorities by assuming their national costume.'[50] Again, one wonders how this assignment could have been entrusted to someone who happened to be passing through. Of course, it is possible that Gordon was not in secret service and instead an adventurous and brave independent traveler who was willing to undertake the risky mission for the sake of his government.

Gordon passed the Ottoman camp and reached the Russian head-quarters at Sistova on 3 May 1812. There he was able to convince the commandant of the Russian headquarters, a colonel of Cossacks, that he was on a special mission for the British Minister at Constantinople. He was transported by the Russians to Bucharest and was able to meet in private with Italinsky on 9 May. Gordon convinced him of the authenticity of his identity and mission 'by unripping my cap + displaying your Signature,' as he later reported to Stratford. He then delivered Stratford's communication about the Austrian proposal to the Ottomans. 'His first observation was that the information, with respect to the measures of the court of Vienna, was very important. . . ,' Gordon reported.

Later that day Gordon was conducted to General Kutuzov who asked him one question: 'whether I thought the Porte was more disposed to connect itself with France than to be on terms of Friendship with England or Russia.' Gordon accurately replied that he thought the Ottomans wished above all to maintain their neutrality. He stayed seven days at Bucharest during which Italinsky explained to him the Russian negotiation positions. Their main problem was that their large 'body of Troops was kept in the [Danubian] Provinces, who might undoubtedly be of much more use elsewhere.' Peace with the Ottomans was urgently needed, Italinsky explained, in order to free up these troops to face an invasion by the French.

Italinsky had sufficient time to inform his superiors at Petersburg about Gordon's visit and receive a response from Count N. P. Rumiantsev, the Russian foreign minister. Italinsky showed this letter to Gordon, who later reported it to Stratford:

> the Count signified to Mr. Italinski, that the Emperor had been pleased to approve entirely of his conduct in not refusing himself to the correspondence which the Minister of his Britannic Majesty at Constantinople had opened with him, + charged him to cultivate + continue that correspondence, for which, Mr. Italinski assured me, the Russian Court was very grateful towards you.[51]

Gordon returned to Constantinople on 28 May 1812.[52] Stratford had thus achieved his goal of sharing with the Russians the new intelligence about the French–Austrian overture to the Ottomans. It was indeed a bold and important move.

8

The day before Gordon had reached the Russian headquarters at Sistova on 3 May, the Ottomans had somehow learnt of his secret mission. The Reis Efendi immediately instructed the Grand Vizir at the Ottoman headquarters to detain Gordon and prevent his mission to the Russians. Stratford learnt of this development the same day and sent Pisani to appeal to the Reis Efendi. The dragoman intercepted the Ottoman statesman at 5pm just as he was coming out of his office to go home. 'I stopped him before he got on his Horse,' Pisani reported to Stratford that evening, '+ begged him, in the most pressing manner, to detain the order at least till to-morrow, that I might return to him ... He said the order was already sent off; and that "it was a shame and a Sin even for us to act in this way." He said this, + got on Horseback to go away.'

Pisani thought that the Tatars who were responsible for delivering the order had not yet departed and it was thus still possible to detain the order. Therefore 'I hastened to the Reis Efendi's House, where, after waiting some time, I was admitted into an interview with him in one of his private Rooms.' Pisani read out Stratford's full statement to him but the Reis Efendi was unmoved by it:

> Nothing would do. He positively asserted that the Order is gone and that it is absolutely impossible to recall it; that he is convinced in his own mind that you knew of Mr. Gordon's going to Boucarest, + that he is bearer of letters from you to the Russians; that, whether these letters be of a tenour favourable to unfavourable to the interests of the Porte, this last is much hurt at your having concealed the thing from her....

The Reis Efendi declared that due to this incident 'the Porte's confidence' in Stratford was now 'essentially altered' and it 'will refrain from making any communication to you in future of what may occur with Russia.'[53]

Stratford was appalled by the Reis Efendi's reaction. He was tired of being held in suspicion by the Ottomans and now being told off and even accused by them of engaging in 'Sin'. On 3 May he instructed Pisani to go to the Ottoman Foreign Office and read out:

> I am much hurt at the Reis Efendi's conduct yesterday – But it is the reward I might have expected. Let the Porte look

to it .... we shall see whether my insult is to be shewn to an Englishman with impassivity. For the consequences of this, the Reis Efendi will I insist be answerable .... if this *absurd* occasion of quarrelling with me had not presented itself, some other would have been found.[54]

The next day Stratford sent an even more forceful message:

I cannot submit to expose myself at every moment to the caprices + suspicions of those whom no assurances can convince, + no services make grateful. If the Porte suspects me on one subject today, tomorrow She will find some other ground of suspicion ... so long as the Porte persists in the suspension of confidence communicated by the Reis Efendi, so long shall I suspend all confidential intercourse with the Porte on every other subject, as well as on that particularly specified by him.[55]

Stratford could easily have found himself finished at Constantinople one way or another. He probably expected that he was. But a few days later the Ottomans again dropped all hostility toward him and even gave their approval to his secret communications with the Russians. 'The suspension of confidence was retracted with more formality than it had been declared...' Stratford informed Castlereagh on 19 May 1812. 'I have since seen the Reis Efendi and entered into such further explanations, as appear to have completely effaced every unpleasant impression; and I am desired by no means to discontinue the secret Correspondence with our friends at St. Petersburg....'[56]

But later that same day the Reis Efendi changed his mind again and demanded to see the texts of the secret communications sent to Stratford by the Russians at Bucharest. Stratford refused and the Reis Efendi again declared he would meet with him no further. Stratford immediately sent Pisani off to deliver another protest: 'If the Reis Efendi continues suspicious of me and my Government, not only is it useless for me to interfere in the affairs of the Porte with

Russia, but an interference, so suspected, is inconsistent with the character and dignity of my Sovereign.'[57]

And three days later Stratford declared to the Ottomans that he had reached the final end of patience:

> I have nothing to add about the Russian business. The conduct of the Porte has made me indifferent to it. I see plainly that by acting for her service I only expose myself + my Government to every sort of caprice + insult. We have sacrificed too much to our regard for this Empire. It is time to provide for our own interests elsewhere. There are others who will better appreciate the friendship of England. The Porte will learn her errors when it is too late.[58]

The Ottoman fluctuation was due in large part to the tense diplomatic situation. An attack by Napoleon was expected at any moment. The Ottomans and Russians were trapped in the ultimate *real politik* game of waiting for the other to cave in under the pressure. As each became more desperate for peace, each became more sure the other would blink first. As the stalemate continued, the tension rose even higher.

Stratford was caught up in a gyration of interests at the very centre of European diplomacy on the eve of continental war. The Ottomans would warm to him whenever they felt close to an agreement with the Russians and thought that his lobbying them could be useful in overcoming a final obstacle. And the Ottomans would turn against him and threaten to cut him off diplomatically whenever they felt pessimistic about the negotiations, blaming the British minister for poisoning them and suspecting him of working in secret agreement with the Russians. By May 1812 all these tensions had become so high that the Ottomans were swinging back and forth by the day.

Right at this time, at the beginning of May, the Russians finally moderated their negotiating position with the Ottomans, reducing their territorial claims in the Caucasus and along the Danube. Russian General Kutuzov was eager to reach agreement, especially as he had received information that the Tsar was on the verge of replacing him at the negotiations because the lack of progress. A few days later, on 9 May, the Ottoman government instructed its plenipotentiaries at Bucharest to reach settlement as soon as possible.[59] This move was due to new intelligence the Ottomans had received (perhaps a piece of Russian misinformation) that the French and Russians were about to revive their alliance. The Grand Vizir, Ahmed Paşa, and Galib Efendi had long wanted to conclude the peace and they seized the new opportunity.

The Russians may have also been motivated at this time, as the British certainly were, by new information about Napoleon's plan to attack Russia and then take Constantinople. 'By the best intelligence received from Paris,' wrote Edward Cooke, Castlereagh's under-secretary at the Foreign Office, to Robert Liston while he was still on his way out to his new post at the Ottoman capital, on 15 May 1812:

> there is every reason to believe that the ultimate Object of Bonaparte's is the taking of Constantinople and placing himself on the throne of Constantinople. He had packed up with his equipage his coronation robes + Imperial Crown, + had a large attendance to his Army, which seems destined for some new establishment. His intention is to make a strong and sudden attack on Russia, + then to offer Her advantageous terms of peace, on Her consenting to assist Him in the taking of Constantinople. She is to have the three Greek Provinces – Austria, the Delta of the Danube + Silesia − + he is to be crowned at Constantinople.[60]

Napoleon was indeed fascinated by Constantinople. On 31 May 1808 he wrote to his ambassador at Petersburg, Général Caulaincourt, 'The base of the grand question is always this: Who shall have Constantinople?'[61] And years later, during his exile at St. Helena, on 28 April 1816, he told the Count de Las Cases that:

> I might have shared with Russia the possession of the Turkish empire. We had oftener than once contemplated the idea, but

Constantinople was always the obstacle that opposed its execution. The Turkish capital was the grand stumbling-block between us. Russia wanted it, and I could not resign it. Constantinople is an empire of itself. It is the real keystone of power; for he who possesses it may rule the world.[62]

CHAPTER 6

THE TREATY OF BUCHAREST

1

'I have the Satisfaction to inform Your Lordship,' Stratford wrote to Castlereagh on 12 June 1812, 'that a Definitive Treaty of Peace between Russia and the Porte was signed on the 28th Ultimo at Bucharest.' Stratford had learnt the information 'through a confidential Channel' which also supplied a copy of the treaty. This Stratford also sent to Castlereagh.[1]

The treaty consisted of 16 patent articles and two secret articles.[2] Article IV established the European boundary between the two empires to run along the Pruth and Danube Rivers.[3] Article VI established the Asian boundary in the Caucasus at its *ante bellum* location, with the Russians returning all captured '*Fortresses et Chateâux*'. And Article VIII reaffirmed Ottoman authority over Serbia while establishing some autonomy and amnesty for those who had been asserting their independence. A great diplomatic victory for the Ottomans was that the treaty did nothing to change or challenge the status of the Straits.

'Your Lordship will observe,' Stratford also wrote to Castlereagh about the treaty, 'that the whole is already ratified by the Russian Commander in Chief and the Grand Vizir; it now remains for the respective Sovereigns to give their ratification, but some hesitation which I perceive on this Subject at the Porte does not leave me entirely without uneasiness.'[4] A problem indeed still remained.

It stemmed from the second of the two secret articles, which provided the Russians with certain military privileges in the Caucasus. Even though the *ante bellum* border had been restored by Article VI, the second secret article allowed the Russians to maintain a munitions magazine that they had built at the mouth of the Phasis River, and to employ a specified strip of coast along the eastern shore of the Black Sea as a military 'harbour' (*'échelle'*) in order to resupply its army in Georgia. But the Sultan strongly objected to and refused to sanction the second secret article, as was discovered by the historian of the treaty, F. Ismail. 'It has become manifest that the Moscovites' interest in the Anatolian question lies in the conveyance of munitions,' the Sultan wrote to the Grand Vizir. 'Their aim hereafter is to conquer Georgia, Iran, Abkhazia and Circassia totally, and to execute the designs they have long harboured against the Ottoman Empire.'

The Sultan therefore ordered the Grand Vizir to renounce this secret article. But Ahmed Paşa resisted. The Russians had based their concession – relinquishing significant conquests in the Caucasus and the reestablishment of the *ante bellum* border – on the Ottomans' concession of the second secret article. Ahmed Paşa thought the exchange fair and justified in order to secure the treaty and achieve the peace before an invasion by France. Galib Efendi agreed, but the whole treaty was now in real danger of being lost.

The Sultan reprimanded the Grand Vizir and also directed that Stratford should be invited to write 'secretly' to the Russians in order to lobby them to drop their insistence on the second secret article. Stratford was also to be requested to relate to the Russians that, should they not comply, the Ottomans were likely to drop the whole treaty.[5]

Before agreeing to lobby the Russians, Stratford first attempted to lobby the Ottomans. He met with the Reis Efendi in the first days of June 1812 and implored him to seize this last chance for peace. The Reis Efendi responded by again accusing Stratford of being in secret collusion with Russia. Stratford reported to Castlereagh:

Your Lordship will perhaps be surprised to learn that that instead of receiving from them any expression of thankfulness for the effect produced by my letters, I met with nothing but jealousies, Suspicions, and insults. So disgusting was their behavior, that nothing but my resolution not to allow any secondary considerations to divert me from the great object in view, could have enabled me to endure it for a moment.

Stratford allowed a few days to pass but he found that 'the reserve of the Turkish Ministers on the whole question of Peace with Russia continued to increase. I was obliged to entertain the most unpleasant apprehensions' that the Ottomans may indeed reject the whole treaty. Stratford therefore met again with the Reis Efendi on 5 June 1812 and conceded to the Ottoman request that he send a letter to Italinsky in Bucharest in which he advocated the elimination of the second secret article. 'I thought it really of consequence if possible to dissuade the Russians from insisting upon the [second secret] Article respecting the Phasis,' Stratford explained to Castlereagh, 'not only because the Porte so strongly objected to it, but in order to show His Majesty's regard for Persia, and thereby to strengthen our interests in that quarter, as well as to put an additional check upon the progress of the Russian arms on the side of Georgia. . .'[6] So Stratford actually shared to a degree the Ottomans' concern about Russian expansion into the Caucasus. Years later his career's focus would be to support the Ottoman Empire as a bulwark against Russian expansion and interruption of the British route to India.

Stratford was pessimistic about the stalemate and thought it very likely that everything was lost. But he dutifully still worked to save the treaty. On 11 June he sent Pisani to the Ottoman Foreign Office to urge them again not to reject the whole treaty due to their objections about the second secret article. Pisani related that 'His Majesty's Government would deeply regret if the Porte were to refuse the conclusion of peace for that sole reason.'[7] And again on 13 June he sent Pisani to say that 'It would be madness to think of refusing to ratify it, if the Russians absolutely refuse the change desired. . .'[8] At the same time Stratford was still urging the Russians to drop their insistence on the second secret article. In a meeting at Constantinople with the visiting Russian councillor of

state, Bulgakov, on 12 June 1812, Stratford defended the
Ottomans' position and declared that they could never agree to
the second secret article because it was so threatening to their
regional military interests. But the Russians would not relent and
they even concluded, according to F. Ismail, that the opposition to
the second secret article came more from the British, worried about
their route to India, than from the Ottomans.[9] Stratford could do no
more about the secret article or the treaty. The Ottomans believed
he was in collusion with the Russians, and the Russians believed he
was in collusion with the Ottomans. His role had come to an end,
but the main diplomacy had already been played out.

Even though the treaty remained unratified by the two
sovereigns because of the impasse over the second secret article,[10]
its signing by the negotiators at Bucharest back on 28 May had
immediately produced two vital international developments. It had
induced the Russians to start the removal of their many thousands
of troops[11] from their Danubian border with the Ottomans for
redeployment to new positions against the French. 'The Tsar was
ready to meet the invasion,' suggested R. B. Mowat in 1924, 'but he
would not have been in a good situation, had not the Treaty of
Bucharest (May 28, 1812) put an end to his long-drawn-out and
harassing war with Turkey.'[12] The treaty signing had also convinced
the French, according to Mowat, of the failure of their diplomatic
offensive to draw the Ottomans into an alliance with them and the
Austrians against the Russians.[13] On 24 June the French crossed the
Neman River and began their epic war with the Russians.

In his excellent study of the treaty, the historian F. Ismail
concluded:

> The Treat of Bucharest was of immense significance for it gave
> Russia the immediate advantage of concentrating her forces
> against the French, thus contributing to the ultimate defeat of
> France, and it enabled the Ottomans to extricate themselves
> from a potentially disastrous war with but a slight loss of
> territory. It was further significant because it became the basis
> of future Russo-Ottoman relations.[14]

2

Stratford learnt on 18 June that Robert Liston had recently landed at the Dardanelles and would arrive in Constantinople about a week later.[15] On 25 June, the day after the beginning of the French invasion of Russia (and before news of which had reached Constantinople), Stratford sent a final message to the Ottoman government in which he expressed his frustrations for the recent past and concerns for the near future:

> If Russia be overcome, there is no other Power on the Continent capable of coping with France. All will then be more or less at the Mercy of Buonaparte ... The general Conscription will then be effectively organized, and France will really become, as described by the French Government itself, a vast impregnable fortress placed in the Center of the World, whence it will send forth its innumerable Armies, in all directions to subjugate mankind. The Porte, situated as her European Territories are, may depend upon being one of the first to be sacrificed, let her conduct towards France be what it will.
>
> In that Case, England, obliged to abandon all hope of preserving the Independence of Europe, will find it necessary to provide for her own Security by adopting a new System. She will be obliged to act upon the principle of perpetual war with the present Government of France ... She will find herself under the necessity of treating as Enemies all those Nations which are weak enough to submit to the influence of France, and to whose blindness and irresolution the evils suffered by the Continent will in that case be to be attributed. This System when once put in Motion will admit of no pause, of no Relaxation![16]

'No pause' and 'no Relaxation!' – these were fitting final words for Stratford's first mission to the Ottoman Empire and a proper mantra for his whole career.

Three days later, on 28 June 1812, Robert Liston finally arrived at Constantinople. Stratford delivered to him 'the Ciphers and Official Correspondence of His Majesty's Embassy at this Court, together with the unexchanged Ratification of the Separate and Secret Article of the last Treaty [of the Dardanelles] exactly as I received it from Mr. Adair.'[17] Stratford wrote his final dispatch to the Foreign Office in London on 3 July and concluded it with praise for his faithful friend and assistant:

> ... Mr. David Morier, who, during the two years that I have acted as His Majesty's Minister Plenipotentiary at this Court, has assisted me in the discharge of my publick Duties with a degree of Zeal, Ability, and Diligence to which no commendation of mine can do justice.[18]

'Our interests have been placed in very able hands,' Liston reported to Castlereagh on 11 July. 'And particularly in the latter times, Mr. Canning's interference in the negotiations for a peace between Turkey + Russia seems to have been managed with equal skill, energy + discretion, and − if we may judge by the Letters from Petersburg − with complete effect.' Liston also appreciated Stratford's organizational skills. 'The papers and official correspondence have been put into my hands in a state of order and correctness, which I have hardly ever witnessed.' And he praised David Morier for his Turkish language skills and for his 'manners', 'prudence' and 'propriety' and promoted him to Consul General at Constantinople.[19]

3

'A little patience, my dear mother, and I shall soon be with you, and you may believe me when I say that my heart yearns for the happy moment,' Stratford wrote home in June 1812. The day of departure from Constantinople finally arrived on 12 July. Stratford and Morier sailed in a Turkish ship across the Sea of Marmara to visit Bursa (as Lady Hester had advised) and Mount Olympus on the way to the Dardanelles. There Stratford boarded the *Argo* and sailed home. 'The sense of emancipation was very agreeable,' as Stratford recalled in his memoir.[20]

In December 1812 Cambridge University awarded Stratford 'by Royal Mandate' degrees of both bachelor and master of arts in recognition for his services 'occupied in the king's affairs' at Constantinople.[21] Castlereagh provided Stratford with time off to rest and then appointed him Envoy Extraordinary and Minister Plenipotentiary to Switzerland in 1814 and also employed him at the Congress of Vienna.

On the way out to the Congress, Stratford stopped in Paris where the victorious Russian Tsar Alexander 'sent for me, and by way of expressing thanks for my exertions in favour of peace at Constantinople,' as Stratford later recorded in his memoir, 'offered me the decoration of one of his orders, which I could not accept, and then a diamond box with his picture, which I was expected not to refuse.'[22]

At the Congress of Vienna Stratford's function was purely administrative and 'I had no place in the list of plenipotentiaries, and still less any voice in their official deliberations,' as he explained in his memoir. But he did experience the dramatic moment in the proceedings when Napoleon's escape from Elba suddenly became known:

I was twice invited to assist at the Board of the General Conference, and on one of those occasions the discussion or rather the conversation which took place brought Prince Talleyrand to the foreground … Napoleon's return from Elba was known. How were the Allies to deal with him? Was he to be opposed as a legitimate enemy, or was he to be outlawed as one beyond the pale of humanity? Talleyrand … took no part in the debate, if debate it could be called. He sat for some time absorbed in thought, and twisting a piece of scaling-wax with his fingers. He then rose slowly up, paused a moment at the table, let the wax drop dead from his hand upon it, and, with a countenance which seemed to say, 'It's all over,' moved his chair aside and disappeared by the nearest door.[23]

Several months before Stratford went off to Switzerland he was invited to the home of his former superior, Wellesley, whose son happened to be a friend from school. Stratford accepted the invitation but found that he could not fulfill it:

> the Marquis's high reputation had naturally great attractions for any young man brought up at Eton and looking for a political career, but his conduct during my mission to Constantinople had made so deep an impression on me that I could not overcome my repugnance to see him. I so far yielded to my friend's solicitation that I went with him reluctantly to Apsley House, but at the foot of the staircase my complaisance stopped short, and pleading an insurmountable objection I turned doggedly away.[24]

4

Despite the immediate advantages the Ottomans gained by the treaty, opposition to it remained fierce at Constantinople. Tension was high and took extreme and unusual forms. In July 1812 several cases of plague broke out. General Robert Wilson, a British military attaché passing through Constantinople at this time on his way to Russia, wrote: 'The Turks have an old saying that "when the Ottomans are at peace with Russia, plague re-appears;" and this prejudice, unfortunately for reason, has acquired proselytes by the symptoms that have shown themselves in the last few days...'[25]

By 17 September 1812 the Grand Vizir would be deposed and, as Liston reported, 'sent in the first instance on a provincial commission of inferior consequence: There is even some apprehension that he may lose his head.' His deputy was also dismissed, as Liston further described:

> The Grand Vizir and his lieutenant + friend the Caimakam agreed in strongly supporting the measure of a peace with Russia, + as that Peace is considered by a majority of the people as being less favourable than it ought ultimately to have been, + at all events as humiliating to the Ottoman pride, many persons are of opinion that the disgrace of the ministers

in question may be looked upon as a sacrifice made the Grand Signor to the feelings + the prejudices of the publick.

Also removed from office was the chief dragoman of the Porte, Demetrius Mourousi, 'as the Family of Morusi are supposed to be particularly devoted to Russia...'[26]

Liston continued to record growing Ottoman sentiment against the treaty. He reported on several large fires in the city, one in Balat on 26 September 1812 in which 20,000 houses and shops were destroyed, and one in Galata on the night of 5–6 October which burned for seven hours and consumed 5,000 structures. Arson was strongly suspected in both cases. Liston informed Castlereagh on 8 October that '... a surmise is naturally excited that both fires have been symptoms of publick discontent, particularly among the Janizaries.'[27]

On 18 October Liston noted in Constantinople:

a general feeling of regret and humiliation at having lost so large a portion of the Turkish possessions, + at having lost it *without necessity*: for an universal opinion begins to prevail ... that had their negotiators at Bucharest stood out a little longer, the critical state in which the Emperor Alexander found himself with regard to Bonaparte would have induced him to consent to the restitution of all that he had taken during the war.

Another large fire had recently broke out at the capital and this was 'thought by many to have been connected with the same sentiment, similar savage marks of dissatisfaction are still predicted...'[28]

And on 12 November 1812 Liston reported:

The Rulers of this country continue to feel deep regret at having made a disadvantageous peace + sacrificed (as they now think, *without necessity*) an essential part of the Turkish dominions. They have appeared for some time past sunk into a state of sullen dissatisfaction with themselves, + of rancorous animosity towards Russia, of which it is not easy to foresee the consequences.[29]

A few days later, on 17 November, Liston received the sad news that the chief dragoman of the Porte, Demetrius Mourousi, 'has been cruelly massacred at Shumla, by orders from hence.'[30] By 9 December Liston had ascertained the gruesome details and learnt more tragic news: the execution also of Panagios Mourousi, the deputy dragoman of the Porte with whom Stratford had had many dealings, including over the outrageous assignment of how deal with Wellesley's rejection of the Sultan's gift to Adair. For Demetrius Mourousi 'there was no regular Executioner on the spot, the poor man was cruelly butchered, and might in fact be said to be *cut to pieces*,' as Liston's report detailed:

> A very few days after, his younger brother Panagios, who acted for a considerable period as Deputy Dragoman of the Porte in the capital ... was invited by a civil message from the Ottoman Ministry (sent to his Villa on the banks of the Bosphorus) to repair to the Porte ... Panagios obeyed this insidious summons with trembling suspicion. He entered the boat sent for him, but found himself before he landed a State prisoner; + after undergoing a short interrogatory, he was beheaded, and his body exposed on the spot allotted for common Criminals – at the Gate of the Seraglio.[31]

Liston was himself in a dangerous situation. On 25 December 1812 he noted the Ottomans' 'extreme ill-humour with England for having *advised* the conclusion of the treaty ... Their conduct towards me has been very unfriendly...'[32] Stratford had been fortunate to have been relieved of his post and to have departed Constantinople just as the treaty was completed and just before the tremendous stress of the diplomatic situation had exploded and destroyed several of his Ottoman counterparts who had served their nation so bravely and faithfully. His main Ottoman collaborator in peace, Galib Efendi, would be deposed and exiled in 1814 and executed in 1821. In that cauldron of tension Stratford had functioned very effectively, earning the respect of Ottoman, Russian and British statesmen, and perhaps affecting the course of events, even though he had been abandoned by London and was just a few years out of school. This was his real achievement.

5

Many British statesmen and historians have proudly attributed the conclusion of the Treaty of Bucharest to the efforts of their own young minister at Constantinople. Robert Liston was of the opinion, writing to Stratford from Constantinople on 28 August 1812, that 'no one surely will say that you rendered a small service when you brought about a peace, who sees that that peace enables Russia to detach an army ... you have enabled Alexander to save the expense, to spare the blood, to escape the mortality, of a Wallachian campaign.'[33] Lane-Poole claimed that it was Stratford himself who 'by indomitable patience and clear foresight, brought about the end so sincerely desired by all the enemies of France...'[34] And many years later, in 1869, David Morier wrote that Stratford himself was responsible for 'negotiating and effecting the peace between the Porte and the Russian government just in time to release Chichagov's army.'[35] But these opinions were gross exaggerations.

Stratford Canning never conducted any peace negotiations between the Ottomans and Russians in 1811–12, nor was he the hero of the Treaty of Bucharest and nor did he never think or suggest he was. As late as 25 April 1812 he exclaimed to the Reis Efendi: 'Sorry that my means are so small.'[36] They were indeed. An inexperienced lad in his middle twenties from a remote country, especially one who had been completely abandoned by his government, was in no position to produce harmony between fierce and ancient rivals at a moment of supremely complicated intercontinental diplomacy. The master historian of the Treaty of Bucharest, F. Ismail, declared that 'Contemporaries and historians alike have claimed too much for Canning.'[37] In fact they have claimed the wrong achievement for him.

Stratford's relentless and creative advocacy of peace to both the Ottomans and Russians did likely assist them to negotiate with each other. The Ottomans found him useful in his supporting role in advancing peace and that is why the Sultan pronounced him 'reliable' and invited him several times to participate. The Russians also thought that they profited from Stratford's role, especially his daring secret communication to them at Bucharest in May 1812. This and other initiatives of Stratford, including his bold military move at Napoli di Romania in November 1811, may have provided the Ottomans and Russians with additional impetus to concede points to each other so that they could sign the treaty on 28 May 1812, critically before the French invasion of Russia.

Stratford's real accomplishment was not as grand as being the legendary hero of the Treaty of Bucharest. It was instead a much more human story. Having been thrown up against the world as a youth, assigned against his will to a vital and almost-impossible diplomatic task at Constantinople during a tense and dangerous time there and at a critical moment in European history, he overcame his complete lack of experience and lack of direction from London to make himself useful to his country and to its allies. Stratford was not the force behind the treaty, but he was creative and effective in the only role available to him: as an advocate of peace to the Ottomans and Russians when peace between them was in the interests of both countries and of Great Britain. On 3 August 1812, the *Morning Chronicle* declared in an editorial:

> although no *Ambassador* from this country had arrived there to take part in the negotiations between Russia and the Porte, we had a *Minister* upon the spot, namely Mr. Stratford Canning, who, at a very early period in life, has displayed an ability and zeal in the service of his country, from which many of the elder Members of our diplomacy might not be ashamed to take a lesson.[38]

Stratford's natural earnestness and eloquence distinguished him from the shadowy types who often haunted imperial diplomacy. He was 'sometimes too sharp and impatient,' as David Morier wrote home on 1 May 1812, but he was also 'the most frank, the most loyal, the most upright'.[39] These qualities or at least the appearance of them would always remain one important basis of Stratford's professional value.

PART III

GREEK-OTTOMAN PEACE, 1824–32

Bâb-ı Hümâyûn, the Imperial Gate of Topkapi Saray, and the fountain of Sultan Ahmed III.

CHAPTER 7

RETURN TO CONSTANTINOPLE

1

'Picturesque diplomacy' at Constantinople, as Stratford later recalled it, was followed for him by a decade of 'quiet and rustic diplomacy'.[1] From 1814 to 1823 he served first as British Envoy Extraordinary and Minister Plenipotentiary at Bern (during which he assisted at the Congress of Vienna) and then at Washington.[2] Neither post was nearly as dramatic or meaningful as what he had known at the Ottoman capital. 'I have nothing on earth to do, and as far as diplomacy is concerned, I might as well go to China...' he wrote to his mother from Bern in November 1815. 'In proportion as I get out of work, I become daily more expert in the lordly arts of twaddledom, politeness and gaiety .... we deal much in small talk, we dance, we waltz, and even have given, and think again of giving, balls ourselves.'[3]

In these years, then, Stratford's career was quiet but his personal life was tragic. In June 1815 his older brother Charles, Lieutenant-Colonel and *aide-de-camp* to the Duke of Wellington, was killed at Waterloo. In August 1816 Stratford married Harriet Raikes, the daughter of a former governor of the Bank of England. The Canning and Raikes families had long been close and all were delighted with the pair. But after ten months of 'blissfully happy marriage'[4] Harriet died in childbirth at their villa near Lausanne in June 1817 and the child was stillborn.

Stratford was immediately joined in Switzerland by his oldest brother William; and a close friend from home came and stayed with him until the end of October. He then spent the winter on his own recovering, using the light work-load to relax. 'I have plenty of books within reach,' he reassured his sister, Bess, in a letter of 18 December 1817, insisting that he was doing well. He re-read Gibbon near the very spot where the great history had been written.[5] And he commissioned a monument to Harriet that still stands in the Lausanne Cathedral.

Immediately after Harriet's death Stratford reverted to his old urge to quit his mission and get out of diplomacy. He must have been especially missing home at this time of great loss. Only three weeks after the tragedy he wrote to George and asked for help in securing a government position in London. A few weeks later he sent him another appeal, recounting with an almost resentful tone how George had drafted him into the profession and kept him there against his will. 'It is a matter of fact that my continuance in diplomacy,' Stratford wrote on 27 August 1817, 'not to say my entrance into it, has been purely accidental, and ever in my conception of a temporary nature.'[6] And on 30 September 1817 he wrote to his close friend at the Foreign Office, Joseph Planta, '... I have always preferred home employment to *any* diplomatic situation.... I should, therefore, wish *in the first instance* to exchange it for office with Parliament if that were practicable...'[7]

George's response was sympathetic but also firm. 'The principle of my conduct towards those connected with me in public life...' George wrote to Stratford on 7 October 1818, 'has uniformly been to endeavour to do them not only as much good, but as little disservice as possible. With this view ... I have always been desirous of placing their political fortunes (or of seeing them placed) out of the reach of the precariousness of my own.'[8] George was trying to keep Stratford in the stable career of diplomacy and out of bruising politics. In this respect it was a repeat of the episode almost exactly nine years earlier, after George's duel with Castlereagh in 1809, when he implored Stratford to remain at his diplomatic post in Constantinople.[9]

Stratford complied with George's wishes and as it turned out he did not have long to wait to leave the Swiss mission. In October 1818 he was granted a leave of absence by the Foreign Office. After travels in Italy he returned to Britain in March 1819. In July of that year he returned to his post at Bern but immediately requested permission of the Foreign Office to resign his mission, a move for which he must have obtained prior tacit approval while in London. Within a month his request was officially granted.

A few weeks later Stratford was offered and accepted the mission to Washington. But he was not formally appointed until July 1820, at which time he was also sworn of the Privy Council, and he finally went out in August 1820.[10] He took the post because he saw it as useful in making connections at home and then getting into domestic politics. 'I should prefer the parliamentary to the diplomatic career...' he wrote to a friend on 24 January 1820, 'the American mission is of all others, I think, the one best calculated to bring me into contact with the domestic interests of England, and to qualify me at some future day for being useful at home.'[11] Stratford remained in Washington until mid-1823.

Here Stratford had his first view of the new invention that was to transform his profession. 'The steamboats particularly attracted our attention...' he wrote to his mother in October 1820, a few weeks after arriving. 'The rapidity with which they move against wind and tide is surprizing .... The invention itself is a noble one, and the Americans seem to understand its full advantage.'[12]

Stratford's position was somewhat challenging 'owing to the ill-feeling created by the war of 1812 and the many delicate questions outstanding between the British and American governments,' as was noted in the entry for Canning in the 1911 edition of *The Encyclopedia Britannica*.[13] Nonetheless he soon found the young American capital uneventful both diplomatically and socially. 'Nothing can be quieter than the life we are leading...' he wrote from there in April 1821.[14] Or, as he wrote in November of the same year, 'Washington is not the Island of Calypso...'[15]

During Stratford's mission to Washington, George Canning returned to the Cabinet as foreign secretary in September 1822 after the sad death of Castlereagh. Stratford promptly took advantage of again having George as his official superior at the Foreign Office, requesting a leave of absence from his post on health grounds. This was granted, giving Stratford an early end to his Washington mission. He concluded the embassy in June 1823 and arrived back in London in the autumn seeking a home position. George attempted to secure something for Stratford at the Treasury but he did not gain the consent of the prime minister, Lord Liverpool. One wonders whether George did not try as hard as he might have because he wanted to keep Stratford in the profession of diplomacy, although political appointments are of course never easy to come by.

The post at Constantinople happened to be available. When Stratford had last been there, from 1809 to 1812, he had tried several times to resign his position but always without success. When he was finally replaced he hoped never to return. But now in 1824 Stratford agreed to go back. He was considering a new marriage and the Constantinople position was distinguished and offered possibilities for a secure career in the Foreign Office if he must stay there. Stratford was also enticed by the highest rank in the British diplomatic corps, Ambassador Extraordinary and Plenipotentiary, and a promise from Lord Liverpool elicited by George in March 1824 that he could be the vice-president of the Board of Trade and have a seat in the House of Commons upon his return from the post. Moreover, the Ottoman capital had again become the focus of European diplomacy due to the Greeks' uprising against their Ottoman overlords.

As with the first mission to Constantinople, George seems to have had larger plans for Stratford which he purposely did not share with him. 'Stratford, who is to be Strangford's successor at Constantinople, is now here. I think of putting the Greek Question into his hands...' wrote George Canning to his ambassador at Petersburg in July 1824.[16] George had not only chosen a career path for Stratford, and provided him with a unique education and experience in it, but over and over again he had also kept him from leaving it.

2

The Ottomans and Russians had very nearly come to war in 1820–21 over the Greeks' struggle for independence from the Ottomans. This was avoided in part through the mediation of Britain, which was strongly averse to a major conflict breaking out in Europe and possibly disrupting its commerce on the Continent and its route to India. But blood continued to flow in Greece, where massacres occurred regularly on both sides. In 1824 the Russians produced a memoir or working plan for Greek pacification and proposed a conference to be held at Petersburg in the autumn for the 'Powers' to work out a final plan. All accepted the invitation and George appointed Stratford to be Britain's representative to the conference before taking up his post at Constantinople. But in the summer the Russian memoir was leaked to European newspapers and several of its sections were at odds with the aims of the Greek provisional government at Napoli di Romania. In August the Greeks wrote to George Canning, protesting at what they saw as Russian designs to dominate their situation and requesting that Great Britain defend their interests.[17]

George was never a proponent of conference politics and has been described as having a 'horror of congresses'.[18] More precisely, he had an aversion to being pulled into collective regional policies, and he had always been strongly against participation in Russia's Holy Alliance over the decade since the Napoleonic Wars. George had reluctantly agreed to participate in the Petersburg conference because of his concern about the massacres in Greece and his continued fears about the Russians and Ottomans falling into war and destabilising European politics. After the protest of the Greek provisional government, however, George withdrew British participation on the grounds that the conference lacked legitimacy. 'It was one thing,' George informed the Russian ambassador, Count Lieven, in a meeting they held on 7 November 1824, 'to go on with the Mediation, *in ignorance* of what might be the feelings of the Greeks upon it: but it would be quite another to persevere in it, after so direct and unqualified a rejection of any notion of the kind by them as by the other contending party.'[19]

The Russians were upset by the British withdrawal and George was faced with a small but significant diplomatic conflict. It was an early episode of the British–Russian imperial competition, the modern phase of the so-called 'Eastern Question', which would shape European diplomacy for the remainder of the nineteenth century. For centuries the Russians had sought to secure their route to the Eastern Mediterranean via the Turkish Straits; and for decades the British had sought to secure their route to India via the Eastern Mediterranean and the Ottoman Empire. But it was only during the politics of Greek independence in 1824 when these imperial ambitions began to conflict significantly.

George decided that Stratford would still conduct his mission to Petersburg, in the capacity of special ambassador, so as not to offend the Russians further. But Stratford was instructed only to exchange diplomatic overviews (as well as to negotiate British–Russian border disputes on the west coast of North America), and not in any case to participate in the conference. On the way out to the Russian capital Stratford was to confer with Prince Metternich in Vienna. He was to inform the Austrians and Russians that Britain was, as his formal instructions read, 'earnestly and sincerely desirous of restoring tranquility to the East of Europe. . . .' Stratford was to explain that Britain was in favour of making an 'amicable intervention' on behalf of the Greeks but in order to do so 'a previous and publick disavowal of Force by all the other Parties . . . is an essential and indispensable condition.'[20] After the mission to Petersburg he was to take up his new post at Constantinople.

3

'You have a bug on your sleeve,' Metternich informed Stratford at their first meeting in Vienna in late December 1824. 'Whether he meant to try me,' as Stratford later recalled the incident, 'or to provide for his own security I know not, but the remark was not pleasing, and I could only defend myself at the expense of the hotel.'[21]

During the meetings Stratford determined that, 'the secret aim of Prince Metternich' in advocating the Petersburg conference was 'to discourage the Greeks, and to impede whatever progress it may be in their power to make towards the establishment of their national

Independence.'[22] In their meetings Stratford tried to impress upon Metternich that '... we were prepared to assert our own line if Austria and her Northern allies took measures to put down the liberal spirit then working in Europe.'[23] So on the one hand, George and Stratford did not want the Ottoman Empire being threatened and dragged into war over Greek independence; but on the other, they did sympathise with the Greek cause and wished to ensure that it was not repressed or controlled by Russia and Austria and their Holy Alliance against revolutions.

Stratford felt he had not made much progress with Metternich and he left Vienna for Petersburg on 7 January 1825. The land-journey took 22 days and was difficult. Roads were poor and hotels often unclean. Stratford's carriage overturned on route with one passenger being 'thrown head over heels – or rather wig over boots – into a neighbouring field, and I received the distinction of a slight contusion,' as Stratford wrote to his mother.[24]

In Warsaw Stratford met the Russian Grand Duke Constantine, who governed Poland for his brother, Tsar Alexander. 'He took me apart after dinner,' Stratford recorded in his memoir, 'and talked with rapid utterance on a great variety of topics .... I had enough to do in listening, and when at length the one-sided conversation ceased, my brains were in a whirl. Too much sail, I thought, for the ballast; too little coherence and discipline for a disorderly rabble of ideas.'[25] Stratford had witnessed here the unfortunate result of Constantine's confusing upbringing. He and Alexander had been removed from the care of their parents by their grandmother, Catherine the Great. Under her guidance, special tutors had relentlessly plied them at a too-young age with Enlightenment rhetoric that had no firm base in their personal experience.[26]

Stratford finally arrived in Petersburg at the end of January 1825. He knew that the Russians were still annoyed by George's refusal to participate in the conference. Therefore he expected from them, 'a strict reserve towards Me Concerning the Affairs of Greece...' as Stratford reported to George on 29 January 1825.[27] This proved correct. The talks amounted to nothing and Stratford spent most of his time aggressively sparring with the Russian foreign minister,

Nesselrode.[28] He eventually departed in the third week of March 1825. These talks were historically relevant for their unfortunate and unusual after-effect.

Stratford seems to have badly taxed Nesselrode in their meetings, and perhaps without the best motivation. His aggressive interchanges may have served as a cover for the weakness of his position, as Britain had originally agreed to attend the conference but then backed out. And Stratford knew how to employ a forceful and relentless style when he was being denied a diplomatic goal. Wearing down counterparts was part of the diplomatic repertoire and this suited an intense or overbearing aspect of Stratford's personality. Throughout his career his colleagues were sometimes also worn down by his relentless capacity for work. Seven years later, in 1832, the Russians took the rare and extreme step of withholding their *agrément* for Stratford's appointment as the British ambassador to their court. The scandal of 1832 would be recycled during the Crimean War, when Stratford was widely (and falsely) accused of pushing the Ottomans into the conflict in personal retribution for the Russians' earlier rejection of him.[29]

4

Stratford's relentlessness had done him no favours with the Russians but perhaps it won the day for him upon his return to London. Before Stratford had set out on the mission to Vienna and Petersburg he had been courting Eliza Alexander, the daughter of James Alexander, an East India Company merchant and MP for the notorious rotten borough of Old Sarum. But Eliza was much younger, only 18 years old, less than half Stratford's age. She rejected him at first and he had conducted the mission to Petersburg with heavy heart. But he persisted and Eliza finally consented after Stratford's return to London. They were married on 3 September 1825. 'Thank God we now live in better times,' George wrote to Stratford a week before the wedding. 'May heaven bless You – and give you support + comfort in acting – as you most certainly do – *right*.'[30] Even though Stratford was already middle-aged when he married Eliza, they would enjoy 55 years of happy union.

When Stratford had first gone out to Constantinople in 1808 he was just a couple of years removed from Eton, and he was very much on his own, especially after the departure of Adair in 1810. Now he was older and experienced; he had benefitted from the long respite of 'quiet and rustic diplomacy' at Bern and Washington; he was married and thus no longer had to fear the terrible loneliness he had previously known at the Ottoman capital. Stratford still enjoyed the prestige he had earned from the timely signing of the Treaty of Bucharest in 1812, and George now was back in office as foreign secretary. Even though Stratford still hoped the mission would be short – 'The sooner it begins, the sooner, I trust, it will end,' he wrote to his mother[31] – and he still wanted to get out of the Foreign Office, he was well-prepared to address Europe's most pressing diplomatic problem, the 'Greek Question'.

5

'I hope to save Greece by the agency of the Russian name upon the fears of Turkey without war,' is how George Canning had summarised his policy toward the Greek struggle.[32] He wished to cultivate the pressure being applied by the Russians in order to inspire the Ottomans to accommodate the Greeks. He was concerned about the severity of the on-going fighting and was sympathetic to the Greek cause, being in the tradition of British philhellenism and having received serious training in the classics at Eton and Oxford. In 1824 the Ottoman government induced its Paşa of Egypt, Mehmet Ali, to send his son, Ibrahim, and his army into Greece to suppress the uprising. The fighting was fierce and both George and Stratford were influenced by rumours about how Ibrahim planned to remove the Greek population into slavery and replace them with Egyptians and other Muslim peoples. 'I begin to think that the time approaches when *something* must be done,' George wrote to his ambassador in Paris in October 1825.[33] A few months later, in January 1826, George expressed to Stratford, who was on his way out to Constantinople, his concerns about:

the manner in which the war is now carried on in the Morea [the Peloponnese peninsula] – the character of barbarism and *barbarization* which it has assumed. Butchering of captives we have long witnessed on both sides of the contest . . . . the selling into slavery – the forced conversions – the dispeopling of Christendom – the recruiting from the countries of Islam – the erection in short of a new Puissance Barbaresque in Europe. . . .[34]

George had to weigh his sympathy with the Greek cause against his fear of a war breaking out between the Russians and Ottomans. 'War, once begun, would spread through Europe...' as George wrote in his instructions to Stratford for the mission to Constantinople, dated 12 October 1825.[35] George believed that war would lead to the destabilisation of politics on the Continent, drag Britain into conflict, produce a Russian victory over the Ottomans and put them in a commanding international position, including a likely disruption of the British route to India. He also instructed Stratford:

> You must remind the Turkish Minister on how slender a thread the peace with Russia hangs. You must represent to him the danger of affording to the Court of St. Petersburgh a convenient opening into a War, into which, for the sake of Greece, she would be glad to find an opportunity of interfering...[36]

George wished to enact a British mediation between the Turks and Greeks before the Russians could enact their own mediation or intervention. But if this should not be possible, George was not completely against joining the Russians in order to move against the Ottomans in support of the Greeks.

Most policy is to a degree conflicted and rarely pure in its goals. But George was especially conflicted and unclear in what he ultimately wanted to achieve concerning the Greek struggle. C. W. Crawley, the leading historical authority on the diplomacy of the Greek uprising, found that 'There is no public or private utterance preserved in which Canning gave any clear indication of the goal of his policy in Greece...'[37]

Stratford of course faced the same challenge as George: how to weigh personal sympathies for the Greeks against strategic interests of Britain that dictated working to support the Turks against the Russians. While still at Washington, in September 1821, Stratford had written home to George about the Greek struggle:

> To me, as an ancient sojourner at Constantinople, the struggle is full of interest: but I have not yet persuaded myself that the Greeks have a chance of recovering their freedom .... I speak of probabilities – as a matter of humanity I wish with all my soul that the Greeks were put in possession of their whole patrimony and that the Sultan were driven bag and baggage into the heart of Asia...[38]

And on 30 July 1821 he had written to Joseph Planta, 'The poor Greeks! I have almost a mind to curse the balance of Europe for protecting those horrid Turks.' Again to Planta about the Greeks on 1 October 1821:

> I wish to God it were possible to wring a concession of territory for their separate and independent establishment out of the Porte. There are plenty of rogues among them, but they are entitled to our compassion and I wish to heaven that the interests of Europe would allow of letting the Russians loose *tout bonnement* on the Sultan and his hordes.[39]

A few years later when Stratford was taking up the 'Greek Question' under George, he directly addressed the issue of how to balance personal sympathies against professional interests. In a mission statement that George instructed him to make before going out to Vienna and Petersburg in 1824, Stratford wrote: '... sentiments of humanity, and the natural sympathy between a people in the possession of liberty and a people struggling to obtain it, must not be allowed to operate to the exclusion of all other considerations.'[40] So no matter how Stratford felt personally about the Turks, Greeks, Russians or any other people, his prime function now and throughout his career was to defend and promote the Ottoman Empire in order to maintain a strategic balance of power between it and the Russian Empire and thus secure Britain's interests, including her imperial route to India.

6

The Ottoman perspective on the Greek struggle is well represented in an interesting record made by Stratford's predecessor at Constantinople, Percy Smythe, the sixth Viscount Strangford. On 25 July 1821 he held a comprehensive discussion with the Reis Efendi at his Bosphorus residence. The next day he sent a long report on it to the Foreign Office in London. Even though the discussion was from 1821, it can be considered a valid expression of how the Ottomans saw the situation still in 1826.

The Reis Efendi declared, Lord Strangford recorded, that his government had been obliged:

> to punish with severity some Traitors of distinguished rank in the Greek Church; and that we did so, in their quality of *Rebels*, and not in that of *Christians* .... A Rebellion was proclaimed, the results of which, if successful, would have been the destruction of the Moslem Faith .... our Religion was in danger. We did not hesitate to avow it. With us, the Religion and the State are identified, and the experience of Ages has taught us that to save the one, we must appeal to the other.

The Reis Efendi also clarified that 'we have never the intention, falsely imputed to us, of exciting a general persecution against those who differed from us in religious opinions. Such a proceeding would have been contrary to the Letter and the Spirit of our holy Law.'

The Reis Efendi further explained the Ottoman view that the Russians were using religion as a 'pretense ... to mask the injustice of the most unprovoked Aggression (should Russia really seek for War) that had ever occurred.' He then made an analogy with the Napoleonic Wars:

> I remember, said the Reis Efendi, when all of Europe complained of Napoleon Bonaparte ... He, too, knew how to proclaim grand and specious principles, and the liberty of the Seas, and the tyranny of the English, were to *him*, what the liberty of Religion and the tyranny of the Turks, are now, to the Emperor Alexander. What would Europe think of us, if we were to say to Russia: 'The Greeks, who possess the same faith as you do, have destroyed (as is the fact) many of our Mosques, have murdered our Clergy, with the most dreadful tortures, have violated their wives and abused their children, and unless you rebuild these Mosques and make reparation for these insults in Eight days, we will declare that your existence is incompatible with the safety of our Religion, we will make war upon you and we will call upon the Mussulman States of the world to make Common Cause with us against you.'[41]

7

Stratford was appointed Ambassador Extraordinary and Plenipotentiary at Constantinople, the highest rank of the British diplomatic corps, on 10 October 1825.[42] He and Eliza arrived at the Dardanelles in February 1826 and he immediately rode by horseback up to Constantinople. 'Descending a hill near Rodosto after dark my hack stumbled and pitched me over his head: I received no hurt from the fall, and my attendant, a Janissary, displayed his zeal by picking me up with the most affectionate alacrity,' as Stratford recorded in his memoir. He rode along the Theodosian Walls and 'just as I turned around the last tower to get into the town at the head of its harbor, a large horned owl, enlivened by the dusk, hooted from the ivy in which it was nestled.'[43] Stratford found it an ill omen for his return to Constantinople.

He had his audience of arrival with Sultan Mahmut II in Topkapi Saray at the end of March 1826. Very unusually Stratford was not required to disarm before the ceremony. Stratford modestly reported the event to George: 'I can only attribute this distinction to accident; but the circumstance has attracted public notice, it having been the first occasion for Centuries on which an Ambassador has been allowed to stand before the Sultan's throne with a sword by his side.'[44]

During his first months back at Constantinople, Stratford was unable to achieve anything diplomatically concerning Greek independence. Part of the problem was that he had momentarily lost his diplomatic leverage with the Ottomans because of a shrewd diplomatic move by the Russians. The new Russian Tsar, Nicholas, who had come to the throne just as Stratford was arriving at Constantinople, announced that Russia would not go to war over Greek independence. The apparent removal of the Russian threat of aggression for a time reduced international tension concerning the Greek situation.

Stratford worked constantly but could make no progress at all. At the end of his first month back in Constantinople he was reassuring George that, '... you must be aware that the Citadel of Turkish Diplomacy is only to be assailed by regular approaches.'[45] But after two more months of toiling Stratford seems to have become completely discouraged. 'I am nearly dead of fatigue and anxiety,' he wrote to his friend at the Foreign Office, Joseph Planta, on 29 April 1826, '... and never certainly had man so complete a failure in all his undertakings as I have had since my arrival here.'[46] The mission continued without success and on 4 June Stratford wrote to George:

> These rascally Turks continue as impracticable as ever. They are so not only about Greece but in every matter of business that one has to transact with them. They are much worse than when I was here last; and I feel that, with every advantage of station and political circumstance of a general nature, I have infinitely less influence than when I was a beardless minister here fourteen years ago .... One almost longs to bring the reckoning once for all to a good settlement with them.

Stratford was at such a loss in dealing with the Ottoman government at Constantinople that he considered appealing directly to Mehmet Ali. 'Would it be impossible to enlist the Viceroy of Egypt. . .' he also wrote to George, 'by holding out to him the prospect of a pashalik in Syria, in place of the Morea, and some assistance, if he behaves well, in his shipbuilding schemes?'[47]

Stratford's inability to achieve anything over these first few months back in Constantinople was not surprising. The 'Greek Question' was so complicated and full of animosity that a diplomatic solution at this point probably did not exist. Neither the Greeks nor the Turks would make concessions; both preferred a fight to the death. The imperial interests of Britain (maintaining its route to India) and Russia (establishing a route to the Mediterranean) were in such strategic conflict that the two powers could achieve no coordinated position despite their common desire to support the Greeks. 'When I look back after an interval of forty years, to the whole of the circumstances, it appears to me quite clear that the success I so ardently desired was a simple impossibility,' Stratford recorded in his memoir.[48] But at that moment the situation was completely changed due to a political *force majeure* at Constantinople.

CHAPTER 8

THE DESTRUCTION OF THE JANISSARIES

1

'The Janissaries are up' Stratford was informed by one of his assistants in the middle of the night of 14–15 June 1826. The ancient elite guards of the Ottoman court had attacked the headquarters of the Janissary *Ağa* and the official residence of the Grand Vizir. For decades the Janissaries corps had clashed with the reform programme of Sultan Selim III, especially with his efforts to supplant them with the creation of a new elite guard. This eventually resulted in the bloody Janissary revolt of 1807–08 and included the execution of Sultan Selim III and Mustafa. Now in June 1826 the same tensions over the reforms of Sultan Mahmud had produced another Janissary uprising.

Stratford immediately wrote out a dispatch for the Foreign Office in London and sent it off with the diplomatic messenger, whom the embassy had managed to call back even though he had set off in the evening. Stratford then dressed and went out to the embassy garden and (as he related almost 20 years later to A. H. Layard when they were sitting in the same spot, and as Layard reported in his memoir), he:

> spent many hours ... listening to the continued discharge of musketry on the opposite side of the Golden Horn ... and was

waiting the result of the attack upon the Janissaries with the utmost anxiety, as there was every reason to believe that, had they [the Janissaries] proved victorious, they would have fallen upon the quarters of the city inhabited by Europeans. . . .[1]

Later in the day while still in the garden (back during the Janissary uprising), as Stratford recorded in his memoir:

I perceived that some one from behind was lifting the skirt of my coat. On turning I recognized the commander of our Turkish guard, himself a Janissary, almost on his knees in a posture of supplication. There was no need of language to tell me that the revolt had failed, and positive intelligence soon followed to confirm that impression.[2]

The *Vaka-i Hayriye* or Auspicious Event, as the Janissary uprising and the disbandment of the corps came to be known, was not completely surprising to Stratford. His first mission to Constantinople had occurred in the wake of the Janissary revolt of 1807–08 and he had spent his first few months at the Ottoman capital in 1809 researching and writing a special report on the revolt for Robert Adair.[3] He had also referred to the theoretical prospect of a new Janissary revolt in his 1824 mission statement commissioned by George.[4] Furthermore he felt that 'their punishment as a body' was somewhat timely and even deserved, as he noted in his memoir: 'They had become the masters of the Government, the butchers of their sovereigns, and a source of terror to all but the enemies of their country.' But at the time of the revolt in June 1826 there was so much 'bloodshed and suffering' in the streets of Constantinople that 'Political considerations swayed me less powerfully than the sympathies of humanity. . .' as Stratford wrote further in his memoir.

The mere name of Janissary, compromised or not by an overt act, operated like a sentence of death. A special commission sat for the trial, or rather for the condemnation of crowds. Every victim passed at once from the tribunal into the hands of the executioner .... The Sea of Marmora was mottled with dead bodies.

The reign of terror also reached into the British embassy and Stratford defended against it. 'Not a day passed without my receiving a requisition from the Porte calling upon me to send thither immediately the officer and soldiers comprising my official guard,' Stratford further recorded in his memoir. He did not believe that any of them were involved in the revolt and:

I was pretty sure that they could not repair to the Porte without imminent danger of being sacrificed. I ventured therefore to detain them day after day, first on one pretext then on another, until, at the end of a week, the fever at head-quarters had so far subsided as to open a door for reflection and mercy.

Stratford then complied with the order to send them to the government but had one of his dragomans accompany the men and:

gave every assurance on their behalf which I was entitled to offer. The men were banished from the capital but their lives were spared, and many years later I was much pleased by a visit from their officer, who displayed his gratitude by coming from a distance on foot to regale me with a bunch of dried grapes and a pitcher of choice water.[5]

2

'To-day have been strangled forty-seven individuals of whom four Chiorbajis and seven Ustas,' as Bartholomeo Pisani, still Chief Dragoman of the British Embassy, reported to Stratford on the first day of the Janissary revolt and its brutal suppression, 16 June 1826. Pisani described how the standard of Muhammed was taken from its repose in Topkapi Saray and displayed at the Mosque of Sultan Ahmet, this being an official proclamation of a state of war. Corpses were piling up in front of the Mosque, on the ancient Hippodrome of the city (which was very close to the Janissary barracks). 'No quarter is given to anyone . . . . The name of Janissary is held in abhorrence by every rank; and it is credibly asserted, that Sultan Mahmud's resolution is to suppress the whole corps, and that name to be effaced for ever from the annals of the Empire.'[6]

Stratford also provided portraits of the bloody scenes in his daily reports to the Foreign Office. 'The events which have occurred in this City during the last eight and forty hours,' he wrote also on 16 June, 'are likely to be attended with very monumentous consequences to the Turkish Empire.' Stratford was correct. In the long run, the elimination of the arch defenders of the Ottoman *ancien régime* would help to open the door to military and other kinds of reform. In the short run, the Ottoman government and society were significantly destabilised by the Janissary revolt and its aftermath. This was one of the prime historical factors – along with the destruction of the Ottoman fleet at Navarino in August 1827 and the Russian invasion of European Ottoman territory in August 1829 – which would move the Ottomans to agree to Greek independence by 1832.

'I informed you some weeks ago,' Stratford continued in his 16 June report to George, 'that the Sultan had issued commands for the introduction of a new form of discipline among the Janissaries.' The reform consisted of 'the adoption of a particular uniform, the exercise of the musket and bayonet as practised in the Egyptian army. . .' This sparked 'suspicion and discontent' among the Janissaries. On the first day of the revolt, many of them had taken refuge in their barracks, which the Sultan then ordered destroyed. 'It was here that a Butchery began which has not yet entirely ceased,' Stratford wrote:

Many hundreds of the mutineers perished in the Barracks. Of those who endeavoured to escape the greater number were shot as they came out. Some prisoners were made and their fate was referred to the Sultan, who ordered their instant execution on the plea of their not having surrendered before the attack. Some fugitives got clear of the City, but orders have been issued to pursue and put them to death. Others, since the gates were shut, have concealed themselves within the walls. Proclamation has been made that no one is to harbour a Janissary on pain of death. Parties of armed men parade the Streets, and seize all suspected persons most of whom, on being taken before the Grand Vizirs, are immediately strangled, and their bodies thrown out for public exposure.

Stratford further described how foreigners were forbidden from appearing in the streets, all the gates of the city except one were closed, and all shops and government offices were ordered shut. 'Under these circumstances it is no easy matter to obtain information of what is going on.' He explained in his dispatch that he had sent out to reconnoitre several Turks who were in the employ of the embassy. Stratford did not yet have enough solid data to detail the number of 'mutineers' or of those slain. According to hearsay, 1,200 had been killed and 'The immediate cause of the revolt is said to have been a blow administered to one of the recruits by the Arab appointed to instructed them in the new exercise'. Many people suspected the Sultan 'of having excited the present resistance, or at least of having allowed the revolt to ripen for the purpose of crushing the Janissaries completely and establishing his favourite system on their downfall.' Stratford also reported that in the foreigners' quarters of Galata and Pera the Christian population had not been threatened.[7]

'It falls to my lot this day' – Stratford rather dramatically declared in his next dispatch, on 17 June 1826:

> to record one of the most remarkable events which have occurred in the history of this eventful empire. The Janissaries have shared the fate of the Strelitz. Their institution is completely abolished. The very name of that Body, which existed nearly five centuries, and which but yesterday was formidable, is consigned by Proclamation to infamy, and, if possible, to oblivion.

Stratford was making a valid historical comparison with the Russian palace guards and elite troops, the *Streltsy*, who, like the Ottoman Janissaries, had often toppled rulers and had resisted military modernisations. The *Streltsy* uprising of April–May 1682 at the Kremlin had terrorised Peter the Great when he was only ten-years-old. He formally eliminated the corps when he solidified his rule in 1689.

Stratford reported:

> The sentence of abolition was read to day in the Mosque of Sultan Ahmet, by the *Imaum*, or Chaplain, of the Seraglio, in presence of the Sultan Himself and before a great concourse of people. It was afterwards proclaimed throughout the City by public criers. The *Hatti-scheriff*, or Imperial Rescrift, which was read before the Sultan, stated that His Highness during twenty years had bourne with the insolence and contumacy of the Janissaries, that they had slaughtered two Princes of his blood, and that now, unreclaimed by his patience, having openly defied his authority, and committed the most atrocious excesses, they merited an exemplary and merciless chastisement at his hands.

After the pronouncements, the Holy Standard was removed from the Mosque and returned to Topkapi Saray, the gates of the city were opened and orders were issued for the shops to resume services.[8]

Five days later the uprising was completely finished but the 'reign of terror', as Stratford termed it, showed no sign of respite. Stratford reported on 22 June 1826 that:

> the executions and deportations continue to a most painful extent. Whatever motive influences the Sultan's mind, whether it be vengeance of whether it be policy, it seems to be the determination of His Highness not to leave his work unfinished. Rank, Poverty, age, and numbers are alike unable to shelter those who are known as culprits or marked as victims....

Suspected sympathisers with the Janissaries were rounded up daily. Past records and involvements were scrutinised. Denunciations abounded. False confessions and false testimony were forced:

> Respectable persons are seized in the street and hurried before the Seraskier or the Grand Vezir for immediate judgment. There are instances of elderly men having pleaded a total ignorance of the late conspiracy, and being reminded of some petty incident which happened twenty years ago in proof of their deserving punishment as abettors of the Janissaries. Whole companies of labouring men are seized, and either executed or forcibly removed from Constantinople. The Boatmen and Porters, who are chiefly Janissaries, are particular objects of suspicion and punishment.

A dragoman of the Porte had confidentially informed the British embassy that 6,000 Janissaries had been executed, not including those who had perished in the destroyed barracks. Stratford had also learnt that, 'The entrance to the Seraglio, the shore under the Sultan's windows and the Sea itself are crowded with dead bodies – many of them torn and in part devoured by the Dogs!'[9]

Six days later, on 28 June 1826, 'butchery still continues, and no one seems yet to foresee the close of it.' According to reconnaissance Stratford had elicited through connections around town, 8,000 people had been executed and 18,500 had been banished from the capital:

> The day before yesterday one of my Interpreters beheld the body of a man, nearly eighty years of age, stretched out, after decapitation, at the gate of the Seraglio. Another, to give an idea of the barbarous way in which the condemned persons are dispatched, saw six individuals engaged in strangling a criminal with his face upwards in the public street.[10]

3

For weeks after the Janissaries' uprising and the subsequent reign of terror against them, Stratford and his family and staff had been trapped in the British Palace in Pera. 'The horrors that have taken place during the last fortnight,' Stratford wrote to Planta on 1 July 1826, 'are enough to petrify a person of modest sensibility.' But even aside from the Janissary events, the mission disagreed with Stratford and he now badly regretted that he had agreed to come out again to Constantinople and had subjected his young wife to such an ordeal. He still worked constantly but could achieve nothing diplomatically. There were outbreaks of plague in Pera and also in Therapia on the Bosphorus where the British embassy *yali* was located and whither they had hoped to flee from the political terror. And the embassy building where they had been effectively quarantined for weeks was 'literally tumbling down'. Stratford declared to Planta that: '. . . I am dead sick of the whole concern, as I protested to you that I should be. I slave like a horse, + can do no one satisfactory thing of any sort or kind. The tide is too strong against me!' His wife Eliza was 'clearly suffering a good deal. . .' in what was probably a reference to her early pregnancy and related sickness while the reign of terror swept through the city:

> I look forward with anxiety to all, poor girl! that she has to go through. – Seriously, I never was more distressed in the whole course of my life . . . In short, my dear Planta, there is a fatality attached to this place, + I have fallen upon evil times. Remember my telling you when you first suggested the idea of my coming here that I should only come out to lose that one little bit of credit which I have gained in the course of my life!![11]

Stratford was referring to his achievements at Constantinople in 1811–12 and the signing of the Treaty of Bucharest in late May 1812 just before Napoleon's invasion of Russia. These were now, he feared, to be overshadowed by his professional failure on the present mission. Stratford was having a drop in morale. He could not resist blaming Planta for getting him to agree to the mission, as he had also previously blamed George for steering him into diplomacy and keeping him there against his will and sending him out to Constantinople twice. All Stratford wanted was to get out and return home. It was a repeat of his mood 14 years earlier on the first mission to Constantinople. Then, as now, he was convinced that he was trapped in an impossible position and was bound to fail, when actually he stood at the centre of meaningful diplomacy and would eventually realise his goals.

Stratford had to wait probably more than two months to receive Planta's prompt and touching response. Planta wrote on 4 August:

> How I have thought of You and pitied You and Your poor wife in having to witness such dreadful scenes as have been lately acted under Your Eyes! Are they at an End? and have You at least moved off from them to a more quiet abode? While I feel most fully the Misery to which You must have been put by the state of the publick Affairs at Constantinople, I cannot quite agree with You in the View which You are inclined to take of the unimportance of Your Situation; or of the Chance of Your present position at Constantinople rather depriving You of, than augmenting, Your Reputation. Your Despatches by the last messenger were of a most interesting Character and were extremely well drawn up, and Your Paper on the Affairs of Greece is one of the most masterly performances we have seen for some time. Therefore do not think that Your Exertions are thrown away, much less that they are to tend to Your Discredit.[12]

Planta was a true friend and he was completely correct — more than he could have imagined — in his belief that Stratford would find success on the mission and that this would enhance his career.

Blood continued to flow in the streets of Constantinople throughout the summer and into the autumn. Stratford reported to George on 12 August 1826: 'No one feels secure .... a reign of terror, which was expected to be short in proportion to its violence, is prolonged indefinitely.'[13] In September a report on the situation was submitted by one of the student interpreters of the British embassy, Richard Wood. He detailed numerous horrors including fires, arrests, purges, exiles, executions, tortures, desertions, mass inscriptions from the countryside. 'People in general apprehensive of Russian war. Sultan is for war, ministers for peace .... Much strangling. General discontent. Reaction hoped for even by quiet Turks.'[14]

War with Russia was a real possibility now as the Ottoman Empire was in a weakened and vulnerable position because of the Janissary events. On 7 October 1826 the Ottomans wisely avoided war by signing the Treaty of Ackerman which ceded the Principalities to Russian protection and which *inter alia* confirmed (as earlier provided by the Treaty of Bucharest) that foreign merchant ships engaged in trade with Russia should have freedom of navigation in all Ottoman waters, including the Black Sea, the Danube and the Straits. Sultan Mahmud's repudiation of this treaty in December 1827 would lead to war with Russian a few months later.

By August 1826 Stratford and Eliza had managed to escape the embassy building in Pera and to take up residence in Therapia on the Bosphorus. To get out of town and onto the water was a great relief and they stayed several months. 'Our commonest mode of exercise,' Stratford wrote to his mother on 21 October 1826:

is either a walk on the garden terrace, where the air at this time of year is delightful, and where we enjoy the most charming views in the world, or a row to the opposite coast in one of the prettiest boats that eye ever beheld .... The constant passage of ships and boats is a never-failing source of interest and amusement.

But the reign of terror was still on and one senses that, no matter the beauty and quiet of their new setting, Stratford could not relax. 'Within the last few days fresh horrors have taken place in the city,' Stratford wrote further to his mother. 'It is said that a conspiracy had been discovered, and that armed parties of insurgents are in several parts of Asia Minor. Executions and banishments are again therefore resorted to by the Government.'

Even before the uprising, Stratford had been unable to achieve any progress on the Greek Question. Now during the state emergency no diplomatic business at all was taking place and he was deeply frustrated. He still hoped to get out of Constantinople and to quit diplomacy but he also wanted to complete his mission and do something about the Greek situation and to have an achievement that would further his career and allow him to settle at home. 'For my own personal wishes and feelings,' he wrote to his mother, 'the most agreeable moment will be that which releases me from the bondage of diplomacy. But the release to have all its sweetness must come after the performance of duty.'[15]

4

Another reason why Stratford and Eliza were so eager to return home was that they were now expecting their first child. To be located far from home and in the midst of a reign of terror, all while a child was due, must have been terrible for them. In the winter, probably in December 1826 or January 1827, the child was born prematurely and died a few weeks later. Joseph Planta wrote in condolence to Stratford on 23 February 1827:

The premature Birth of the Child gave me Alarms .... and I confess I was always inclined to believe that the poor little Child would probably not live. For the subsequent account therefore of its Death, I felt more prepared. I anxiously hope that the Grief to You + more especially to its Mother, caused by this Event will, by the Effect of time, pass away; and that when you receive this Letter, her health will be essentially re-established .... I trust that her + Your trials are now drawing to a close; that all the future will be much more cheerful than the past; and that most *certainly*, you have gone through the worst.

Planta's letter also provided Stratford with probably his the first knowledge about another tragedy that would soon overtake him, concerning George Canning. Planta wrote:

> our poor dear Master (Your Cousin) has had an Illness . . . . from the End of January unto this day he has been there [Brighton] for the most part in Bed. He had been bled, and cupped, and cupped again + dosed with Calomel, put into Vapur Baths + drenched with Bark in its strongest form; and yet, notwithstanding all this, I hear from Persons who saw him two days ago that he has not lost much strength or flesh, and that his Spirits are very good. He comes to town tomorrow.[16]

Meanwhile Stratford still could not achieve anything diplomatically with the Ottomans concerning Greek independence. He was completely pessimistic and wrote to Planta on 25 February 1827:

> . . . I am exceedingly puzzled. I can form no idea of the probable duration of the Greek Business. I mean that part which I should like to bring to a conclusion . . . . I can only say I shall think myself not only the most fortunate but the most miraculous of Diplomats if I am destined to be the successful mediator of the Bases of pacification between Turks + Greeks. . .

Stratford wrote that he would agree to spend another year in town if he could achieve a settlement because, '. . . I never could leave Constantinople with a better grace than upon the accomplishment of so difficult + excellent a work.' But he still wished to get out of Constantinople and to quit diplomacy in general. 'Return to Christendom + employment at home are still my favourite objects. . .' The city was still reeling from the destruction of the Janissaries and Stratford remained concerned. 'Should the dangers increase at any time to an alarming degree, it will of course be my wish + my duty to provide for Eliza's removal to a place of safety.'[17]

Stratford's situation remained the same throughout the spring and summer: stuck in diplomatic limbo, waiting for the terror to pass, fearful for Eliza's health. He was suffering from occasional 'languor of body, and depression of spirits to a painful degree,' he confessed to his mother in a letter of 5 April 1827:

> ... my Greek negotiations must end before long in one way or another, and I look forward to the moment when I shall at length be able to leave my cares – at least those of Constantinople – behind me, and realize, *perhaps*, my long cherished hope of settlement in England. By dint of banishments and decapitations the Sultan has managed to keep his capital quiet. You might almost hear a pin drop in the streets. But depend upon it, the whole empire is going to destruction as fast as it can gallop. Though all is quiet, the Government appears to be in constant apprehension of plots and disturbances.[18]

Despite his continuing illness, George Canning became prime minister on 30 April 1827 after the fall of Lord Liverpool's government. Stratford learnt of the news no later than early June. 'I need not tell you how much I rejoice at George Canning's elevation...' Stratford wrote to Planta on 11 June 1827. Nonetheless this, for him, was a time of horror: living through the reign of terror at Constantinople, mourning the loss of his child and worrying over the health of Eliza. Stratford's first wife, Harriet, had died after losing a child in birth, and the pain of this previous tragedy must have contributed to his present anxiety about Eliza. He also remained despondent about word from London concerning his release from the Constantinople post. 'I am living in hourly expectation of a Messenger,' he wrote to Planta, 'but so many hopes have been disappointed that I know not where to place my reliance.' He declared that his situation at the Ottoman capital was 'attended with more anxiety + humiliation than I have ever before experienced in diplomacy. Depend upon it that we cannot remain as we are without disgrace, even if we could with safety.'[19]

Planta responded on 11 July 1827, assuring Stratford that:

> I have not failed to bring Your name before our Chief; and
> his view seems always to be that after You have completed
> what You have to do on this most difficult + arduous
> Subject of Greece, You should return home and that he
> should then find employment for You here, as we had always
> intended.[20]

So Stratford was again, as in 1810–12, unable to quit Constantinople
until he could find a solution on his own to an almost impossible
diplomatic situation. And then he received the tragic news.

5

'GEORGE CANNING IS NO MORE!' announced a bulletin in
the London village of Chiswick on 8 August 1927,[21] the place and
date of George's death. 'We lament to state that Mr. Canning expired
this morning ... at 10 minutes before 4 o'clock.'[22] *The Times*
observed the next day that Canning 'is the last of five who may
be said to have perished at their posts within the last 22 years – all,
with the exception of Mr. Perceval, sinking under the toils and
cares of office, or under vexations incidental to it, and operating
on already shattered constitutions. The names of Pitt, Fox,[23] and
Liverpool, and Canning, are warnings to political ambition in this
country, of the end which too often betides it.'[24] As Britain fought
her way through the Napoleonic Wars and then began her century
of massive empire, the concerns of state multiplied and statesmen
became over-burdened.

On the evening after George's death, plans were made in
government to send a special messenger to Constantinople in order to
notify Stratford as quickly as possible but for some reason this was
not done, as Stratford was later informed by a family friend.[25] He
therefore learnt of George's death only on 5 September from a
dispatch via the French embassy mails.[26] He had had no idea that the
illness was serious and therefore, '... the news of his death took me

by surprize,' as Stratford recorded later in his memoirs, 'and at a moment of careless relaxation when I was wholly unprepared for so great a shock.'[27]

Joseph Planta wrote to Stratford on 10 August that the 'blow is so stunning that one hardly collects one's Senses under it ... a Poignancy which it is impossible for me to describe. So rapid was the Progress of the Malady that the poor Sufferer was hardly ever free from Pain till within six Hours of his Death.'[28]

'Oh! my Stratford, what a blank is left, a blank which it is impossible to fill up,' wrote Stratford's oldest brother on 15 August 1827. Harry Canning had nobly struggled with the family finances after the early death of their father and thus never had a chance to develop his own career. But George then rescued him with an appointment as British consul at Hamburg and there he had a long and pleasant life. So Harry also had a special connection with George and mourned his loss. And he sympathised with Stratford's position: far from home in a difficult posting, out of touch, unable to learn the news until later, deprived of his mentor and government patron. 'I pity you from my heart,' Harry wrote further to Stratford, 'who at this moment are ignorant of the great event + have all the sorrow to endure. I believe it will affect you more sensibly than any of us, as to you at this moment the loss is probably of the utmost consequence....' Harry felt that his own position at Hamburg was safe but he could see that Stratford's situation was much more tenuous. 'For myself I do not expect that this event will cause any change in my situation. I shall probably be permitted to jog on here for the present | as long as I like; but you have something to do.'[29]

Stratford was in shock for weeks over the news. He wrote to Planta on 1 October:

To me, whose eyes have held no part of the mournful scene, the whole appears as a hideous dream, and my mind had scarcely yet satisfied itself of the reality. Yet real, alas! it is .... I am now more anxious than ever to get home; and not the less so on Eliza's account, who (I mention it in *strict confidence*) shews suggestions of being in a situation, which makes it my duty not to expose her to any unnecessary risks. The fact is that we have all been under anxiety about our Ladies; and although the *corrected* Language of the Reis Efendi has been such as to justify our detaining them till now, my Russian Colleague has two masked vessels before his door on the Bosphorus for the eventual removal of his family, and Sir E. Codrington has very considerably sent up the best vessel he can spare to Tenedos for mine ... It results from these circumstances that my situation is in every respect a critical one.

Stratford was also upset about the inconsiderateness of the Foreign Office in London. 'Lord Dudley [the foreign secretary] should have sent me a Messenger on Mr. Canning's death; or at least as soon as the Government was tolerably settled again. Such missions discredit and embarrass me, especially at a crisis like this. . . .'[30]

Stratford was completely frustrated and discouraged. He was worried for his wife, his family back home, his mission, his professional reputation and career prospects. The loss of a connection at the top of government made it even more unlikely than ever that he and Eliza would be able to quit Constantinople. And soon another crisis would be upon them.

CHAPTER 9

THE BATTLE OF NAVARINO

1

'An Express from Smyrna brought us this morning intelligence,' Stratford wrote to Dudley on 1 November 1827, 'of the total destruction of the Turkish and Egyptian fleets on the 20th ultimo in the port of Navarino by the combined Squadrons of England, France and Russia .... The event which has burst in upon us so suddenly is of too extraordinary a character to admit of our calculating its effect with any degree of precision.'[1]

The Battle of Navarino (also referred to as Navarin and Navarine, located on the southwest coast of the Peloponnese), was the last major naval battle fought entirely between sailing ships. It would completely change the course of the Greek Question and radically alter Stratford's fate. The background of 'the untoward event', as King George IV would describe it,[2] was based on a contradictory diplomacy. The British and Russians on the one hand were united in wanting to promote Greek independence, but on the other hand they were divided on the prospect of war with the Ottomans. The Russians were ready for it, but the British dreaded it, fearing that such a war would destabilise the politics of the continent and interrupt their route to India.

In the past year the military situation had swung in the Ottomans' favor. Back in 1824 the Ottoman Paşa of Egypt, Mehmet Ali, had agreed to send to Greece his highly effective troops, which he had trained in Western military methods. His son, Ibrahim, led a flotilla of 63 ships and 100 transport ships carrying 16,000 troops, launching from Alexandria in July 1824.[3] This had culminated in a series of important Ottoman victories in Greece over the first half of 1827.

The British, French and Russians responded by concluding the Treaty of London on 6 July 1827, George Canning being one of its architects. This was primarily an agreement for enacting an armistice in Greece and preventing the Egyptian and Turkish fleets from resupplying their forces on the Greek mainland. The 'important part of the treaty', as C. W. Crawley observed, was its article which spelt out that if the Ottomans should not accept allied mediation after one month, the Powers would send consuls to Greece and thus effect a *de facto* recognition of Greek independence. This article also provided for joint allied naval action to maintain an armistice between the Greeks and Ottomans. Instructions sent a week later to allied ambassadors and naval commanders in the region further directed that if the Ottomans were to refuse the armistice, then the allied naval squadrons were to unite themselves in order to prevent supplies reaching Ottoman forces in Greece.[4]

An Egyptian fleet of about 100 warships departed Alexandria for Greece on 5 August 1827. Also headed to the area was a Turkish fleet which had recently launched from Constantinople and consisted of 16 warships. The British and French squadrons that had been dispatched to the region in order to enforce the Treaty of London, under the command of Vice-Admiral Edward Codrington (one of Nelson's captains at Trafalgar),[5] and Rear-Admiral Henri de Rigny, sailed together to the capital of the Greek provisional government at Napoli di Romania in order to make a show of support against the approaching Egyptian–Turkish flotilla.

As a possible conflict loomed, both Codrington and de Rigny were justifiably confused about their military situation. The Treaty of London was a complex concoction. It attempted to apply diplomatic and military pressure on the Ottomans in order to assist the Greek cause but it also simultaneously sought to prevent the outbreak of hostilities. Crawley observed that, 'The Treaty was, perhaps inevitably, a compromise between a strictly impartial mediation and an open intervention on behalf of the Greeks; but it led to a great deal of sophistry and puzzled the admirals not a little.' The subsequent instructions sent out to the commanders about how to enforce the treaty at sea were also confused and vague.[6]

Seeking clarification, the French and British commanders wrote to their ambassadors at Constantinople in August 1827.[7] A joint protocol was prepared by the ambassadors on 4 September 1827.[8] But before this Stratford, not wanting to waste time, had sent his own instructions to Codrington as early as 3 and 11 May, and also on 19 August and 1 September 1827. These stark directives are of prime historical importance in the much-debated question of who was responsible for the outbreak of hostilities at Navarino, and they are examined below.

The Turkish fleet that had left Constantinople reached the bay of Navarino in the second week of September 1827, when it combined with the ships of Ibrahim which had already arrived in the bay. Meanwhile the British and French squadrons combined with the Russian and later began cruising off the southern Peloponnese.[9]

The situation was tense at Constantinople, as an engagement by the opposing fleets was expected. Each of the British, French and Russian ambassadors at Constantinople had made secret provisions for smuggling out their families should circumstances dictate this necessary. 'Apprehensive that it will shortly become necessary for me to provide for Mrs. C.'s safety, + that of her female attendants, in case of matters taking a still more unfavourable turn at this Court,' Stratford wrote to Codrington on 1 September 1827 in a communication marked 'Private + most Confidential', 'I have to request you will let me know by the earliest opportunity whether you are likely to be able to spare a frigate for their conveyance from the Dardanelles to Corfu in the course of this month, + if so, how soon.'[10]

Throughout September 1827 Stratford together with the French ambassador, Guilleminot, and the Russian, Ribeaupierre, continued to hold conferences with the Reis Efendi, Pertev, but these 'proved to be a mere loss of time,' as Stratford recorded in his memoir.[11] As the autumn began and the stormy season approached, both the Allied and Ottoman fleets faced certain danger if they did not find shelter. The closest satisfactory harbor in the region was Navarino,[12] where the Ottoman ships were already at anchor. The three Allied commanders together decided on their own to take their squadrons into Navarino. On 20 October 1827, while the Allied and Ottoman ships were all at bay together and all armed and ready, someone fired a shot and this immediately ignited a firefight.[13] The Ottoman flotilla was completely destroyed, with almost all ships sunk and 6,000 killed and 4,000 wounded, according to Codrington's estimate. The allies lost no ships and their casualties totalled 174 killed and 475 wounded.[14]

The British newspapers were soon full of accounts and questions about Navarino. The ultra-populist newspaper *John Bull*, which was often devoted to denigrating British statesmen, blamed the battle on the aggressive stance of the Allies. Its editorial of 14 November 1827 read:

We shall cry out – Oh, what barbarians! when we shall hear that Mr. Stratford Canning is confined in the Castle of the Seven Towers, and every Frank in the Turkish dominions is cut to pieces: yet this act, however cruel, would not be so treacherous as the attack upon the Turkish fleet in Navarin, without previous notice, and with the advantage of passing the forts and batteries erected for their protection. It is almost immaterial which side commenced the fire – it was the inevitable and pre-determined consequence of *taking that position*.[15]

The Times reached a very different conclusion in an editorial the same day:

In one respect, this battle is advantageous to the Turks; for we believe that if it had not taken place, – if the Turks had gone on evading the demands of the Allies, and they temporized instead of acting, – it would have been difficult to prevent Russia from espousing the cause of Greece singly, and in her own fashion, by

passing the Pruth [River], and marching an army into
European Turkey.[16]

But this is precisely what the Russians did only two years later,
approaching within 70 km of Constantinople in August 1829. This
Russian invasion, together with the elimination of the Janissaries in
1826 and then the destruction of the Ottoman fleet at Navarino in
1827, may be considered the major practical developments which
motivated the Ottomans to agree to Greek independence by 1832.

2

Stratford's role in the Battle of Navarino was central, much more so
than his role in the Treaty of Bucharest in 1812, for which he has
always remained far better known. He several times on his own –
without specific verification from London or agreement from his
French and Russian counterparts at Constantinople – advised Vice-
Admiral Codrington in forceful terms how he should conduct his
squadron in engaging the Ottomans. What precisely was Stratford's
historical role or responsibility in the battle?

In early May 1827, when Codrington and his squadron were still
located at Malta,[17] Stratford began imploring him to send ships to
the Archipelago in order to prevent the Turkish and Egyptian
squadrons from resupplying Ottoman troops in Greece. Stratford
sent a directive to Codrington marked 'Secret' on 3 May 1827.
Declaring himself:

> ... unwilling to leave too much to chance where so many
> important interests are at stake, I deem it an indispensable duty
> to give you this early notice of my position, + to suggest the
> Expediency of your coming for a time into the Archipelago ....
> I have no doubt that the Turks will make the strongest efforts of
> which they are capable against Greece during the present
> Campaign ... All my endeavours to bring about an
> accommodation between the two parties at war have hitherto
> failed of success....[18]

And on 11 May Stratford strengthened his call to Codrington to bring the squadron in:

> The high + menacing language employed by the Turkish Ministers ... obliges me to follow up my Letter of the 3rd instant with a more urgent application for your appearance in the Archipelago with as large a portion of your Squadron as you can possibly spare from other important services .... you will probably agree with me in thinking that it is our duty at so important a crisis to leave as little as possible to chance ...[19]

At the same time that Stratford was sending these forceful directives to Codrington, he was also writing in similarly strong diplomatic terms to George in London. 'The situation of the Embassy is really distressing, not to say critical,' Stratford wrote on 30 May 1827. 'If the Turks persist in their obstinacy, I wish that you would think seriously of changing the ambassador, not into a minister plenipo., but into the lowest kind of chargé d'affaires, with orders, known also to the Porte, to communicate constantly with the admiral of the squadron cruising in the Archipelago.' And Stratford wrote again to George on 12 June 1827: 'I submit with all humility whether it would not be better for the Greeks as well as for ourselves that we should either at once proceed to measures as coercive as possible short of war, in support of our proffered mediation, or frankly relinquish the proposal ...'[20]

On 19 June Codrington took his fleet out of Malta and headed east.[21] Stratford responded to Codrington on 2 July 1827 that: 'I ... look forward with satisfaction to the prospect of your early arrival in the Archipelago ... Your presence there in the critical circumstances of the time cannot be otherwise than highly serviceable ...'[22] However, Codrington was delayed from taking up his military position by some unknown complication. He therefore decided first to put in at Smyrna in order to facilitate communication with Stratford.[23] The ambassador actually expressed relief at this turn of events because in the interval he seems to have become nervous about his having authorised or inspired Codrington's operations in the Archipelago without confirmation from London.[24]

Codrington remained in the vicinity of Smyrna from the end of July until the beginning of September 1827. During this stay he had time to consult with his French counterpart, de Rigny. It was from there on 16 August 1827 that Codrington wrote to Stratford in his own name and also in de Rigny's about their confusion over the new Treaty of London and how they should enforce it at sea:

> Neither of us can make out how we are by force to prevent the Turks, if obstinate, from pursuing any line of conduct which we are instructed to oppose, without committing hostility .... The subject presents difficulties in whichever way we look at it, as such a business necessarily must ....[25]

Stratford was already in discussion with his French and Russian counterparts at Constantinople about how to advise their naval commanders concerning rules of engagement with the Ottoman squadrons. But he continued to advise Codrington on his own before these talks were concluded. On 19 August he sent Codrington an especially forceful directive concerning military engagement:

> you are not to take part with either of the belligerents, but you are to interpose your forces between them, and to keep the peace with your speaking trumpet, if possible, but, in case of necessity, with that which is used for the maintenance of a blockade against friends as well as foes; – I mean *force*. This is my individual impression, but, as I said before, I will talk it over with my [French and Russian] colleagues, and in some shape or other inform you of our common opinion on the Subject....[26]

On 1 September 1827 Stratford wrote to Codrington that he had discussed the issue of engagement with his French and Russian counterparts at Constantinople and they would issue a joint response

to their naval commanders 'in a few days'. But Stratford of course did
not stop there because:

> ... I am unwilling to lose the present opportunity of stating to
> you briefly my own impressions, which seem to be nearly the
> same as those of my colleagues. On the subject of collision, for
> instance, we agree that although the measures to be executed by
> you are not adopted in a hostile spirit, and although it is clearly
> the intention of the Allied Governments to avoid, if possible,
> anything that may bring on war, yet the prevention of supplies,
> as stated in your instructions, is ultimately to be enforced, if
> necessary, and when all other means are exhausted, by cannon-
> shot. ... [27]

Concerning this 'cannon-shot' directive by Stratford, Crawley
claimed that, 'Codrington repeated this phrase to all his captains';[28]
and Temperley more specifically noted that, 'The substance of this
communication was embodied by Codrington in a General Order to
the British Squadron, which he dated the 8th September, the day on
which he received it.'[29]

In all of this time, both Stratford and Codrington were acting on
their own initiatives as neither had received clear instructions from
London about how to act concerning the Ottoman fleets. This silence
was no doubt in part due to the conflicted nature of Allied policy
toward Greece, as well as to George's illness and death and then a
sluggishness of policy during the transition to a new leadership of the
government and at the Foreign Office.

3

Many have interpreted Stratford's 'I mean force' directive of 19
August 1827 and 'cannon-shot' directive of 1 September as evidence
for his responsibility for the Battle of Navarino.[30] Codrington
himself did so during an investigation conducted by Dudley a few
months after the battle.[31] Canning denied such responsibility in his
later memoir.[32]

These two directives of Stratford to Codrington in the crucial weeks before the battle are certainly important but they are also difficult to assess. This was a most complicated diplomatic and military case and any evaluation of it must take into consideration Codrington's expression to Stratford on 16 August 1827: 'The subject presents difficulties in whichever way we look at it, as such a business necessarily must ...' This opinion was still valid a century later and it was verified by the British military historian, J. Holland Rose, writing in 1927 for the 100th anniversary of Navarino: 'Even now the immediate causes which produced that collision between the forces of West and East are shrouded in mystery.' This remains true today and it is still not possible to answer definitively what Rose identified as the prime historical question of Navarino: 'In short, was there on one side, or on both sides, a desire to let the guns speak, or did they in that tense situation "go off of themselves"?'[33]

While there can be no doubt that Stratford strongly advocated aggressive measures, the degree to which he influenced Codrington is not as clear as many historians have claimed. But it is entirely possible that he was largely responsible for Navarino. If he indeed was, his aggressive stance and directives can perhaps in part be explained by the tremendous pressures he faced at that time. He was after all forced to make an immediate decision completely on his own, demonstrating one of Monsieur de Callières's dictums on the methods of the diplomat, published in 1716: 'there are even pressing and important occasions when he is sometimes obliged to make up his mind in the field, & to enact certain *démarches*, without waiting for the orders of his master when he is unable to receive them in time.'[34] And Stratford took this responsibility onto himself in 1827 when he was conflicted, agitated, worried and grieving.

On the one hand his sympathy with the Greek cause, his frustrations with the diplomatic stalemate, his being '... unwilling to leave too much to chance where so many important interests are at stake' (as he wrote to Codrington on 3 May 1827), and his desire to achieve a great diplomatic breakthrough which would allow him to establish himself once and for all in a new career at home – all of these likely suggested to him that the military initiative should be seized and not lost. On the other hand, Stratford had to be fearful of sparking a war between the Ottomans and Russians which would run counter to British interests. Such a move could have finished off his career with his own government, especially as he had no authorisation from it to undertake such action. It could have also placed him and his wife in a highly dangerous situation with the Ottoman government and Constantinople masses.

Deciding such a question of peace and war must have itself weighed heavily on Stratford. But there were of course other sources of great tension for him at this time. He and Eliza had recently suffered the tragedy of their child's stillbirth, and her health remained a concern. Having just lived through the reign of terror against the Janissaries must have also taken a great toll on both of them. The long war with the Greeks also continued to produce many grisly scenes, even at Constantinople. As Stratford reported to Dudley on 21 August 1827, just days before he made his two key directives to Codrington, 'Several hundred pairs of ears, described as being transmitted by Ibrahim Pasha, were exhibited at the Porte a few days ago.'[35]

4

When the news of Navarino reached Constantinople in the first week of November 1827, it '... blazed abroad in all its terrible proportions,' as Stratford described the situation in his memoir. 'Half a century sooner and a residence in the Seven Towers, or something worse...' would have been the fate of the allied ambassadors. 'Escape, had we thought of it, would have been impossible. We could not have gone ourselves and left our countrymen at the mercy of a resentful Sultan. Besides I had sent to the admiral a few days before the only armed vessel at my disposal, knowing that he was in want of such a craft ...'[36] Stratford had ordered the frigate *Rifleman* from the Dardanelles back to Codrington at Smyrna on 16 October 1827 – as it happened, just four days before Navarino occurred – because he did not want to detain it further without use.[37]

Stratford also recorded that the Sultan:

... was furious, and his first impulse, as we were afterwards informed, was to hold the ambassadors responsible for what had occurred. Our persons were respected, but at night our houses were surrounded by military patrols. Our dragomen were summoned to attend at the Porte ... Not knowing what was to follow, I burnt that same night a number of papers ...[38]

The Ottoman government also imposed an embargo on all European vessels landing in Ottoman ports.[39]

The emergency situation was changing on a daily basis, even hourly. Stratford wrote to Dudley on 6 November 1827 that just the day before '... it was believed that the Porte had determined on a rupture of diplomatic relations with the Three Allied Powers, and was only hesitating as to War.' But the situation had improved and '... appearances are more in favour of a pacific Decision than they were yesterday.' Stratford also conveyed to Dudley his concern that the Ottoman government may completely cut off the British embassy's communications. If this were to happen, Stratford felt that it would be 'out of the question for us to remain in the Country...' His overall conclusion for the moment was that 'the Porte is still in doubt as to the line which it ought to take.'[40]

At 10pm that same day (6 November) Stratford again wrote to Dudley that it seemed likely that he and his French and Russian colleagues would quit the city within days due to both security and political concerns.[41] 'Suffice it for the moment to say that present appearances are greatly in favour of our embarking before the close of another week, though we do not contemplate the adoption of such a step without making a last effort to bring the Porte to a sense of her situation and true interest....' Stratford also expressed concern for the fate of the British officials, subjects and property remaining behind when he would leave. 'The apprehension of a seizure of all property belonging to the French, Russian and English has somewhat abated today but I do not feel at all confident that the measure, however impolitic in the end, may not be adopted by the Turkish Government.'[42]

Stratford and his French and Russian colleagues continued to press the Ottomans to agree to the terms of the Treaty of London and to Allied mediation concerning Greece. Negotiations to this end were conducted in the weeks following Navarino but still without result. The Ottoman position was stated in vivid terms by the Reis Efendi in a long meeting which he held in his home with Stratford on the evening of 16 November 1827. 'The dominions of the Porte, he said,' as Stratford reported to Dudley the next day, 'were held by conquest effected under the sanction of God, and by what right, he asked, could any foreign Power interfere in their concerns? If England had rebels of her own to deal with, what would she say to any Foreign Power who presumed to interfere in their behalf?'

The Reis Efendi then portrayed the conflict as follows:

Greece was a house full of Scorpions whose owner was unjustly prevented from cleaning the tenement of its noxious inhabitants; the Mediation [proposed by the allies] was a gangrene which threatened, if once received into the frame, to destroy the whole body politic of the Empire; the Empire itself was a Vessel filled with milk and water, which the introduction of a foreign ingredient was sure to separate and to corrupt.

The Reis Efendi also expressed concern that if Greece were to be free, 'the Turks should be excluded from Greece while the Greeks were allowed in common with the Turks to enjoy property and the free exercise of their worship throughout the Sultan's Dominions.'[43]

After nine more days of fruitless negotiations between the Ottomans government and the allied ambassadors, 'We came to the conclusion,' as Stratford recorded in his memoir, 'that the only course which offered a chance of gaining the object of the Treaty without going to war, was a rupture of diplomatic relations and consequently the retirement of the three embassies.'[44] The Allied ambassadors informed their Ottoman counterparts on 24 November 1827, at the end of a five-hour meeting with the Reis Efendi, that if their demands for mediation concerning Greece were not accepted by the Ottoman government within 48 hours, they intended to ask for their passports (which were held by the host government by old tradition), quit their posts and break diplomatic relations.[45] The deadline passed and the Ottomans refused to supply the passports on the grounds that the ambassadors were acting without justification and without any written orders from their home governments.

5

The situation was 'delicate and hazardous', as Stratford observed in his memoir:

> It was also attended with much inconvenience and embarrassment. We were acting under a heavy responsibility towards our respective Governments. We had to provide for the protection of the merchants, for the conveyance of the official correspondence, and for the safety of the crown property which must be left behind. We could not foresee into what fanatical agitation the Musulman populace might be thrown by our departure.[46]

Stratford was also concerned about how his radical decision to quit his post and break relations would be received in London. He assured Dudley in a dispatch of 28 November 1827 that he had made '... with my Colleagues every possible effort, and every reasonable sacrifice to overcome the scruples and apprehensions of the Porte.' But now nothing more could be done and '... I fully expect to embark for the Dardanelles in the course of three or four days.'[47]

Stratford had already begun seeing to the practicalities of closing the embassy, of providing for its local staff and for remaining British subjects, and of getting out of the country with his family and attendants. He explained to Dudley in a separate dispatch also on 28 November 1827:

> On our part we conceive that, in going away ourselves we are bound to order the principal persons in the employment of the

Embassies to leave the Country also. There are others of inferior note, to whom as to the Merchants we think that the choice of staying may be left at their own discretion. It will be our object to make the best arrangement that we can for the protection of such individuals as determine to stay. We recommend them to His Excellency the Netherland Ambassador, who has consented to take them under his charge, unless some unexpected impediment should be raised by the Porte....[48]

Stratford gave the embassy dragomans a choice of either departing the country with him or remaining behind.[49] He also prepaid their salaries for the month following his departure.[50] Stratford arranged for at least one of his dragomans who was remaining in Constantinople, G. Calavro Imberto (and perhaps for others also), to be provided with an honorary title and with diplomatic status at the Netherlands embassy.[51] Stratford also provided Calavro Imberto with access to 3,300 piastres for 'purposes intimated in my last letter' plus an 'amount of eight hundred piastres I leave with you as a small fund out of which you may assist any poor British Subject who after my departure may stand in need of charity.'[52] He also directed the dragoman to maintain the payment of 'several salaries.'[53]

The Ottoman government withheld its consent for Stratford's arrangements with the Netherlands ambassador. It was also still refusing to let the Allied ambassadors have their passports and would not give them official permission to sail through the Straits.[54] The Ottoman government agreed to provide a residence permit ('*teskere*' in Turkish, and '*Carte de Sureté*' as the government referred to them in French) to any subject of the powers who had reason for remaining at Constantinople.[55] At this point the Ottoman government gave no assurances about protection for Ottoman Christian subjects.

Just before departing, Stratford met with the leading British merchants who were remaining behind at Constantinople and '... he assured them that all his endeavours would be used to restore peace,' as later reported in a London newspaper, 'and that their interests, under all circumstances, would be the object of his peculiar solicitude.'[56]

The majority of British merchants in Turkey were located in Smyrna, the international trade capital of the country. They had begun carrying out emergency plans as soon as they had heard about Navarino. The Lloyd's agent at Smyrna recorded the situation just after word of Navarino had arrived, in a letter of 5 November 1827 which was printed in *The Times*. Here it was noted that British and French trading houses had immediately removed as much property as possible from warehouses to merchant vessels in the port. These merchant ships were under protection of nearby American, Austrian, and Dutch warships and marines. The Ottoman governor of the city 'has promised to give ample time for embarking all persons and property, even should war be declared.'[57]

The British merchants of London were also suffering from the diplomatic crisis at Constantinople. On 3 December 1827 the news of the Ottoman embargo on foreign ships 'diffused much alarm this morning in the city, and business commenced consequently in the Money-market with very adverse appearances,' it was reported in *The Times*. The Stock Exchange was 'a scene of great confusion.' Markets were shaken also by the news that the Allied ambassadors had been denied their passports by the Ottoman government. A brief rally was knocked down by a false rumour which suddenly began to spread in London that the Russian ambassador at Constantinople, Ribeaupierre, 'had been sent to the Seven Towers ... the Stock-Exchange relapsed into a state of panic and distrust.' *The Times* summarised the situation: 'The speculators on both sides of the question have seldom been placed in a more critical situation than at present, it being obvious that every hour may bring either some act of submission on the part of the Sultan, or an utter defiance to the Ambassadors of the Allied Powers.'[58] Here was an early example of market volatility created by rapidly changing word of a distant developing international situation.

6

With departure imminent, Stratford was concerned that the Ottoman government may 'actually impede our Embarkation or passage thro' the Straits,' as he wrote privately to Codrington on 6 December 1827.[59] But further delay was impossible. On 7 December the windows of the British embassy chancery were closed up with bricks in order 'to prevent accidents from fire' as one of the staff recorded.[60] The next day, 8 December, Stratford boarded a ship with his large party after having walked down to the Bosphorus from the embassy in Pera. Stratford reported to Dudley that, 'The Porte adheres to its plan of not affording us any facilities for our passage through the Straits; but we have been assured confidentially that no opposition will be made.' So right up to this moment on board ship, Stratford and his party were still not completely sure that they would be allowed out of the country. Stratford also detailed in the dispatch that, 'The French Ambassador [Guillleminot] is already on board [his ship]. M. de Ribeaupierre [the Russian Ambassador] has not yet sailed from Buyukdere and the wind, which is favourable to us, is against his departure.'[61]

For the British and French the wind and weather had turned just right on 8 December for a stealthy walk down the hill of Pera from their embassies to their ship and then a surreptitious flight south toward the Dardanelles. There would be some complication for the British on the sail down and then more than a little drama to be played out in order to pass the Ottoman fortresses and enter the Aegean. Stratford provided a vivid account of the escape in his memoir:

On 8 December I embarked on board a small merchant vessel previously hired for the purpose. My wife went with me. Our companions were numerous – secretaries, attachés, consuls, interpreters, followed by our respective servants. We had to walk a considerable way through the town. It was already dark when we started. It blew hard from the north, and rained plentifully. We had the streets in consequence to ourselves; there was no hindrance to our exodous, and the wind, though strong, was favourable. The French ambassador had weighed anchor an hour or two before us,[62] but we passed him in the night and were the first to reach the Dardanelles.

On the route down the Dardanelles the British vessel ran aground but was swiftly restored. At the Ottoman castles of the Dardanelles, at the junction with the Aegean, they faced a serious challenge of getting past customs officers and the Paşa of the Dardanelles, without being discovered as the escaping British embassy. While the inspecting officers were entertained on deck with coffee, Stratford went ashore and met with the Paşa:

> who treated me as a mere English traveller with becoming hospitality. The windows of his Excellency's apartment looked out upon the water, and when I saw that our vessel had cleared the line of his guns, I told him who I was, and I explained the circumstances under which I had left Constantinople. He took my communication with Turkish gravity, and personal good humour. It looked as if he had received orders to let us pass; but perhaps he had been left in ignorance and only gave us the benefit of his Government's silence.

Stratford was then allowed to rejoin the ship. Despite fears about pirates operating in the area, they safely reached the bay of Vourla outside of Smyrna.[63]

7

Here Stratford transferred to the British frigate *Dryad*. He conferred with the French Ambassador Guilleminot and Rear-Admiral de Rigny about whether to enact a 'Blockade of the Dardanelles'. They together decided that this 'would not be an advisable measure at the present moment,' as Stratford wrote on 21 December 1827 to Codrington (who was not in the region), as they were concerned that available British and French forces may not be sufficient to enact a blockade. And they still hoped that the Ottoman government might radically change policy soon because of its weakened military position after Navarino.[64] The British and French ambassadors also decided here '... to wait at Vourla till they receive news of the departure of M. de Ribeaupierre before they set out for Corfu.'[65]

The British merchants at Smyrna addressed a special letter to Stratford on 16 December 1827 in which they requested assistance with their emergency situation. On 19 December Stratford announced arrangements 'for sending Vessels of War in succession at short intervals to the Dardanelles for the purpose of giving convoy to the trade for Smyrna.'[66] Then on 21 December he directed the British consul at Smyrna, Francis Werry, to call together the British merchants and to read to them a communication from him (as he was diplomatically prevented from leaving the British frigate *Dryad*). In this, Stratford assured the merchants that he would make 'every effort to procure to the English commerce...' He provided a word of comfort to the merchants in declaring that he believed they '... have no reason to fear any attack on the part of the Turks.' But he also did warn them that they should also prepare for the possibility of a 'decisive rupture', meaning a declaration of war between the Ottomans and British.[67]

After the departure of the allied ambassadors from Constantinople, the Sultan '... peremptorily ordered that all Franks who had no stated business in the capital, should leave it,' according to a British visitor to Turkey, Aldolphus Slade, 'and freighting two vessels, he caused them to embark at a day's notice. This harsh measure was excused on the plea of their being dangerous as spies.'[68] Dragoman Calavro Imberto reported to Stratford from Constantinople on 11 February 1828 that the Ottoman government had already 'ordered away' a significant number of non-Muslim Ottoman subjects of Constantinople. 'The most part of them were obliged to leave this Country and others to hide themselves for some time ...'[69]

On 22 February 1828 *The Times* published a letter composed by a British merchant which was dated 'Constantinople, Jan 8.' and referred to 'lists' of names of foreign nationals to be deported:

The proceedings of the Government in reference to those persons intended to be sent away, and those allowed to remain here, have continued much in the same spirit with which they commenced, and the lists seemed, a few days ago, to be completely decided on ... the names of no less than 101

English, Ionians, and other persons, under protection, have been set down for removal, and about as many French subjects. Owing to the departure previously of most of the Russian subjects, very few of that nation remain to be sent away.[70]

8

Almost immediately after the departure of the Allied ambassadors, the Ottomans and Russians fell into a collision course for all-out war. When Ribeaupierre and the Russian embassy left the Ottoman capital on 16 December 1828, they made an unusual demonstration. A German newspaper reported it from Constantinople the next day:

> Before the Russian Embassy quitted the Hotel [embassy building], the Imperial arms were taken down. This step, which was not taken by Baron Kroganoff [Stroganov],[71] when he left Constantinople, nor by the English and French Ambassadors on the present occasion, caused some sensation here ...[72]

On 20 December 1827 Sultan Mahmud II issued a *Hatt-ı Şerif* which repudiated the Treaty of Ackerman of 1826 and declared that 'as the object of the enemy was to annihilate Islamism and to tread Muhammedanism under foot, the faithful, rich and poor, high and low, should recollect that it is a duty to fight for their religion, and even willingly to sacrifice property and life in this vital struggle.'[73] This decree remains somewhat puzzling. It may have been something of a generic formula for rallying the people in a time of crisis. However it was certainly bellicose in word. The Russians then took advantage of the 'very injudicious manifesto proceeding from the Sultan Mahmud to declare war against the Porte,' as Stratford described the developments.[74]

'What possessed Mahmut II to go to war, unprepared as the empire was for another confrontation on the Danube?' asked the historian of Ottoman wars, Virginia Aksan. 'Most contemporaries concluded that there was little else he could do, as the empire was faced with dissolution on all sides...'[75]

After the exchange of various communications, the Russians declared war on the Ottomans on 25 April 1828. Word of this reached Constantinople on 15 May but intelligence had already been received there on 12 May that five days earlier a Russian army consisting of 120,000 troops with 300 guns had begun crossing the Pruth River into Ottoman territory.[76] The precise date of the Ottomans' formal declaration of war has not been determined.[77]

Fronts were eventually opened in both the Principalities and in eastern Anatolia. The war was a disaster for the Ottoman Empire. On 20 April 1829 the Russians entered Adrianople, or Edirne, the old European capital of the Ottomans which they had held uninterruptedly since the year 1365, located only about 130 miles west of Constantinople. On 8 September 1829 the Russians established a military line which stretched from a point on the Black Sea coast only 60 miles from the opening of the Bosphorus all the way west to the Aegean Sea.[78] They would also reach Çorlu, only 60 miles directly west of Constantinople.[79]

On the verge of having their capital invaded, and under fears of an uprising by former Janissaries and their supporters, the Ottomans accepted the punishing Treaty of Adrianople on 14 September 1829. This sanctioned effective Russian domination of the Principalities and navigation of the Danube, reopened the Straits to all commercial traffic, and required the Ottomans to pay a war indemnity to the Russians. A kind of autonomy of Greece was also promised. While this did not officially achieve a Greek independent state, the Russians' advance to the gates of Constantinople in September 1829 may be considered, along with the Janissary uprising in June 1826 and the Battle of Navarino in October 1827, the prime strategic developments which prompted the Ottomans to agree to Greek independence in 1832.

CHAPTER 10

'LAST ACT OF THE GREEK DRAMA'

1

After having conferred with his French and Russian colleagues at Vourla and attended to the security of the British merchants at Smyrna, Stratford returned home via Corfu, Ancona and Paris. He crossed the Channel from Calais to Dover on the afternoon of 25 February 1828, immediately 'proceeded as far as Sittingbourne, in Kent, where he slept' and early the next morning he set out for the capital, as the *Morning Chronicle* covered his journey.[1] 'On reaching London my first care was to know how I stood with the Government,' Stratford recorded in his memoir.[2] Having broken diplomatic relations, left his post and returned home, all without direct authorisation, he expected to face a significant amount of questioning and perhaps even reprobation from his superiors and he immediately reported to them in person, as the *Morning Chronicle* also noted:

> Mr. Stratford Canning, on his arrival in town, proceeded to the residence of Earl Dudley, in Arlington-street, and had an interview with the Noble Earl for near two hours. On leaving his Lordship, Mr. Canning visited the Duke of Wellington at the Treasury, and had a long conference with his Grace. Mr. Canning afterwards transacted business for a considerable time at the Foreign Office.[3]

Dudley, Wellington (now in the Cabinet and soon to be prime minister) and later the King all expressed complete approval for Stratford's actions. He described in his memoir:

> Assured by facts rather than by words that the Government had no intention of blaming me either for leaving Constantinople or for returning to England without orders, I felt nevertheless a natural curiosity to know what impression had been made at the Admiralty by Sir Edward Codrington's reports. Sir George Cockburn was then high in office at the department and to him I addressed my inquiry. On the first intimation of my object he exclaimed, 'You need not give yourself any trouble about the matter. We understand perfectly well how it all happened' referring to the battle of Navarino and implying that the responsibility of that event and its consequences lay in no degree either on me or my colleagues.[4]

With the outbreak of war between the Russians and Ottomans in spring 1828, Stratford was eager to press the advantage in order to secure full Greek independence. He firmly advocated sending British and French military forces to Greece, but this was rejected by government. Dudley, whom Crawley described as the 'most indolent and eccentric of foreign ministers,'[5] did not support Stratford's call for action in Greece, and he then left office by June 1828. The Duke of Wellington, now prime minister, and Aberdeen, the new foreign secretary,[6] also did not agree with Stratford's aggressive plans.

In early July 1828 Aberdeen sent Stratford to Greece to negotiate with Greek, French and Russian representatives about how to realise an independent Greek state.[7] Aberdeen also had in mind (but did not yet provide instruction to this effect) that Stratford would, after the negotiations in Greece, return to his post at Constantinople along with his French colleague in order to reestablish relations and thus provide the Ottomans with diplomatic leverage against the Russians. The Ottomans were keen on the return of the ambassadors for precisely this reason.[8]

Stratford arrived in Corfu on 8 August and here spent two weeks studying the political situation and waiting for the arrival of his former Constantinople colleagues, Guilleminot and Ribeaupierre.[9] The meeting place was then set at Poros, a small island near Hydra. Stratford set off for there on 25 August 1828, along the way undertaking discussions with the Greek government.[10] He also stopped at Navarino on 5 September 1828 and there met Ibrahim Paşa, the Egyptian invader of Greece and later of Anatolia. He had been camped with his troops at Navarino for several months while waiting to be transported back to Egypt, according to an agreement he had signed with Codrington. Stratford did not have any particular business to discuss with Ibrahim and he sought the encounter probably because he wished to meet and assess the famed warrior. He described the encounter in a letter to his wife, dated 5 September 1828:

> I have just been making acquaintance with Ibrahim pasha. Figure yourself a fat short man, sitting like a Christian with his legs down, a large clear blue eye, a high forehead, a brownish reddish beard straggling from beneath a face much marked with small-pox, and the whole appearance, in spite of shortness and corpulency, that of an active intelligent man, full of enterprize, subject to humours good and bad, and eager for instruction. . . .[11]

The negotiations at Poros were slow and difficult. The problem was not with the Greeks or with the French and Russian representatives but rather with the British government, which was averse to applying any pressure to the Ottoman Empire, in contrast to Stratford's suggestions. 'I hope they will be satisfied at home, though I hardly expect it,' Stratford wrote to his wife on 15 December 1828. 'They want settlement and peace by short cuts, but it cannot be.'[12]

The Poros negotiations concluded without agreement and in December 1828 Stratford went to Malta and then Naples to spend the winter there while waiting for instructions from the Foreign Office. He was deeply discouraged about his lack of prospects to conclude the peace and also about his career situation now that the

Poros mission had failed and Greek independence seemed as distant as ever. He was now overcome with regret at ever having returned to Constantinople to address the Greek Question. On 17 January 1829 he unburdened himself in a private letter to Joseph Planta:

> You may remember how often I have wished to break this Turkish chain, which seems to wind about me in proportion as I struggle to escape from it. There are moments, and those not unfrequent, when I reproach myself with the weakness of having surrendered my own judgment to advice of friends last year. I have worked harder than I ever did before; I have endeavoured in every instance to judge with soundness and honesty; I have suffered many privations – and what are the rewards? – blame and suspicion.[13]

2

Stratford and Aberdeen were at odds concerning two key strategic points. When Aberdeen had sent Stratford to Greece in order to conduct the negotiations, he had specifically noted in the formal instructions for the mission that, 'One of the most important and difficult questions for discussion will be the line of frontier to be proposed for the new state [of Greece].'[14] Stratford, Guilleminot and Ribeaupierre had agreed at Poros to approve a Greek border from the Gulf of Volo to the Gulf of Arta, an area beyond the Morea. This border recommendation was accepted by the French and Russian governments; but the British government sought to limit the territory of the Greek state strictly to the Morea and the Cyclades and thus it did not approve the proposal.

The other point of disagreement between Stratford and Aberdeen concerned the blockade of the highly-strategic island of Crete. Stratford wished to maintain the blockade in order to protect the Greek population of the island from the Ottoman troops stationed there. Aberdeen wished to lift the blockade because he specifically did not want the island falling under the military control of the

Greek provisional government. Aberdeen had written to Stratford on 2 October 1828:

> There are so many reasons for not meddling with Candia [Crete] that it is not necessary to state the most powerful of all; which is, a determination not to see an island of such paramount importance + commanding the whole of the Levant, in hands hostile to Great Britain. That such will be the case with the Greek State, I have little doubt. Even if not under the control of Russia, the sight of the superior wealth, happiness, + prosperity of our Ionian islands, will for years produce hatred + jealousy among the continental Greeks.[15]

Aberdeen therefore had ordered that the blockade was to be lifted. But Stratford believed that this move would endanger the local Greek population; and he therefore, with the concurrence of his French and Russian colleagues, refused to carry out the order. Aberdeen was irate at Stratford's move and a tremendous row broke out between them. This would involve serious and undiplomatic accusations by both men in their dispatches to each other. Submitting by mutual consent to a kind of binding arbitration conducted by Joseph Planta, they eventually agreed to remove their harsh words from the official archival record of the Foreign Office. But the row also resulted in Stratford making a conditional offer of resignation from his mission in January 1829. Aberdeen accepted this on 28 March 1829 and replaced Stratford with Robert Gordon, Aberdeen's own brother.

Stratford received Aberdeen's notification to this effect and his recall home around 10 April 1829. 'When I read half of it, I threw it on the ground and stamped on it,' as Stratford wrote to a friend. 'But I picked it up again and read the rest; and then I thanked my God that the Government did not *dare* to ask me to do such work as they had given that fellow [Robert] Gordon.'[16]

Stratford wrote to Planta on 27 April 1829 that he was relieved to be off the mission because he could not faithfully represent Aberdeen's line and also because he did not desire:

... either to take part in a wretched result, or to be suspected of not having been zealous enough in trying to bring it about ... I would at this moment most willingly go to Constantinople, if Government were to find sufficient motives (as I cannot but think they will before long) for acting in a resolute straightforward manner.[17]

Another possible reason why Stratford was pleased to be released from the mission was that he may have believed that his superiors were attempting, as Crawley stated was indeed the case, to make him 'the scapegoat for the result' of the failed negotiations over Greek independence.[18]

The careers of Aberdeen and Stratford would continue to intersect over the years and the two statesmen would clash many more times. Aberdeen would serve again as foreign secretary from September 1841 to July 1846,[19] which coincided with Stratford's next mission to Constantinople. And they would have extremely complex dealings during Aberdeen's tenure as prime minister from December 1852 to January 1855 during the Crimean War.

3

The conflict between Aberdeen and Stratford concerning the Greek Question was based on both professional and personal differences. Aberdeen and Wellington wished to limit the Greek state as much as possible in order to accommodate the Ottoman Empire against the Russians. Stratford was in general more favourably inclined toward and willing to work for the Greek cause, even though he was weary of war breaking out between the Ottomans and Russians and was strongly devoted to maintaining the Ottoman state as a bulwark against Russian expansion.

In considering Aberdeen's quality as foreign minister, it is perhaps sufficient to note the observation of Joseph Planta, who was ever sober in his evaluations and also had the benefit of the ultimate insider's view of operations at the Foreign Office. There he had just concluded 25 years of service, first as a clerk, précis writer and private secretary from 1802 to 1817 and then as the Permanent Undersecretary of State from 1817 to 1827.[20] A few months after Aberdeen came into office as foreign secretary, Planta wrote to Stratford on 26 October 1828: 'The present Chief of the F.O. is very kind + civil to me, + seems to withhold no Information from me – but *swaying Decisions* is another thing.'[21]

This tendency of Aberdeen was clearly evident in his attitude toward Greece and Turkey. He had been famous for his philhellenism as a youth during the Napoleonic Wars. But when serving as foreign secretary, he threw all his support behind the Ottoman Empire, turned against Greek independence, forced Stratford out of the Greek Question and replaced him with his own brother. Then, after the Russo-Ottoman War of 1828–29, Aberdeen completely gave up his hopes and support for the Ottoman Empire and again decided to embrace the Greek cause. Aberdeen's own son who was also his literary secretary, Arthur Gordon, the later Lord Stanmore, wrote a biography of his father in 1893 in which he stated: '... the conclusion of the Treaty of Adrianople led Lord Aberdeen at once to abandon the hope he had entertained of finding in Turkey any effectual resistance to the progress of Russia.'

Arthur Gordon also reprinted a private letter by Aberdeen to his brother at Constantinople, Robert Gordon, the replacement for Stratford, written after the Treaty of Adrianople and clearly demonstrating Aberdeen's complete rejection of the Ottomans:

> You know that to preserve the Porte substantially entire was my great wish. But the instant that the Russians had arrived at Adrianople and we saw of what the Turkish Empire was composed, I changed my views, and determined to lay the foundation, if possible, of making something out of Greece . . . . I now look to establish a solid power in Greece with which we may form a natural connection, and which, if necessary, we may cordially support in the future.

Aberdeen now supported the full independence of Greece 'and that its frontiers should receive a considerable extension...', as Arthur

Gordon confirmed.[22] In other words, Aberdeen completely came around to Stratford's position on Greece soon after terminating him. Robert Gordon, whom Lord Melbourne found to be 'tiresome, long and pompous',[23] followed his older brother in completely turning against the Ottomans shortly after having strongly supported them.

While Aberdeen was subject to 'swaying decisions' (as Planta observed), there was something seemingly monomaniacal at work in Stratford Canning's actions: he was prone to attach himself fiercely to singular issues, relentlessly concentrating on them and driving them through at all costs. And yet he was also able to understand and hold complex and subtle positions. He never varied in his support for Greece and eventually oversaw Greek independence. At the same time, he was also a consistent advocate of support for the Ottoman Empire in order to maintain the state as a bulwark against Russian expansion. This was a somewhat conflicted and most complicated dual policy, one which would have been most easy to abandon, but Stratford consistently maintained it. During Ibrahim Paşa's invasion deep into Anatolia in the 1830s, Stratford would be the first and by far the strongest European voice calling for immediate military support for the Ottoman government against its rebel governor.[24]

4

Stratford returned to London in mid-1829 as a virtually dismissed ambassador. This put him in an especially bad mood concerning his career. He blamed his whole experience in diplomacy for his present difficult situation: lacking an established position at home even though he was already 42 years old, married and now with a child; being too old to enter a new profession; and all this after he had performed supremely at Eton and had begun Cambridge, which would have surely opened a home profession or political career to him if it were not for George Canning's having sent him on the Adair mission to Constantinople in 1808 and then kept him in diplomacy. 'His absence from home in early youth and the independent position he had held much before the usual age, had in fact disqualified him for the career of a parliamentary party man,' as was correctly noted in the entry for Stratford in the *Encyclopedia Britannica* of 1911.[25]

Stratford's ill-feeling now toward his diplomatic service seems to have been exacerbated when Aberdeen lodged him with a heavy and tedious assignment in the autumn of 1829: writing up the British case in a dispute with the United States concerning its northern border, to be arbitrated by the King of the Netherlands. While Stratford was still working on this, in December 1829 he was invested as a Knight Grand Cross, Order of the Bath in recognition of his public services in diplomacy (perhaps an expedient move by the government in response to his being popularly regarded as a hero of Navarino). But this honour did not overcome Stratford's resentment against his diplomatic career. He wrote to his wife on 11 December 1829, a few days after the conferment of the knighthood:

> ... I am sometimes half tempted to blaze out against the waiters and cooks who seem to have an understanding together for the trial of my patience. Yes; Sir Stratford! No; Sir Stratford! You must not surprized of I go back to Windsor and beg his Majesty to unknight and unriband me ... The North American papers have half killed me. I worked at them yesterday, by tongue and pen, from breakfast-time till two at night.[26]

After his unfortunate experiences with Aberdeen, and lacking George Canning's guiding hand, Stratford now attempted to quit diplomacy and pursue his old dream of becoming a home statesman. He sat in the House of Commons first for the notorious borough of Old Sarum, officially from April 1828 to 1830 (even though he was on the diplomatic mission to Poros for much of this time, from July 1828 to mid-1829). 'I was indebted for the seat to my father-in-law, Mr. Alexander, who jointly with his brother, the East India director, possessed the nomination at Old Sarum,' Stratford wrote in his memoir. 'I cannot say that I was much attracted by the honour of representing the rottenest borough on the list. But several considerations pleaded in its favour. The seat was free of expense ... it bound me to no party ... it also relieved me from responsibility to the constituent body. My constituents were eleven in number. They voted in obedience to their landlord. Not one of them did I ever see.'[27]

Stratford took the oath of office on 3 April 1828 and made his first speech in the House of Commons on 13 May. This was in support of a pension for George Canning's widow. He spoke on inspiration, without plan or preparation, and performed poorly. 'I was kept back by something under the name of shyness or timidity. . .' he described in his memoir. 'It cost me a good deal to walk up the House. To go above the gangway was for some time simply impossible.'[28] Charles Ellis, the devoted family friend and lieutenant to George Canning, found Stratford's first performance a 'sad failure' and noted that 'with his expectations of success as a parliamentary speaker, the disappointment must have been very severe.'[29] He who was so at ease and authoritative in speaking with a sultan or a king had severe stage-fright in front of a group of his parliamentary colleagues.

Stratford's seat at Old Sarum was retaken by his father-in-law's brother in 1830. He therefore tried his luck with the Leominster electorate but quickly abandoned the attempt. Southampton, Marlborough and Liverpool (for which George Canning had once sat) were all considered in quick succession but each of these also realised nothing.[30] Finally he resorted to the convenience of another rotten borough, Stockbridge. 'My return was secured by the payment of a thousand pounds to Mr. Vizard, the attorney,' Stratford explained in his memoir. 'Considering that the borough figured in Schedule No. 1 of Lord John Russell's Reform Bill, and consequently that my seat was not likely to be good for more than one or two sessions, the price was sufficiently high.'[31] Stratford was indeed the final sitting member, from 1831 to 1832. His beginning at politics was progressing in a far less distinguished manner than had his diplomatic career.

Aberdeen remained in office as foreign secretary until November 1830 when he was replaced by Palmerston.[32] 'In the autumn of 1831 Lord Palmerston proposed that I should go on a special mission to Constantinople,' Stratford recorded in his memoir. 'His object was to obtain an additional extent of territory for the new and independent state of Greece.'

Stratford was reluctant to return to diplomacy and Constantinople. It was a hard life and, as he recorded in his memoir, 'My wife's
health was a subject of anxiety.'[33] But various factors now
temporarily brought him back to diplomacy with the Ottoman
Empire. He was already becoming disillusioned with his new career
in politics.[34] The prospect of securing Greek independence remained
attractive to him and now seemed within the realm of possibility: the
warring had ceased, both sides were worn out by the ten-year struggle
and desired resolution. Palmerston was a figure he deeply respected
and felt comfortable with. Friends suggested to Stratford that he
owed it to himself, to his government and to the Greeks to seize the
opportunity. Even Robert Adair, who himself had so disliked the
post in 1809–10, advocated now to Stratford that he had to take it
again. Adair wrote to Stratford on 18 November 1831:

> I have read so much in the newspapers about your going to
> Constantinople that I cannot help hoping there may be some
> truth in it. 'Hoping' you will say is a barbarous word from a
> friend, especially from one who remembers how much you used
> to dislike that place even in better times; but as there seems to
> be now one more chance for the poor Greeks, and as you are the
> only person who can lay hold of it and turn it to account for
> them I must be just, and so pass sentence upon you in their
> name as well as in that of your country.[35]

5

Stratford thus returned to the Ottoman capital for his third mission
there, arriving on 28 January 1832.[36] 'I was now on the scene of
the action…' as he described in his memoir.[37] Despite all of the
frustrations and inconveniences of working in international relations
and residing far from home, he was still drawn to diplomacy at
Constantinople.

He had been away for more than two and a half years. Many
changes had taken place. On 2 August 1831 a massive fire in the

diplomatic quarter of Pera had destroyed all the embassies except two, consumed 10,000 Turkish homes and made 80,000 residents homeless. 'You know that the Palace is burnt down,' Stratford wrote to Adair in March 1832 about the old British embassy building, which had been planned and founded by Lord Elgin in 1802. The scene of 'so many pleasant hours of diplomatic dalliance with Pisani and Chabert' was now 'a shapeless mess of ruins! My head quarters are at Therapia.'[38]

Sultan Mahmud II had pushed ahead with reforms after the destruction of the Janissaries in 1826. Stratford described some of the changes in a private letter he addressed to Palmerston on 14 February 1832:

> The Turks have undergone a complete Metamorphosis since I was last here, at least as to costume. They are now in a middle state from Turbans to hats, from petticoats to breeches. How far this change may extend beneath the surface I will not take upon myself to say. One of the Turkish Ministers who was Reis Efendi in 1827, took care to tell me that they are only changed in dress, – quite the same, he could assure me, in everything else . . . . The great difficulty consists in effecting such a change in the internal administration as may bring out the resources of the Country, which nature has favoured in every way; and make them convertible into means of national defence. Can the Qur'an stretch to this point? Will the ever-watchful Eagle of the North [Russia] allow it? I should say 'Yes' to the former question more readily than to the latter. Meanwhile, *Taxes, poverty,* and *discontent.*[39]

Stratford wrote to Palmerston concerning Ottoman reform again on 7 March 1832 in a long dispatch marked 'Confidential'. Now he seemed rather more impressed with the achievements of Mahmud II, such as his having broken the hold of several old and entrenched orders which had fiercely resisted modernisation. 'The Pashas of Bagdad and Scutari, the famous Ali of Ionnina, the Dére-Beys or feudal Lords of Asia Minor, the Janissaries, and finally the Albanian Chiefs, have all in succession sunk beneath the weight of his sceptre,' Stratford wrote to Palmerston. 'To these may be added the Mamlukes, who were treacherously butchered in cold blood by the present Viceroy of Egypt, acting under the sanction, if not at the instigation of the Sultan, and the Wahabees, who were subsequently reduced to insignificance by the forces of the same Pasha.' Stratford also called for the creation of a definite and clear British course of action toward Ottoman reform: '... I think the time is near at hand, or perhaps already come, when it is necessary that a decided line of policy should be adopted and steadily pursued with respect to this Country.'[40]

Stratford was still anxious and conflicted about being back in diplomacy. He had gone out to Constantinople on his own, leaving Eliza at home because she was expecting a child. He hoped the mission would be short. He wrote to Adair on 29 March 1832:

You do not seem to be aware that I am here only for a special service [to negotiate Greek independence]. The Embassy [to serve as chief of mission] would not suit me at all, and indeed I had much difficulty in making up my mind to come out as I am. I have had my share of this Country; and when one reaches a certain time of life, wives and children cannot be left out of the calculation. My best reward will be to serve the Government by succeeding in this last act of the Greek Drama, and it is only my anxiety to do so to the full that induces me to put up with the large measure of Turkish delays we have already experienced.[41]

Stratford's success now was swift, though complicated. His methods included employing the British embassy physician, Doctor Samuel MacGuffog,[42] as a secret go-between between himself and the Sultan in order to circumvent certain recalcitrant Ottoman ministers. (MacGuffog's clandestine contact was the Sultan's jester, Abdey Bey.)[43] A local Greek was also employed in the same function. A general agreement was reached at the negotiations in the beginning of July 1832 but several details remained. In order to reach final agreement, Stratford enforced a marathon negotiation session lasting 16 hours. When at this meeting progress was stalled on a single point to which the Ottoman plenipotentiary objected, Stratford enacted what he called in his memoir a *'coup de théâtre'*, in which the Sultan secretly agreed to send a messenger to break into the meeting and announce a directive that the point must be overcome. The long meeting was finally concluded and agreement signed by all parties on 22 July 1832 at 3am.[44] Later that day Stratford wrote a private note to Palmerston about the concluded negotiation, which included: 'No man in Christendom can have an idea of what we have gone through. I defy even a Dutch Negotiation to be worse. At length, however, we are fairly delivered of our burthen, and if you are satisfied, I shall soon forget my vexations.'[45]

Stratford had his Audience of Leave with the Sultan on 6 August 1832 at the Istavros Palace near Beylerbey on the Asian shore of the Bosphorus. The Sultan, as Stratford reported:

... was pleased to declare his satisfaction at my personal conduct, honouring me at the same time with the gift of his portrait suspended by a gold chain, and set in brilliants. This mark of His Highnesses's condescension, which is without precedent here, I confess I should like to have His Majesty's permission to accept.[46]

Stratford departed Constantinople on 11 August 1832 aboard the *HMS Bahrain*. 'On reaching the old metropolis in September 1832, my wife received me in our newly bought house, with a boy, newer still, in her arms,' as Stratford wrote in his memoir.[47] Palmerston wrote to Stratford, saying: 'I congratulate you with all my heart upon your safe return from your successful and brilliant mission.' Stratford's close friend, Gally Knight, also wrote to him in praise:

I congratulate you also most sincerely on your success at Constantinople. – Few men have the opportunity of so completely reaping the reward of their rectitude as you have had on the present occasion ... your temporary eclipse, and now – your final triumph – really it is complete in all its parts – and I have a great mind to write the *Canningniad,* an epic in 20 books, to give it immortality.[48]

A special registration of praise for Stratford was made by the eminent French ambassador in London. David Morier, Stratford's dear friend from the first mission to Constantinople in 1809–12, happened to sit next to Talleyrand at a party when news of the general agreement between the Ottomans and Greeks first became known in London. Morier reported the scene to Stratford in a letter of 3 July 1832:

> Sitting next to old Tally yesterday at dinner at Lord Granville's … he informed me of the news just received of your complete success at Stamboul. I can't impress with what sincere delight I heard this Doyen of European Diplomacy speak with admiration of my old master, and attribute to your sole Management so great a triumph in the Science of Negotiation. . .[49]

A few days after returning to London, Stratford wrote to Palmerston on 25 September 1832 in praise of Captain Pigot and the officers of *HMS Bahrain,* which had delivered him home after making an impressive display at Constantinople. He also requested that the Admiralty recognize the ship and '. . . that the First Lieutenant and Senior Midshipman of the Bahrain may be promoted.'[50] And on 25 October 1832 Stratford wrote to Palmerston in support of the claims of the dragomans of the British embassy at Constantinople that government reimburse their extensive losses in the fire of 2 August 1831.[51]

6

Stratford's success in the final negotiation of Greek independence at Constantinople in June–July 1832 was due to his extensive diplomatic skills, as well as to the fact that the Ottomans and Greeks both found him a reliable mediator for peace. Several years after Stratford's death, the *Illustrated London News* declared that the creation of the independent Greek state was 'the brightest achievement of both the Cannings, from first to last.'[52]

But Greek independence was due primarily to three historical events: the elimination of the Janissaries in 1826, the destruction of the Ottoman navy at Navarino in 1827, and the Russian invasion to the gates of Constantinople in 1828–29. These all greatly weakened the Ottoman state and clearly demonstrated to Ottoman leaders that they must enact external peace with their neighbours plus domestic reform, and that this could not occur until the Greek Question had been resolved. Stratford's aggressive role in the events leading up to Navarino – including his 'cannon-shot' directive to Codrington, and then his breaking of relations and departure from Constantinople along with his French and Russian colleagues, to leave the Ottomans to their fate with the Russians – suggest that he was responsible for circumstances in at least two of the three events which led to Greek independence.

When Codrington died on 9 July 1851, the Greek parliament unanimously passed a motion which expressed 'eternal gratitude' to him, and declared him to be an 'illustrious philhellene', both for his role at Navarino.[53] And almost a century after independence, Greek sentiment for George Canning was represented in Athens in April 1931 by the dedication of a statue to him.[54] It still stands there in Canning Square.

When Stratford returned to Greece in January 1842, on his way to begin a new mission at Constantinople, he was greeted as a hero for his efforts during the diplomacy of Greek independence. He was awarded the Greek Order of Saviour but was instructed by the British Foreign Office not to accept it[55] (probably out of concern that doing so would compromise his position with the Ottoman government). And on 16 March 1847 the Scottish philhellene, Edward Masson, noted in his letter to Stratford that in Greece 'the venerated name of Canning is enshrined in the grateful remembrance of every genuine patriot.'[56] Eventually, however, Stratford's role in the Battle of Navarino and Greek independence would be forgotten both in Greece and in Britain. This was probably because George and Stratford were confused in the public mind; because Stratford lived so long, 48 years past the creation of the Greek state and 22 years past his retirement, thus delaying and diluting reconsideration of his career; and also because of the predominance of 'The Stratford Legend' and his general decline as a historical figure. At 'The Navarino Centenary and Greek War of Independence Commemorative Exhibition', held at the Greek Legation in London from 21 October to 11 November 1927, not even one item was devoted to him.[57]

Recognition of the part Stratford Canning played in Greek independence did, however, find an utterly unique form of expression in the Levant. In autumn 1850 Stratford and his family made an excursion from Constantinople to the Greek islands during which they approached Mount Athos by water. The monks, relaxing their tradition of *avaton*, allowed Eliza, Louisa, Catherine and Mary Canning to land at the Holy Mountain and even welcomed them at several monasteries.[58]

PART IV

OTTOMAN REFORM: THE APOSTASY CONTROVERSY, 1843–44

CHAPTER 11

THE CASE OF AVAKIM

1

The negotiation of an independent Greek state brought Stratford renown across Britain and throughout the capitals of Europe. Soon after his return from Constantinople in 1832, he was appointed British ambassador at St. Petersburg, a prestigious post. He accepted the position, possibly indicating his intention to stay in diplomacy and relinquish his dream of being a politician. But the Russians took the rare step of withholding their *agrément* for Stratford's appointment as ambassador to their court. In the days when diplomats were international stars, the rejection became the talk of Europe.

While the Russians' rejection was officially based on a technicality,[1] a rumour quickly spread across Europe that it was due to personal animosity between Stratford and Tsar Nicholas that went back to their meeting at the Congress of Vienna at the end of the Napoleonic Wars. But this encounter in fact never occurred. Another version of the rumour on the same theme pointed to their meeting at the conclusion of Stratford's special mission to Petersburg in 1825. But this encounter also never occurred. Other explanations for the rejection have also been offered.[2] There are indications that the Russian foreign minister, Nesselrode, was the real source of the rejection of Stratford. They indeed had had long and strained dealings at Petersburg in 1825.[3] When in November 1832 the

British ambassador at Petersburg, John Duncan Bligh, inquired about the Russian rejection, Nesselrode responded with 'full justice to the talents and good intentions of Sir Stratford, but said that his suspicious temper and extreme sensitiveness rendered it so extremely difficult to do business with him, that he could not think of it without pain,' as Bligh reported to Palmerston.[4] And according to Cyrus Hamlin, an American missionary who went to Constantinople during the Crimean War where he was associated with Stratford and later founded Robert College, the first American college abroad, the fiction about the personal dislike between Stratford Canning and the Tsar originated with Nesselrode himself.[5] Furthermore, Canning and Nesselrode had the profiles of possible rivals: they were close in age, both had entered diplomacy about the same time and both would remain in it until the late 1850s.

2

Over the first half of 1833, Stratford undertook at Palmerston's request a special diplomatic mission to Spain. While on the mission, he seems to have reverted to his old urge to enter politics. In March 1833 Stratford declined Palmertson's offer to appoint him ambassador there. 'I wished to obtain a seat in Parliament, but could hear of no suitable opening,' he wrote in his memoir. His father-in-law and wife were against his entering Parliament because this would require the relinquishment of his diplomatic pension. But he still pressed ahead with his desire to be a home statesman. In late 1834 he received an invitation from Lord George Bentick to sit with him together for King's Lynn, in Norfolk. Stratford took up the seat the next year and remained in it through November 1841.[6]

'It is curious that during his diplomatic career he was constantly hankering after Parliamentary distinction,' as a British newspaper of December 1888 assessed Stratford's career:

> To say the truth, his talents were not such as would command success in debate. His powers of speaking would probably have

improved by practice, but he was not suited for party warfare. He was far too independent and too imperious, and the man who baffled Continental statesmen by his rigid honesty and wrung concessions from Turks by force of character, was out of place in the strife of parties and war of tongues.[7]

Indeed, throughout his tenure in the House of Commons, Stratford spoke little and failed to distinguish himself or receive a ministerial position. He was again disappointed in 1841 when the new Peel government merely renewed an offer of the general governorship of Canada, which had been previously made in 1835, and then suggested the treasurership of the Queen's household.[8] Neither of these were the kind of substantive position of home statesmanship that he sought, one which would place him in the centre of action in London and allow him to express himself about the life of the nation.

Stratford now finally admitted to himself that this aspiration was misplaced. And he had also suffered from the loss of his diplomatic pension. He therefore addressed Peel in 1841 with a request to be reinstated to diplomatic service. 'Lord Aberdeen then sent for me,' as Stratford recalled (Aberdeen had again become Secretary of State for Foreign Affairs in September 1841),[9] 'and his first words were, "I have now an embassy to offer you, but one, I fear, which you will not like." "Perhaps your lordship will tell me what it is," I replied. "Constantinople," was his answer. "With your lordship's permission I will take forty-eight hours to consider it."' This 'new banishment', as Stratford put it, he now accepted.[10]

He left Britain in November 1841 and made a visit of several weeks to Greece, where he was feted and honoured by the Greek state for his role in Greek independence.[11] He then arrived at the Ottoman capital in late January 1842.

3

Stratford had been away from Constantinople for almost ten years and the interval had been eventful. Upon departing in 1832, he had strongly advocated to the British government that it support the Ottomans against the threat from Ibrahim Paşa of Egypt.[12] Palmerston ignored this advice, for reasons which remain unclear.[13] Ibrahim's massive invasion ran deep into the heart of Anatolia and even threatened Constantinople itself. Desperate, the Ottomans did the unthinkable and in 1833 turned to their old rivals. The Russians sent warships into the Bosphorus to support the Ottoman government and the two powers signed a treaty of friendship at Hünkâr Iskelesi on the Asian shore of the strait.

The greatest spur to comprehensive reform is the threat of losing national sovereignty. The Ottomans had originally begun their reform programme after suffering a disastrous war with the Russians in the 1770s, during the Europeans' partition of the state of Poland. The early stages of Ottoman reform led to fierce politics and Janissary uprisings which had toppled several sultans, including Selim III, the father of modern Ottoman reform. More calamities followed over the following decades which further weakened the Ottoman state: the stalemate war with Russia in the Danubian Principalities 1806–12; the British breaching of the Dardanelles and appearance at Constantinople under Vice-Admiral Duckworth in 1807; the Greek uprising beginning in 1820; the Janissary revolt of 1826 and their subsequent bloody elimination as an order; the battle of Navarino and the loss of the Ottoman fleet in 1827; the Russian invasion to the gates of Constantinople in 1828–29; the invasion of Ibrahim Paşa in 1832–33 and then the sight of Russian warships in the Bosphorus as the guarantor of Ottoman sovereignty. The spectre of becoming a vassal of Russia, or of experiencing a partition by several different powers such as Poland had experienced in the 1770s, was real. In 1839 the Ottomans launched their modern reform movement, the *Tanzimat*, enacted under the direction of their leading statesman, Mustafa Reşit Paşa, and his *Gulhane* decree.

The sight of Russian warships in the Bosphorus in 1833 also enacted a reform in international relations. It woke Palmerston and the British to the prospect, about which Stratford had previously warned, of the Russians gaining sway over the Ottomans and interrupting the British route to India. This was the first major international development of the modern phase of the so-called Eastern Question or *Question d'Orient*, the imperial competition among the Powers, and especially between the British and Russians, for leverage in the Levant. Stratford would become the central figure of this rivalry because of his long experience at the Ottoman capital and his consistent support for the Ottoman reform movement. And just one year after returning to the Ottoman capital, he was to play an interesting role in a key event which stood at the intersection of domestic reform and international relations.

4

One day in the summer of 1843, Stratford was riding from the diplomatic quarter of Pera to his residence on the Bosphorus when his carriage was unexpectedly stopped by several Armenians, 'throwing themselves before the wheels' and then pleading to speak with the ambassador, as Stratford later detailed in his memoir. They begged him to intervene on behalf of their young relative Avakim, who was scheduled to be executed in a matter of days by the Ottoman government in punishment for the religious crime of apostasy against Islam.[14]

Stratford complied with the request but was unsuccessful and Avakim, who was recorded by the British to be 'of eighteen or twenty years', was executed on 22 August 1843. A report on the precise details of the case was compiled on Stratford's directive by the Oriental Secretary of the British Embassy, Charles Alison, and enclosed in a dispatch to Aberdeen of 27 August 1843. The report in part read:

Case of Armenian Avakim, son of Yagya, of the parish of Top Kapousee [Topkapi].

About a year and a half ago Avakim having had a drunken quarrel with some neighbours, was sentenced at the War Office to receive 500 bastionadoes.

Fear and intoxication induced him to become a Mussulman, and he was conducted on the spot to the Mehkemé where the name of Mehemet was given him.

Some days afterwards Avakim repented of what he had done, and fled to Syra, from whence he returned a few months ago.

About three months ago, while returning from his sister's house . . . he was recognised by the Kolaga [*Kol-ağası?*] of the quarter, Mustapha, and denounced at the War Office of having renegaded from Islamism. He was then submitted to the most cruel punishment to compel him to re-abandon his original belief, and was even paraded through the streets with his hands tied behind his back as if for execution. Avakim, however, unintimidated by torture or the prospect of death, proclaimed aloud his firm belief in Christianity, and was led forth to suffer on Wednesday last amidst the execrations of the Ulema partisans . . . . A petition of the Armenians for the corpse was rejected, and it was after three days exposure cast into the sea.[15]

The Times later reported on the incident, providing gruesome details:

The poor man's head was cut off, and, his whole body being exposed in the market-place, the head was placed between the knees, with the cap or hat upon it, to add to the indignity with which it was desired to visit upon him the penalty of the offence. The mob of Constantinople, always to the last degree superstitious, fanatical and brutal, indulged in atrocious gesticulations and pleasantries on the subject; and for some time it was impossible for any Frank, especially if he was attached to the suite or household of some one or other of the European Ambassadors, to show his face in the public streets without being reviled or heeted at or even pelted, by a vile rabble of beggars, disbanded soldiers, &c. . .[16]

There are three other contemporary accounts of the case of Avakim, as detailed in a study of the apostasy controversy undertaken by Turgut Subaşı in 2006. One was by a French author, Gérard de Nerval, who happened to be visiting Constantinople at the time of the execution. He saw Avakim's body in the *Balık pazarı* or Fish Market of Pera, the diplomatic quarter, and was then told the story by an Armenian shopkeeper. Subaşı noted:

> According to this Armenian, Avakim had been found three years previously with a Turkish woman, and as a non-Muslim he would have been sentenced to death, whereas a Muslim would have been subjected to a beating only. He therefore became a Muslim, but later repented and went to the Greek isles, where he renounced his new religion.[17]

Subaşı also uncovered another published account of the event, provided in 1871 by the Armenian Patriarch of Constantinople, Avadis Berberyan, in his *History of the Armenians*. This account, according to Subaşı, was concerned mostly with the diplomacy of the controversy. It claimed that 'The elders of the Armenian Church did not intercede for him because that would have been an insult to Islam, but they advised Avakim's parents to petition the Russian Ambassador. When he had read their letter, the Russian ambassador sent them to Canning.'[18]

Subaşı also conducted archival research concerning the event and uncovered four relavent primary documents produced by the Ottoman government in 1843, all before the execution took place. According to them, in Subaşı's description, Avakim, a bootmaker, undertook a completely legal conversion to Islam on 11 March 1842. The Sharia Court had previously determined that Avakim was not a minor and not coerced into his conversion. He had recited the required statement of faith, the *Kelimeteyn-i Şahadeteyn*. He requested to change his name to Mehmed. His conversion documentation was officially stamped, signed and witnessed.

Subaşı also found among these documents a record that:

> Avakim was a relative of one of the servants in the British
> Embassy ... For Canning's sake, it was decided [by the
> Cabinet] to bring Avakim before the court once more and to
> give him one last opportunity to change his mind. If he refused,
> the sentence was to be carried out openly to show others that
> Islamic Law is fixed and cannot be altered.[19]

No corroborating evidence has been located in the archives of the
British Foreign Office that Avakim was related to a domestic servant
in the British embassy. Nonetheless, the Ottoman archival
documentation uncovered by Subaşı is important for its evidence
that Avakim made a completely willful, legal and regular conversion
to Islam, in contrast to other accounts that he was coerced into this
while intoxicated.

5

The capital punishment of Avakim for apostasy from Islam in 1843
was not a novel event in the Ottoman Empire. On 25 May 1830 a
young Greek, Matteo, was executed in the city of Smyrna, according
to *The Times*, for abusing Islam. He had converted to Islam while a
slave as a minor. Many years after running away from his owner, he
recanted his conversion and was executed for it.[20] In fact, religious
conversion had long been an issue in relations between the European
and Ottoman governments. As Stratford pointed out to the Foreign
Office in London on 23 August 1843, two articles of the British
capitulations with the Ottoman Empire addressed the fate of
property belonging to 'any Englishman who should turn Turk'; and
the French capitulations contained an analogous article.[21]

During Stratford's first mission at Constantinople, on 8 September
1810, he had requested his chief dragoman, Bartholomeo Pisani, to
report to him on the practice of the Ottoman government in
handling non-Muslim subjects who wished to convert.[22] Presumably

Stratford had been inspired to make such inquiry by a case he was then considering.

On his next mission to Constantinople almost 17 years later, in June 1827, Stratford unsuccessfully attempted to gain the release of several Ottoman Jews who had been converted to Christianity and 'baptized at their own request' by an English Clergyman and then were imprisoned by the Ottoman government for a term first of six months and then of three years.[23]

In December 1838 *The Times* reported that Sultan Mahmud II had issued a decree that any Christian subject of the Ottoman Empire who officially declared his intention of adopting Islam 'shall be committed to the charge of the patriarch or of his delegates [of his community], and suffered to remain under custody for the space of 40 days.' After that period, if the individual should still profess his desire to convert to Islam, it would be allowed.[24]

In some Muslim societies today punishment for apostasy remains an important and controversial subject.[25]

6

The day after the execution of Avakim, on 23 August 1843, Stratford sent a confidential directive to his chief dragoman, Frédéric Pisani (nephew of Bartholomeo Pisani, Stratford's former chief dragoman at Constantinople, who had died in 1826.)[26] Frédéric Pisani was, 'an old, honest, and faithful servant of the British Government,' according to A. H. Layard who had arrived at Constantinople earlier in 1843.[27] Stratford's written directive to Pisani, which he was instructed to read to the Grand Vizir in person, included:

I have received your report of the young Armenian's execution, and it has filled my mind with sorrow and abhorrence ... The law which has now shed the blood of a Rayah may in future be levelled at a foreigner and that foreigner, an Englishman .... Let the Ministers of the Porte look to it in time. They would then have others than Rayahs to deal with.[28]

Stratford had in mind the theoretical but not unrealistic plight that might befall a visiting British subject who had originally been Muslim but had later converted to Christianity. 'If any of His Majesty's numerous Mohametan Subjects were to come into this country,' he wrote to Aberdeen in his dispatch of 27 August 1843, 'and be exposed to the danger of decapitation for a change of religion, I should need your Lordship's commands to induce me to acquiesce in his execution, or, even without that danger, to admit the transfer of his allegiance from Her Majesty to the Sultan.'[29]

In fact an apostasy case involving a British subject had actually already occurred on Stratford's present mission, as he reported to Aberdeen:

> The British subject, a Maltese, returned to the Catholic faith a few days after he had declared himself a Turk, and he was privately conveyed out of the country .... had the man been arrested after his recantation, I should perhaps have been reduced to the necessity of putting all to hazard in order to snatch him from the hands of the executioner.[30]

Two days after the execution of Avakim, on 24 August 1824, Pisani met the Grand Vizir, Rauf Paşa, communicating Stratford's message. He then wrote a report on the meeting. According to this, Rauf, despite having 'a horror of even putting a fowl to death', reiterated his previous assertion that 'positively neither the Ministers nor the Sultan could have saved the life of the Armenian.' He described the 'laws of the Qur'an' as:

> inexorable both as respects a Mussulman who embraces another religion, and as respects a person not a Mussulman, who, after having of his own accord publicly embraced Islamism, is convicted of having renounced that faith. No consideration can produce a commutation of the capital punishment to which the law condemns him without mercy.

Rauf Paşa also said that the only way for the accused in such a case to escape capital punishment was to embrace Islam; and that when the Ottoman government provided Avakim with opportunity to do so, he declined and was therefore executed.

In response to Stratford's request for information 'as to what would occur if a foreigner, an Englishman, for instance, were to be placed in similar circumstances,' Rauf Paşa stated, 'I really do not know what would become necessary in such a case if a foreigner were concerned; I am ignorant as to what is said in the law as regards a Frank who should be compromised by the circumstances which caused the Armenian, who was a Rayah, to be condemned to death.' Rauf Paşa then concluded the meeting with Pisani by saying, 'Present my compliments to the Ambassador, and tell him that I appreciate his humane and well-intentioned sentiments, but that what has occurred was a misfortune for which there was no remedy whatever.'[31]

Stratford later noted in his memoir that, 'It was clear from the first that the better minds among the Turkish ministers revolted from such sanguinary acts.' He listed the Grand Vizir, Rauf Paşa, as being against the execution and 'The Foreign Minister [Rifaat Paşa] expressed equally humane and equally discouraging opinions.' The religious leader of the city, the Grand Mufti, was also against carrying out the execution, as Stratford recorded.[32] He officially reported to Aberdeen in his dispatch of 27 August 1843 that '. . . Nafiz Pasha, the President of the Council, was the chief obstacle to mercy.'[33]

7

Stratford had still not yet received any response or instruction from London about the apostasy controversy, but this did not prevent him from pressing forward in a decisive manner by sending his protest to the Ottoman government and by imploring his European colleagues at Constantinople – the ambassadors of Austria, France, Prussia and Russia – to do likewise. All were eventually authorised by their governments to comply.

The French ambassador, de Bourqueney, sent his dragoman to communicate to the Ottoman foreign minister an official protest against the execution. The meeting was held on 17 October 1843. In his verbal reply to the French protest, Rifaat Paşa explained to de Bourqueney that his government had carried out the execution because, '... nothing could be alleged against a judgment founded upon the express will of God.'[34]

Aberdeen eventually sent Stratford instruction on how to handle the apostasy controversy, on 4 October 1843. In this Aberdeen noted that the government 'highly approve' of the ambassador's line and authorised him to continue with it.[35]

Pisani met Rifaat Paşa on 3 November 1843 and reported to Stratford the same day that the Foreign Minister confidentially agreed to comply with Stratford's request. Rifaat Paşa provided Pisani with an unofficial assurance that the Ottoman government would instruct all local officials to deliver up to central authorities anyone who wished to renounce Islam, and that capital punishment would not be carried out against such individuals. Pisani wrote in his report that 'Rifaat Pasha added, that the Porte can give no written answer respecting this affair without compromising itself...'[36]

Stratford decided to accept Rifaat Paşa's unofficial assurance of 2 November 1843 and not to press for an official, written prohibition against further executions of alleged apostates. But Stratford remained unsatisfied and two weeks later he wrote Aberdeen, 'It remains indeed to be considered whether it would be prudent ... to insist upon receiving a formal answer.'[37]

CHAPTER 12

DISPUTATION ON QUR'ANIC THEOLOGY

1

Despite Rifaat Paşa's assurance, 'another religious execution has recently taken place in the Pashalic of Brussa [Bursa],' as Stratford received intelligence at the beginning of December 1843 and reported to Lord Aberdeen.[1] Further confirmation of this came from his consul at Bursa, Sandison, on 9 December, as well as from Monsieur de Cordoba (probably a merchant friend of the British embassy) on 6 December. 'A young Greek turned Turk in a moment of ill temper,' reported de Cordoba, 'having come to himself, he went to a priest and evinced a desire to return to his faith.' After returning to Christianity, the young man, reported to be 22 years old, was arrested by government authorities and eventually hanged.[2]

On 16 December 1843, Stratford instructed Pisani to meet Rifaat Paşa again in order to communicate Stratford's request that the Ottoman government issue an 'assurance' – meaning, a formal, written declaration – that it would end capital punishment for apostasy.[3] But the Ottoman government refused to comply with the request.

Aberdeen again sent Stratford confirmation of his line, on 16 January 1844. He also instructed him to meet in person with the Sultan to communicate most directly the request for an official and written declaration ending capital punishment for aspostasy.[4]

When Stratford himself met Rifaat Paşa on 9 February, he exhibited Aberdeen's instruction and the minister read it over. 'Having finished it, he rose from his seat rather abruptly, without saying a word, and left the room for a few minutes,' as Stratford recorded. When Rifaat returned, he informed Stratford that he would have to consult with his government before he could formally respond. But he did offer right away to give his:

> observations as occurred to his mind .... he then proceeded to draw a strong line of distinction between custom and divine law, intimating that a practice derived from the former might be abandoned to meet the wishes of Europe, or even of Great Britain alone, but that a law, prescribed by God himself, was not to be set aside by any human power; and that the Sultan in attempting it might be exposed to a heavy, perhaps even to a dangerous, responsibility.[5]

Rifaat Paşa's argument was a repetition in similar terms of what he had said the previous October to the dragoman of the French Ambassador, de Bourqueney.[6] It was also related to what he had said to Pisani in their meeting on 3 November 1843: '... that the Porte can give no written answer respecting this affair without compromising itself...'[7]

The Times of 15 April 1844 was certainly correct in observing that, 'The practice of putting to death relapsed apostates is undoubtedly an act of intolerable barbarity, and it appears not to be sanctioned by the Qur'an, any more than the not very distant practice of burning heretics was justified by the divine precepts of the Gospel.'[8] What, therefore, was the reason that Rifaat Paşa and his colleagues condoned such harsh punishment when they themselves abhorred it? They may have been motivated by the worldly concern that if they undid the severe punishment against apostasy, it could possibly destabilise their political standing by inciting conservative elements of society. Furthermore, it would have been reasonable for them to fear that if one part of the law of their religion, which was also the law of their state, were undone or left open to challenge, then many other challenges to the law and the authority of the Ottoman Empire might have been invited. The empire was ethnically very diverse – the Turks were only one of its many peoples – and it was also geographically long and unwieldy. Islam was one of the main sociological factors which united the empire culturally and legally. The Ottoman ministers therefore might reasonably have feared that if they were to abrogate the law against apostasy, the government would be, as Rifaat Paşa had put it to Pisani, 'compromising itself' and undermining its own authority. On the other hand, it would also have been reasonable for Ottoman ministers to fear that depending on such a harsh method, one very much based in an earlier era, was a poor method of maintaining the stability of their state and society.

Stratford had great experience in dealing with the Ottomans and he recognised here that for both spiritual and practical concerns Rifaat Paşa and his colleagues were highly unlikely to be moved in this matter by any amount of exhortation offered by the other European Powers. As a diplomatic approach was thus not possible, Stratford hit upon a completely different method: he took the issue literally into his own hands.

<h1 style="text-align:center">2</h1>

'It so happened that on leaving my bed one morning,' Stratford recorded in his memoir:

> I remembered that some one had given me a French translation of the Koran. Where to find it was the question. My search was amply rewarded, not only by finding the book, but on opening it to fall at once upon a passage which made me think that Mohammed in condemning renegades to punishment had in view their sufferings in a future state and not their decapitation here.[9]

Stratford's account of opening the Qur'an to precisely the correct passage concerning apostasy sounds suspiciously like an imagined episode of bibliomancy. But he was not prone to exaggeration or confabulation; and he did at the time relate the event to an American

missionary at Constantinople, Willian G. Schauffler, who recorded it
in his Autobiography:

> Sir Stratford, on receiving this communication, went to his
> library, and took down the Koran, at which, he told me, he
> had not looked for years, and on opening the volume, his
> eye lit upon a passage, saying 'that the man who made
> defection from the faith should die, and his soul would go
> to hell.'[10]

Stratford then commissioned a report from his Oriental secretary,
Charles Alison, on this passage as well as any others in the Qur'an
which related to punishment for apostasy. This report was then
presented to Rifaat Paşa. According to Stratford, when Alison
presented the report, the minister was confounded by it and
immediately 'sent for the Imam of his district to continue the
discussion. Neither the priest nor the pasha could make any head
against Mr. Alison's arguments. . .'[11]

Charles Allison's report consisted of several main findings which
Stratford summarised in the dispatch that he sent along to
Aberdeen together with the report. The first part of the theological
argument was based upon the argument: 'It really appears that
the only passages of the Koran which visit apostacy with death,
refer to particular incidents in the career of Mahomet, and have
nothing in view beyond the expression of renegades, who were
in arms and actively opposed to him.' In other words, the law was
now outdated and unnecessary because the religion had become
established and such 'renegades' no longer posed any kind of
institutional threat.

The second part of the theological position of Stratford and Alison
questioned the textual origins and legitimacy of capital punishment
for apostasy. Stratford summarised this as follows:

> The traditions, commentaries, and the judicial opinions
> are invested with less sanctity [than the Qur'an], nor can
> they be received as authorities for executing Apostates from

Islamism ... The *Fetwas* of the Mussulman Doctors are not always consistent with each other. Still less are they infallible...[12]

While Alison's report was based solely on an examination of the Qur'an, he and Stratford theorised that the real basis for the law and punishment against apostasy was from the Traditions, *Sunna*, or possibly another Islamic text. Stratford and Alison therefore apparently attempted to argue to Rifaat Paşa that the 'sanctity' of the law and punishment against apostasy was reduced because it was based on a text other than the Qur'an.

This argument was legitimate theologically (at least in its first part); and it is in fact still maintained today by Islamic 'Modernists' in the following terms, as summarised in a study by Peters and de Vries (1976–77):

No verse in the Koran prescribes capital punishment for the apostate *qua* apostate; on the contrary, verses like K 2:218 and K 3:86–97 clearly envisage a natural death for the apostate. Moreover, K 4:89 and 90 ... verses that have not been abrogated by any other verse, offer proof that only the dangerous, aggressive apostate may be killed. A further argument is that capital punishment for apostasy is founded on two Traditions ... that are contrary to the explicit Koranic rulings of K 4:89 and 90. There exists a much debated controversy on the question whether a Tradition can abrogate a Koranic rule....[13]

Lane-Poole noted in his biography that he was never was able to see Charles Alison's report on his examination of the Qur'an because Stratford's personal archive did not contain a copy of it 'and the rules of the Foreign Office forbid an examination of the original.'[14] But as an arabist and authority on the Qur'an, Lane-Poole was able to undertake his own hermeneutical study of the issue, and he offered the following appraisal: 'Canning was perfectly right in holding that the Koran did not warrant the law. As a matter of fact no passage in the Koran is explicit on the subject of punishment for apostasy.'

Lane-Poole also concluded that the main source for the law and punishment against apostasy was not the Qur'an but:

> ... the body of Traditions (*Sunna*), or unofficial conversations of the Prophet, and the long chain of judgments analogically founded thereon, delivered by eminent jurists. The law of apostasy is perfectly explicit in the Traditions: those who changed their religion were to be killed .... a voluntary male convert to Islam who afterwards apostasized must be killed.[15]

3

Rifaat Paşa responded to Stratford's disputation on Qur'anic theology in a meeting with him and the French ambassador, de Bourqueney, held on 5 March 1844. Fuad Paşa also attended at Stratford's request 'for the interpretation of what passed between us,' as Stratford reported to Aberdeen the next day:

> The Pasha's main position was this: if we refuse, we lose the friendship of Europe; if we consent, we hazard the peace of the empire; you come as friends, and therefore we reckon upon your helping us to find some course by which we may satisfy you without injuring ourselves.

Stratford and de Bourqueney responded in warm terms to the diplomatic expression of friendship but they also communicated, as Stratford reported, 'that although we were not called upon to require an express and formal repeal of the law which they termed religious, we must, at the very least, require an official declaration that effectual measures would be taken to prevent the recurrence of executions for apostasy...'[16]

A few days later Stratford received a draft statement from the Ottoman government which read:

> As the law does not admit of any change being made in the enactments regarding the punishment of apostates, the Sublime

Porte will take efficacious measures, the measures which are possible, in order that the execution of Christians who, having become Mussulmans, returned to Christianity, shall not take place.

Stratford found the statement conditional and vague and thus 'We refused to take it, because it is not satisfactory,' as he informed Aberdeen on 14 March 1844.[17]

Still, Stratford remained optimistic about a successful resolution. 'The Porte, I am satisfied, is prepared to give way in the end, though with much reluctance,' he further reported to Aberdeen. Stratford was also unmoved by predictions of doom should the Ottoman government enact the reform:

Nothing whatever has occurred to warrant the alarming rumours of popular excitement and insurrection diligently circulated, and even countenanced by Rifaat Pasha, some days ago. If my information be correct, there is reason, on the contrary, to believe that not only the Mussulman inhabitants of the capital are sufficiently indifferent to the question at issue, but that many of the upper classes, some of the most distinguished Turkish statesmen, and a few even of the Ulemah are favourable to our view on the subject.[18]

On 21 March 1844 Sultan Abdülmecit issued an 'Official Declaration of the Sublime Porte, relinquishing the practice of Executions for Apostasy'. The declaration read:

It is the special and constant intention of His Highness the Sultan that his cordial relations with the High Powers be preserved, and that a perfect reciprocal friendship be maintained and increased. The Sublime Porte engages to take effectual measures to prevent henceforward the execution and putting to death of the Christian who is an apostate.[19]

At an audience with Sultan Abdülmecit held on 23 March 1844, 'He, in fact, gave me his royal word that henceforth neither Christianity be insulted in his dominions, nor should Christians be in any way insulted for their religions,' as Stratford reported to Aberdeen later that same day.[20] 'He added that he was the first Sultan who had ever made such a concession, and was glad that the lot of receiving it had fallen to me,' as Stratford recorded in his memoir. 'I replied that I hoped he would allow me to be the first Christian ambassador to kiss a Sultan's hand. "No – no –" he exclaimed, and at the same time shook me by the hand most cordially.'[21] A Turkish official participating in the audience related the gesture to the local correspondent of *The Times* who then reported it as '... the first time such condescension had occurred from any descendent of the Othmans on the throne of Constantinople.'[22]

Encouraged by the apostasy reform, Stratford petitioned the Ottomans to enact other legal–social reforms. This included Ottoman recognition of Protestants as comprising a *millet* or officially sanctioned religious community, which was eventually decreed on 26 November 1850.[23] Cyrus Hamlin, the American missionary, declared that this 'change has affected the whole religious constitution of the empire.'[24] During the Crimean War, in 1854, Stratford would petition the Ottoman government to undo parts of its slave-trade.[25]

The recognition of a Protestant *millet* was a component of Stratford's larger reform goal of striving toward religious equality in the Empire. As Temperley observed:

> Stratford's idea of reform was of a purely administrative and humanitarian character. He wished Christians and Jews to be put on an equality with Mohammedans. He wished Christians as well as Mohammedans in the military, naval and civil services; Christian evidence in the law courts; Christian as well as Mohammedan children in the State Schools. He wished a purified civil service, just laws, fair taxes and a balanced budget.[26]

This goal would in fact be adopted as part of the *Tanzimat*, and Roderick Davison found that it was 'one of the most significant aspects of Ottoman history in the nineteenth century that the doctrine of equality did, in fact, become official policy.'[27] There is no evidence which suggests that Stratford was responsible for the Ottomans' adoption of this policy of religious equality. But he certainly was its most forceful and vocal proponent at Constantinople in the years before its implementation, and in the days when most Europeans, including Stratford's immediate superior in London, felt that the Ottomans were completely incapable of undertaking such reforms.

CHAPTER 13

ADVOCATE OF OTTOMAN PROGRESS

1

News of the Sultan's abolition of capital punishment for apostasy quickly spread across Europe. Many considered it Stratford's doing and declared it a victory for Christian or European civilisation. 'This was, without doubt, the most remarkable diplomatic achievement in the annals of Turkey. It was the death-blow to Turkish fanaticism; it levelled the last artificial prop of the Turkish society,' as *The Times* correspondent in Constantinople reported.[1]

But the newspaper's editors in London expressed a very different opinion, which directly matched the line of the government (and thus may have been the result of pressure from that source). The newspaper's editorial of 13 April 1844 declared that British policy should be strictly limited to supporting the Ottoman Empire at all costs and should desist from pressuring the Empire for better treatment of its Christian minorities. The editorial did accept a certain 'sacred duty imposed upon us by Christianity and civilisation, of endeavouring to mitigate the ferocity of fanatical power and the sufferings of those to whom we are bound by their weakness and by our common faith.' But it questioned whether it was prudent to become involved in a domestic religious controversy 'between the Sultan and the Mussulman priesthood, of which he is the head.' The editorial also denounced 'the policy of foreign Ministers' – obviously referring here to Stratford – 'who have seized every unfortunate incident of persecution or local misconduct as an opportunity for acquiring a little national *éclat* at the expense of an humiliation to the Sovereign to whom they are accredited.' Such self-serving interference by ambassadors, the newspaper suggested:

> will end in nothing short of general massacre of the Christians. The horrors of such an occurrence would outweigh all the lives we may have saved; and though foreign diplomatists may coerce the Government of Turkey, they can neither give the law to the mosques nor restrain the passion of the people.[2]

A few days later, on 24 April 1844, *The Times* correspondent at Constantinople reported on a government crackdown against an apparent planned uprising by conservative elements of the city. On the first day, 'some 3,000 persons were arrested, were then bound arm and arm and marched down in many separate divisions to the Golden Horn, where four steamers and three vessels of war were ready to receive them' and delivered them to the Princes Islands in the Sea of Marmora. The arrests continued for several more days 'to the amount all in all of about 15,000 men,' including 'many remaining members of the old Janissary corps, distinguished by the indelible *Janitzany Nishan* on the arm.' It was suggested that 'an alarming conspiracy existed to make an attack on the Frank population, under an idea of influencing in favour of the Divan the religious question lately at issue.'[3]

The editors of *The Times* saw this as proof that Stratford's actions had indeed sparked a backlash against Christians. In another editorial, two days later, they declared: 'Our prognostication as to the probable consequences of the recent interposition of Sir Stratford Canning and M. de Bourqueney ... has been more promptly and directly confirmed than we could have anticipated.' The editorial predicted a possible result of 'intolerable calamities on the Christian population of the empire,' which could then lead 'the intervention of all Christendom, and the very existence of the Turkish empire would be staked on the desperate chances of a religious war.' It also asserted that the Sultan's declaration was actually 'of small importance. It involves no surrender of the religious law of Turkey; and the only engagement taken is that the law shall not be put in force with the least rigour on these relapsed apostates.'[4]

2

Another critic of Stratford's involvement in domestic issues at Constantinople was his government master in London. Aberdeen had previously strongly supported Stratford's stance concerning the apostasy controversy. But he now began to suspect that Stratford had exceeded his authority as ambassador and therefore needed to be reined in.

In his dispatch to Stratford of 20 January 1844, three months before *The Times* editorial, Aberdeen expressed his doubt that the Ottoman Empire was comparable to other states or comprehensible to foreigners; and he suggested that British support for Ottoman reform could prove counter-productive. He wrote: '... after all a question may arise whether it is safe or wise to judge Turkey by the standards of Christian Europe. There appears to be in Turkey a principle of vitality, an occult force, which sets at nought all calculations based upon the analogy of other states....' Aberdeen questioned in the dispatch 'whether by striving too much to accelerate the progress of Turkey, the Powers of Europe, friendly to the Porte, may not defeat their own object.' And he asserted that 'by pressing upon Turkey systems ill-adapted to the wants and sentiments of Her People, the risk is incurred of creating an aversion even to the very name of improvements, and of engendering suspicions...'[5]

In a separate dispatch which Aberdeen wrote to Stratford the same day, he instructed him not to 'stand forth as the avowed protector of the Christian subjects of the Sultan' or to be 'considered as the organ through which complaints of hardships or persecution should be conveyed to the knowledge of the Porte.'[6]

Stratford quoted these two admonitions in a rather indignant response of 1 June 1844. He pointed out that Aberdeen had contradicted himself by previously urging the ambassador to press the Ottoman government for reform, but then later telling him not to be the 'avowed protector' or 'organ of complaints'. Stratford also stated somewhat defiantly that in the Ottoman Empire, 'cases of forced proselytism ... are still frequent' and there also existed other injustice which on its own 'will not subside in a moment, though I firmly believe that its extinction would be no less conducive to the interests of this Empire, than accordant with the best interests of humanity.'[7] Stratford was diplomatically implying, in contrast to Aberdeen's position, that a push for reform was necessary and possible in the Ottoman Empire and that he would continue to attempt to support this movement.

3

Stratford himself saw great meaning in the apostasy controversy. Weeks before a resolution was achieved, back on 10 February 1844, he had written to Aberdeen that, 'never was a greater or more essential service rendered by one Government to another than by the opportunity now offered to the Sultan of placing Himself in real harmony with the powers of Europe, and giving his Empire a degree of security and prospects of improvement...'[8] And on 29 February 1844, Stratford wrote to Aberdeen:

> The Stand... with reference to executions for apostacy from Islamism, will ultimately, notwithstanding the resistance and difficulties to be expected at first, produce, I confidently hope, the most beneficial results, not only as to the particular object of our demand, but in the general policy and administrative system of the Porte.[9]

When Sultan Abdülmecit issued his reform on 23 March 1844, Stratford reported to Aberdeen in exalted and even religious terms:

> I am thankful to your lordship, under Providence, for having made me the humble instrument of contributing, not only to

the abolition of a barbarous practice, but to the establishment
of a great and beneficent principle, without which it may be
safely affirmed that the preservation of this empire for any
length of time is impossible.[10]

And a few weeks later, in his report to Aberdeen of 17 May 1844,
Stratford wrote, in reference to the elimination of execution for
apostasy: 'The bloodless conquests of humanity over barbarism are
those which are the most worthy of Her Majesty's reign and
character.'[11]

Stratford's religious and cultural invocations – his references to his
acting 'under Providence' and as 'the humble instrument' and to 'The
bloodless conquests of humanity over barbarism' – seem to suggest
that when the Ottomans abolished execution for aspostasy in March
1844, Stratford began to see his relationship to the Ottoman reform
movement as divinely inspired. If he did have a messianic vision of
himself here, it could have had roots in his serious religious
upbringing and convictions; or it could have also come simply from
his delight at the outcome. It may have also sprung from the special
attention he received at this time. The reform was a great surprise and
lauded all across Europe. As news of his efforts in the apostasy
controversy spread both across Europe and the Ottoman Empire, he
received and acted on endless appeals for help from minority groups
in the Ottoman Empire;[12] and one British resident of Constantinople, the Rev W. O. Allan, felt inspired to write in a letter home,
dated 7 June 1845, that Stratford 'has earned, and richly deserves, the
honourable title of the Friend of the Oppressed.'[13]

But something else also seems to have been at work here in
Stratford's view of himself and in many others' view of him. Elizabeth
Malcolm-Smith suggested in 1933 that from the early 1840s
Stratford saw himself as a kind of a Moses figure:

He returned to diplomacy with the feeling ever growing that,
like Moses, there was a mission awaiting him .... This time he
went with the conviction that God Himself, and no lesser
power, had called him, and he discovered that his task was to be

the regeneration of the Ottoman Empire. There was to be no looking back. To that task he bent all the energies of his powerful personality.[14]

Another vision of Stratford as Moses came from one of his embassy underlings, Percy Smythe, the eighth Lord Strangford, who had worked on Stratford's staff at Constantinople from 1845 to 1856. In 1862 Smythe wrote to his wife that Stratford 'is not only able, but bound, before it is too late, to survey the world from his height, and to speak of the future with the impartial utterance, like Moses from Mount Pisgah.'[15] *The Glasgow Herald* in its editorial obituary of Stratford on 16 August 1880, also employed a reference to Moses in its observation that Stratford 'certainly did not forget the Ten Commandments' throughout his career.[16]

In June 1891 a British missionary in Turkey, the Rev C. C. Tracy, wrote in his 'Turkish Missions Report', when recounting the history of social reforms in the Ottoman Empire: 'At that juncture came a man sent of God, if ever man was – Sir Stratford Canning. Piteous appeals were made to him. He was a strong, just and God-fearing man.'[17] And on 27 October 1894 in a lecture on Stratford's career delivered to the American Antiquarian Society of Worcester, Massachusetts, the former American missionary in Turkey, Cyrus Hamlin, declared: 'If he could do anything to mitigate persecution he would do it because the persecuted were his fellow-men, and not because they were Protestants. This was the character of his whole official life...'[18]

Stratford was energetic and often successful in his humanitarian activities and not undeserving of being called the 'Friend of the Oppressed' at Constantinople. It is true, as was observed by one American missionary based in Constantinople in 1827, that 'Mr. Canning lent his countenance, perhaps farther than political men are accustomed, to the operations of Bible and Missionary men.'[19] Undertaking humanitarian deeds certainly satisfied Stratford personally, as an end in itself. Yet it was also a useful means for him: a way to see his own work as a diplomat and his country's work as an empire as being divinely or at least benevolently inspired. And this vision was shared by many of his compatriots. 'The British liked to think that their diplomatists behaved better than those of other nations, and found much consolation in the career of the best known of Queen Victoria's representatives abroad – Stratford Canning (Lord Stratford de Redcliffe),' as was noted in a consideration of his diplomacy published in *The Times* in February 1954 to mark the centenary of the Crimean War.[20]

Seeing Stratford Canning as an agent of spreading humanity or civilisation, as 'a man sent of God, if ever man was', as a Moses figure, all demonstrate the method by which many of the British found spiritual justification for their empire. This kind of imperial thinking was considered by the historian of empire, Eric Hobsbawm, who observed:

> All established states put their own interests first. If they have the power, and the end is considered sufficiently vital, states justify the means of achieving it (though rarely in public), particularly when they think God is on their side . . . . Few things are more dangerous than empires pursuing their own interests in the belief that by doing so they are doing humanity a favour.[21]

4

The apostasy episode prompts several questions. What is the historical meaning of Sultan Abdülmecit's elimination of execution for apostasy in 1843–44? What was Stratford's main practical motivation in the controversy? What is the larger historical role and meaning of Stratford's relationship to the Ottoman reform movement? And was he being realistic or prescient when he wrote to Aberdeen in his dispatch of 29 February 1844 that the end of execution for apostasy would 'produce, I confidently hope, the most beneficial results, not only as to the particular object of our demand, but in the general policy and administrative system of the Porte'?

Turgut Subaşı concluded that the apostasy controversy 'enabled Canning ... to strengthen his position in relation to the Porte and thereby to introduce further reforms leading to full equality for Christian

subjects.'[22] Bernadotte E. Schmitt, writing from the perspective of
World War I in 1919, including the on-going collapse of the Ottoman
Empire, declared that 'Stratford and Palmerston, who believed the
regeneration of Turkey possible, were wrong.'[23] Malcolm-Smith,
looking back from the perspective of the late 1920s and early 1930s,
declared that: 'As Reformer of Turkey ... Stratford Canning must be
regarded as one of the splendid failures of history, although his efforts on
her behalf gave the Ottoman Empire a further lease of life.'[24]

Temperley was nearer the mark when he stressed that British
policy in support of Ottoman reform was strictly self-serving and a
means to satisfy British domestic public opinion:

> The obligation to defend Constantinople was at bottom based
> on British interests and on the safeguarding of the route to
> India .... It seemed crude to defend the British Empire on the
> pure plea of *realpolitik*. To this suggestion was added another. If
> England was so interested in the Turkish Empire as to be
> prepared to fight for her, she must be prepared to help her in
> other ways and for nobler reasons. England decided to help
> Turkey reform herself .... this appeal to the public afforded a
> sentimental argument for preserving the Turkish Empire. That
> was the view before the British public. The argument is more
> cynically put by Lord Palmerston in one of his later utterances.
> 'Our power' of maintaining the Turkish Empire 'depends on
> Public Opinion in this country and that public opinion would
> not support us unless the Turkish Government exerts itself to
> make Reforms.'[25]

Perhaps the most valuable observation on Stratford's relationship to
the Ottoman reform movement comes from Michael Warr. His
perspective was not that of a professional historian but of a British
career diplomat who served at Istanbul in the 1960s. Warr realised, as
he put it:

> how many-sided was the foreign contribution towards the
> reform of Turkey. It is thus difficult to say just how much

Stratford personally achieved over reform. All that is certain is that he worked harder at it than anybody else ... It is well to remember that Stratford was not working on an idea [of reform] of his own. He had adopted Mahmoud's idea and, after his death, strove to carry it on.[26]

Actually it was Selim III's idea, which was continued by Mahmud II, but Warr's point here is valid: Ottoman reform was not the invention or accomplishment of Stratford Canning. It was an Ottoman creation and movement, and it was lasting. Stratford Canning supported Ottoman reform, including in the apostasy controversy, because it was in the strategic interest of the British Empire to do so: only a strong and stable Ottoman Empire could stand up to the Russian Empire, check its expansion, maintain peace in the region, and make the British route to India secure.

In general in human relations, and especially in the free-for-all of international politics, the interests of separate parties are often or perhaps even usually in conflict. But on rare occasions they do converge. These moments are precious opportunities for realistic collaboration, perhaps even for something on the order of 'friendship' or as close to that as can occur between states.

5

The elimination of capital punishment for the act of apostasy from Islam should be reconsidered as a critical point in the whole Ottoman reform movement. Many Ottoman leaders and members of the public who eventually supported the reform seem to have been originally reluctant to do so out of concern for the empire 'compromising itself', as Rifaat Paşa had said to Pisani on 3 November 1843, perhaps meaning, risking social and political upheaval and losing the cohesion of religious law. But the reform may have subsequently demonstrated to Ottoman leaders and to the Ottoman public that more fundamental changes to law and society were possible without producing the collapse of order.

Stratford was not responsible for this or any other Ottoman reform. He was clearly in no position to dictate religious law to the

Porte. In arguing that the law against apostasy was based not on the Qur'an but on the interpretations of judges as expressed in the *Sunna*, Stratford had (while not proving or disproving anything) provided a viable and significant retort against the claim of Rauf Paşa that the law was 'inexorable'; and also against the claim of Rifaat Paşa that the law was 'prescribed by God himself' and 'the express will of God' and thus could not be questioned by mortals. Unable to challenge the law against apostasy via political negotiation, Stratford had resourcefully and ingeniously engaged his Ottoman colleagues on their own religious grounds.

Stratford's theological argument certainly could not have significantly swayed the Ottomans and should not be seen as responsible for the reform which soon after occurred. It seems that he did contribute weight to one side of the Ottoman political–religious struggle by bringing the issue to prominence all over Europe. Indeed Subaşı discovered primary documentary evidence to this effect, based upon which he stated: 'The Sublime Porte sent instructions to its ambassadors in the European capitals to contact influential people in order to direct public opinion in favour of the Ottoman government.' Subaşı also located documentation indicating that the Ottoman leaders were aware that:

> The insulting treatment of Avakim's body had made a particularly deep impression on the European public. Although this kind of behavior did not form part of the law, and the Porte had considered punishing it, it did not believe that such action would change public opinion in Europe.[27]

Stratford's real achievement in the apostasy controversy was, first of all, to have represented the line of his government concerning this Ottoman domestic development in a convincing and creative fashion, using all resources available to him, avoiding diplomatic dead-ends and pressing forward where he correctly sensed it was realistic to do so, such as when he conducted his examination of the Qur'an and presented a theological argument to the Ottomans. These were aspects of diplomatic practice.

But perhaps Stratford's most important achievement in the apostasy controversy was his wide vision of the Ottomans and his ability to act on it and express it. He comprehended well and advocated effectively that Ottoman reform was entirely possible and deserved to be supported, at a time when this was strongly or completely doubted by most European statesmen. Upon Stratford's death in August 1880, *The Times* declared, 'It would be a mistake to say that he understood Turkish nature; for he suffered heavily for the confidence he placed in its capacity for reform.'[28] But in fact Stratford did sufficiently understand 'Turkish nature' in order to foresee that fundamental Ottoman reform was possible. Instead of rejecting the Ottomans as otherworldly, he was able to accept and understand them as human beings who were acting upon, not only their own distinct cultural traditions, but also those certain needs, abilities and potentialities that are shared by all people.

It was not ever thus. When Stratford arrived at the Ottoman Empire in January 1809, he was young and brittle. He tended to reject not only the Ottomans but all peoples and most situations which were foreign to him. In 1811 Lady Hester Stanhope correctly identified 'the narrowness of this man's mind.'[29] This condition continued for many more years. While travelling throughout the Polish countryside on his way to Petersburg, for example, Stratford wrote to his mother on 8 February 1825:

> The inns throughout Poland, with the exception perhaps of those at Kracow and Warsaw, are poor and filthy in the extreme, being usually kept by Jews, who are so far from conversion to Christianity that they are scarcely human. After seeing their persons and manner of living one ceases to blame the Government which forbids their residing in towns indiscriminately with Christians, who, by the way, are also sent into the country, but only to be buried.[30]

But after his years and experiences abroad and at the Ottoman capital, he came to understand and empathise with the plight of those different from himself. This included the Jews. When Stratford became active in the House of Lords during his retirement from diplomacy, on 27 April 1858 he spoke there in strong support of the right of Jews to sit in Parliament; and he called for the removal of the words 'upon the true faith of a Christian' from the oath of office, a disability which had prevented elected Jews from taking their seats in the House of Commons. He declared aloud to the Lords that when he was ambassador at Constantinople and had called for Ottoman reforms concerning religious equality, the fact that Britain still did not have Jews sitting in Parliament was 'the subject of remark in Turkey'. He added that nothing would give him greater pleasure now than to have Jews sitting in Parliament, among various reasons 'to show that we in this country had set aside ancient prejudices, which we had unfortunately so long cherished.'[31]

Stratford Canning's journey to the Ottoman Empire occurred not only over land and water but also within himself. In the 'very wide world' of Constantinople,[32] Canning broke through his inner narrowness and achieved a measure of understanding for people different from himself. Given Canning's milieu, such intellectual growth was a significant achievement. However, it was never enough to inspire him to speak or act on behalf of the many who perished and suffered under the British occupation of India.

PART V

THE CRIMEAN WAR, 1853–56

CHAPTER 14

'HEAVEN HELP ME!'

1

Believing or hoping he was 'perhaps never to return',[1] Stratford
Canning began a leave from his post and quit Constantinople for
home on HM Steam Sloop *Scourge* on 22 June 1852.[2] He was already
planning to resign the embassy and this he achieved in London a few
months later, in January 1853. He was now 66 years old and had
arrived at retirement from diplomacy and a relaxed secondary career
in the House of Lords. The previous year he had been raised to the
peerage as Viscount Stratford de Redcliffe after having nearly been
appointed Secretary of State for Foreign Affairs in the new
government of the Earl of Derby.[3] He seemed at this point to have
finally realised his dream of settling at home. But suddenly world
events intervened, his diplomatic career was reactivated, he was
returned to Constantinople and his journey was back on.

The Crimean War is renowned for beginning with the 'Holy
Places dispute' between the French and the Russians over the
maintenance of Christian religious sites in Ottoman Palestine. The
dispute had actually begun in 1842 and ran perennially as a problem
no one thought would ever be solved or would ever cause major
trouble. While it was indeed important in contributing to the
explosion of tensions in 1853, the real spark came not from Palestine
but from Montenegro. In early 1852 the armies of the Ottoman
general Omer Paşa had occupied this region in response to a

nationalist uprising there. These troops remained through the year and there was talk of war between the Ottoman and Austrian empires. Tsar Nicholas wrote to the Austrian emperor, Franz Joseph, that: 'If war by Turkey against Thee should result, Thou mayest be assured in advance that it will be precisely the same as though Turkey had declared war on myself.' On 30 December 1852 the Russians mobilised two army corps in the Danubian Principalities along its border with the Ottoman Empire. And on 13 January 1853, the Russians undertook naval operations in the Black Sea and mobilised two more army corps in the region.

Armed with this new military pressure on the Ottomans, in late January 1853 the Austrians sent a special diplomatic mission to Constantinople under Count Leiningen. He sought the full Ottoman military evacuation of Montenegro and an Ottoman concession that the Austrians should have a guarantee over the rights of the Christian subjects of Ottoman Bosnia. The Ottomans rejected the Austrian demand of the guarantee but they did agree fully to the evacuation of their troops and this was considered throughout Europe to be a major concession. This agreement was reached on 12 February 1853 and on 3 March the Austrians and Ottomans signed a peace treaty. The Russian military movements along its border with the Ottoman Empire and in the Black Sea, and its assurance of support to the Austrians, had been decisive. Franz Joseph wrote to Tsar Nicholas expressing his 'deepest gratitude'. According to Temperley, 'Austria's triumph was complete and served as a model for Nicholas to imitate and to surpass.'[4]

A few weeks later, at the beginning of February 1853, while the Austrian mission to Constantinople was under way, the Russians relaxed their military movements somewhat and sent their own special diplomatic mission to the Ottomans under Prince Menshikov. The formal instructions to Menshikov for his mission, provided by Nesselrode, included obtaining from the Ottomans a ferman, according to Temperley, 'granting and guaranteeing for the future full privileges to the Greek Christians of the Turkish Empire, and acknowledging Russia's right to protect them .... The right itself was to be embodied in a *Sened*, or Convention, "having the force of a treaty.'"[5] The existence of such a right would have provided the Russians with a legal pretext to intervene at will in the domestic affairs of the Ottoman Empire. This in effect would have completely undone British policy in the region, that of maintaining a balance of power between the two empires and keeping secure the British route to India.

In response to the Austrian and Russian extraordinary missions to Constantinople, the British Cabinet swiftly decided in late February 1853 to return Stratford to his old post. He did not seek the appointment, and he was content to begin his retirement and finally settle at home, especially as he was now approaching advanced age. But he agreed to return to government service out of a sense of duty. Stratford was of course the obvious choice to address the developing crisis at Constantinople due to his profound experience there, but a domestic political element was also at play in his reappointment. Both the British political establishment and the public were hanging on his every word concerning the ominous events at Constantinople. As Temperley explained, 'the government were undoubtedly afraid of Stratford. He was capable of making difficulties in England by appealing to public opinion if he remained. The papers called loudly for his recall to Constantinople at the crisis and the government seem quite frankly to have yielded to their pressure.'[6]

The new prime minister, Aberdeen, was Stratford's old rival from the 1820s and the tense diplomacy of the Greek Question when he actually relieved Stratford of his ambassadorship, and then again from the 1840s and the apostasy controversy. James Graham, First Lord of the Admiralty, wrote to Clarendon, the foreign secretary, on 9 May 1853 in reference to Stratford, 'He is a Bashaw – too long accustomed to rule alone. Such tempers and manners are not the pledges or emblems of peace.'[7] In September 1853 Aberdeen, who had previously expressed misgivings about the Turks' ability to enact meaningful reform,[8] wrote to Graham:

I thought that we should have been able to conquer Stratford, but I begin to fear that the reverse will be the case, and that he will succeed in defeating us all .... to contend at once with the pride of the Emperor, the fanaticism of the Turks, and the dishonesty of Stratford is almost a hopeless attempt.[9]

And then Clarendon himself wrote to Lord Cowley on 10 November 1853 concerning Stratford, 'He is *bent on war* ... In short, he seems just as wild as the Turks themselves, and together they may, and will, defeat every combination coming from the West, however well devised it may be.'[10] It was doubtlessly in this light and to this effect that a few days earlier, on 4 November 1853, Clarendon had presented Stratford's dispatches to the Queen, who the next day wrote about them to Aberdeen, 'They exhibit clearly on his part a *desire* for war, and to drag us into it.'[11] Clarendon's predecessor, John Russell, now the leader of the Commons, was also disinclined toward Stratford. As one of Stratford's Foreign Office colleagues at this time, Henry Drummond Wolff, put it: 'I have found as regards ... distinguished diplomatists that there has always been a clique to run them down. Such was the case with Lord Stratford...'[12]

According to Temperley:

> Aberdeen thought he would not be formidable at a distance. It was a typical politician's error. Stratford was far more powerful on the Bosphorus than he could ever be at Westminster. The evil was aggravated because Aberdeen was weak and Clarendon inexperienced, while the two strong men, Palmerston and Russell, were a great deal more bellicose than Stratford himself.[13]

And A. J. P. Taylor was of the opinion that, 'The irritation of, say, Clarendon against Stratford was really that of a man in a state of muddle and hesitation against the man who presented the issues clearly and without pretence.'[14]

On the way out to Constantinople, Stratford stopped for consultations with the governments at Paris and Vienna. A. H. Layard, now a prominent MP, accompanied him as an adviser on the visit to Paris. Stratford was not optimistic about his mission and his concerns at first rested more with the Ottomans than with the

Russians. In early March 1853 he wrote to his wife from Paris: 'The more I hear and the more I reflect on Turkish affairs the less reason do I see to reckon upon any success at Constantinople. France, I think, is inclined to move with us, and I question whether Russia even is ready to bring on a crisis...'

Delayed by the consultations as well as by troubles with trains while crossing the continent, Stratford sailed from Trieste and around Greece to the Dardanelles and up to the Bosphorus. He arrived at Constantinople on 5 April 1853. To be back at the Ottoman capital and in the British embassy seemed unreal, dreamy, daunting. Stratford wrote that day to his wife:

> How strange! and without you? It cannot be, yet so it is. We got into port soon after daylight. A glorious morning – the domes and minarets towering above the mist and over each the crescent glittering in sunlit gold .... At 11 we landed under a salute from the *Tiger*, at Tophana on the place d'armes; a crowd of English, Ionians, and Maltese were collected there. They received me with three shouts, which brought tears to my eyes, and made my horse very skittish! The horse, richly caparisoned, had been sent to me by Rif'at with a dozen kazasses, and up the hill we went, followed by a long train and through the ranks of people greeting the old ambassador. We reached the palace [embassy] in due course; I dismissed my friends with a speech, the pattern of brevity, and here I am, Heaven help me![15]

2

Within only a few weeks of Stratford's return to Constantinople, the Ottomans and Russians were effectively at war. Hostilities were held off until late 1853 but they quickly became brutal. This included both land and sea battles and various long sieges, the most famous of which, that of Sevastopol, lasted 11 months. The war was fought not only in the Crimea but in multiple other theatres: the Danubian

Principalities, eastern Anatolia, the Sea of Azov; and there were even minor events in the Baltic Sea, the White Sea and the Pacific Ocean. Estimates of the total number of deaths from the war vary from over 250,000 to 1 million. New technology contributed to the great losses: it was the first war fought with mass-produced rifles for infantry, and with a prominent amount of steam transport which steadily delivered weaponry and men to the battles.

The war transformed Stratford into a full-time administrator. He was 67 years old and his experience and strengths were of course elsewhere, in the negotiation and mediation of diplomacy. His staff was small but his duties were massive, including the procurement of military materiel, finding labourers, coordinating various kinds of communication, liasing between different civilian ministries and military departments of the British government and between all of them and their Ottoman equivalents, and apparently also oversight of the military hospitals at Constantinople.[16] Part of the problem was his renown after for his long career and experience at Constantinople: everyone assumed that he was all-powerful there and thus virtually all requests for anything that needed to be done went to him.

Lane-Poole assessed Stratford's activity during the War as follows: 'whenever anything was wanted, let it be ever so difficult of attainment, and ever so remote from his own special department, he put his shoulder to the wheel and laboured unremittingly till the work was done.'[17] Stratford himself later testified to a committee of the House of Commons, 'There was one year [during the Crimean War] in which, if I remember right, the number of despatches addressed by me to the Foreign Office alone was about 1,750.'[18]

Even while fully occupied with duties of administration, Stratford continued to pursue diplomacy with the Ottoman government in the form of advocating further reforms. This included his effort in 1854 to stop the trade of slaves taken by the Ottomans from the Black Sea coasts of Circassia and Georgia, which the Russians had evacuated in the war; and also to stop the sale of these slaves in Ottoman markets. This historical episode was thoroughly examined by Y. Hakan Erdem, in a study published in 2011.

Erdem correctly observed that Stratford attempted here to employ the same basic method which he had used in 1843–44 to challenge Ottoman capital punishment for apostasy from Islam: calling into question the theological legal grounds on which the act was based by claiming that it had no justification in religious scripture.[19] Stratford also made strategic arguments to the Ottoman government, stressing that the present military alliance between the Ottoman Empire and their allies in the war would be politically undermined if the Ottomans continued enslavement on the Black Sea coasts. But here Stratford also went to lengths to argue to the Ottoman government precisely why the practice was socially retrograde and harmful to the Ottoman Empire itself. Erdem discovered in the archives Stratford's instructions to his chief dragoman, Etienne Pisani (nephew of Frédéric and grand-nephew of Bartholomeo, Stratford's previous chief dragomans),[20] dated 29 August 1854, to communicate to the Ottoman government a statement against slavery, which read in part:

> ... the privation of liberty, not forfeited by crime, is itself an intolerable evil. But the injury does not stop there; the slave can hold no property; he is a property himself and, worst then all he is bit too often an instrument of vice and sometimes even of crime. His life is at his owner's mercy. If a Christian, his children are born to slavery, as if to reconcile those, who never can be parents, to the mutilation which deprived them of that hope. In one respect there is no difference between negro and Circassian slavery. Black or White, wherever slavery exists, the Whole Society suffers. A Curse is on the trade. Dealer and owner are alike infected by the taint. They treat their fellow creatures like brutes and are themselves brutalized in return.[21]

Stratford's communication also specifically requested that the Ottoman government issue fermans which, in Erdem's description, 'would prohibit the slave trade in the Black Sea as well as the transport of slaves to and their sale within the empire.' Mustafa Reşit Paşa, serving then as foreign minister, agreed with Stratford's opinion. Reşit wrote a brief for the government in which he declared that Ottoman officials' practicing slavery in Georgia was 'against the natural freedom of human beings', appeared 'absolutely hideous in the eyes of foreigners' and was 'among the most pressing public matters'.[22] He therefore brought Stratford's appeal to his government.

The Ottoman council of ministers met to discuss this on 18 September 1854. The government, according to Erdem, 'did not want the Black Sea white slave trade to come to an end on the one hand, it could not say "no" to the allies on the other'. They therefore settled on a 'middle path'. The council recommended the prohibition of Ottoman slavery in Georgia but not in Circassia, as well as taking some measures against the open sale of slaves in Constantinople. These recommendations were immediately approved by the Sultan, who issued fermans to this effect. The council rejected Stratford's demand for ending slavery throughout the empire and merely advised Ottoman officials, as Erdem summarised, 'to prevent open slave sales and confine the trade in slave to private house in a discreet way. It seems that the Ottoman government's perception of what constituted a problem was quite different than that of its allies.'[23]

As with the apostasy controversy in 1843–44, Stratford used his position effectively concerning Ottoman slavery in 1854. In both cases, he challenged the Ottomans on their own religious–legal terms and applied pressure concerning a vital issue of Ottoman reform by bringing it to increased popular and political attention throughout Europe.

CHAPTER 15

'OUR OWN PASHA AT CONSTANTINOPLE'

1

As the Crimean War dragged on through 1854 and 1855, devolving into the bloody standstill of trench-warfare, public opinion turned increasingly against Stratford and he came to be widely blamed for the whole conflagration. John Bright, Liberal MP and the forceful leader of the British anti-war movement, unleashed a tirade against Stratford in an address to the Peace Society held in Manchester Town-hall on 5 April 1855. This attack was fierce and expressed in succinct terms the main charges which were commonly made against Stratford during the Crimean War. Bright declared:

Now, we have, as you know, an Ambassador at Constantinople – Lord Stratford de Redcliffe . . . a man of the very worst temper . . . of direct personal hostility to the late Emperor of Russia. He was appointed many years ago – nearly 20 years ago – to be Ambassador to St. Petersburg, and the Emperor of Russia refused to receive him as ambassador . . . . if the late Government had sought throughout England to find a man particularly and especially disqualified for being Ambassador to Constantinople at this crisis they would above all others, have picked out Lord de Redcliffe. Lord Stratford, during his whole time at Constantinople, while these negotiations were going on, did his very utmost – and his utmost was most successful – to deter, by coercing at one time and by threats at another, the Sultan and the Government of Turkey from making the slightest concession that might have put an end to these difficulties, saved Europe from convulsion, this country from war, and Turkey itself from that destruction which war must inevitable bring upon it. (Cheers.)[1]

Bright's accusation – that Stratford had personal spite toward Tsar Nicholas due to the Russians' having withheld *agrément* for his appointment as ambassador to their court in 1832 – was a popular story in Britain and across Europe, and perhaps the most absurd notion of 'The Stratford legend'.[2] But Stratford was not so petty or undiplomatic that he would treat Nicholas with 'hauteur' in 1815, and in fact they never even met; he was not so fragile that he would hold a personal grudge against the Tsar or all the Russians for being rejected by their government in 1832; and he was not so wildly megalomaniacal that he would seek to make international war in 1853 out of some personal spite, particularly after he had spent his career trying to promote a balance of power between Turkey and Russia.

Bright's further claim against Stratford was that he 'did his very utmost ... to deter' the Ottomans from making peace with the Russians and that he thus forced the outbreak of the war. Historians have generally agreed that Stratford was bellicose and the cause of the war, and they have lodged three specific historical charges against him concerning the outbreak of the Crimean War:

(1) that he forced the Ottomans to reject the demands of the Menshikov Mission in May 1853;
(2) 'that Stratford de Redcliffe passed camouflaged or disguised warships through the Dardanelles and up to Constantinople during the month of June or at other times previous to mid-September 1853,' as Temperley summarised the charge;[3] and

(3) that Stratford was again responsible, in August 1853, for the Ottomans' rejection of the so-called Vienna Note, the emergency peace proposal produced by the European powers (without Ottoman participation) while meeting at the Austrian capital.

These three charges against Stratford were examined by Harold Temperley – or 'exploded' by him, as A. J. P. Taylor put it[4] – in a long and thorough study titled 'Stratford de Redcliffe and the Origins of the Crimean War', which appeared in two parts in *The English Historical Review* in 1933 and 1934; and then in his 'The Alleged Violations of the Straits Convention by Stratford de Redcliffe between June and September, 1853', which appeared in the same journal also in 1934.

Concerning the first charge, Temperley demonstrated that Stratford actually advocated to the Ottomans that they should accommodate Menshikov in order to maintain negotiations and avert war. At the critical juncture of 20 May 1853, Stratford sent a personal note to his old ally, Reşit Paşa, who had just been reappointed foreign minister. Stratford's note, transmitted by his dragoman, suggested to Reşit that he communicate to Menshikov the possibility of 'accommodation of a complete adjustment if the Prince would suspend his departure and negotiate...' Reşit Paşa was already of the same opinion, not because he was following Stratford's advice, rather because this was the path of common sense. But the Ottoman war party had become ascendant and the joint position of Reşit and Stratford was not followed by the Ottoman government. As Temperley summarised:

> Stratford's private advice was, therefore, in favour of retaining Menshikov by a friendly and conciliatory reply. But the advice was not taken, though Reschid seems to have wished to take it .... the Turks did not want to adopt Stratford's hint of asking Menshikov to stay and negotiating further with him .... Menshikov, on receiving this rebuff, broke off all relations finally and departed in dudgeon on the 21st. The very eagles

and arms of Russia were erased from the gates and the walls of the Embassy. A crisis of the first order had arisen.[5]

Concerning the second charge, Temperley showed that 'There was no violation of the Straits Convention by British ships between April and mid-September 1853 ... Stratford throughout showed a greater respect for the Straits Convention than did his own government, or the French Government.'[6] After Menshikov's dramatic departure from Constantinople and the closing of the Russian embassy there on 21 May 1853, the British and French fleets were moved to Beşika Bay, just before the Dardanelles. But this decision was taken by the British and French governments and not by Stratford. 'The British cabinet reached its decision on 30 May, and informed Stratford the next day. It is important to note that it was against the advice of Stratford,' Temperley stated.[7] He also showed that when the fleets arrived at Beşika Bay on 13 June 1853, Stratford refrained from ordering them (as he had been authorised to do by the Cabinet, should he have found it expedient) to cross into the Strait and come up to Constantinople as a show of force. He refrained from this act because he feared it would spark hostilities. Likewise, Temperley demonstrated that when the Russians armies crossed the border on the Danube on 2 July 1853, Stratford advised the Sultan not to respond militarily because he 'preferred moral and not material action ... in May, June, and July he deliberately preferred negotiation to action.'[8]

Concerning the third charge, the Ottomans' rejection in August 1853 of the Vienna Note, 'Everyone, of course, blamed Stratford,' as Temperley put it. Aberdeen, Clarendon and Graham, as has been noted above, were especially forceful in their blaming of him. Stratford doubtlessly preferred a peace proposal which he and the other ambassadors of the 'Powers' had negotiated with Ottoman participation at Constantinople. Nonetheless Stratford in fact advocated to Reschid Paşa on 13 August 1853 that the Ottomans should accept the Vienna Note in order to maintain negotiation with the Russians. Again, Reschid Paşa was in agreement with this path of common sense and he strenuously worked toward this. Temperley

discovered that on 18 August, when it became clear that the
Ottoman government would not accept the Vienna Note, and that
almost no hope remained to avoid war, Reschid's 'eyes overflowed
with tears', as Stratford recorded later the same day.[9]

The next day the Ottomans formerly rejected the Vienna Note.
'During the brief interval that remained Stratford certainly did his
best to damp down the ardour for war...,' Temperley affirmed.
'Stratford's attitude can only be explained by the idea that he
wanted to prevent hostilities from breaking out.'[10] These were
staved off for several weeks but by the end of January 1854 full-
fledged military war had broken out. Stratford then wrote his wife
a letter. This does not seem to be the private writing of a man who
was *bent on war* (as Clarendon had put it in his letter of 10
November 1853) and had just achieved it:

> I thank God that it has been my lot to bring about the last offer
> of peace ... How strangely have things been brought to pass!
> How inconceivable that such an atom as myself should be made
> the rallying point in such a chaos! ... I have never sought this
> distinction; my position here is an accident. I always thought
> that the great struggle of the East would not be in my time,
> and that I was destined only to fall in the ditch that others
> more fortunate in later times might pass over with less
> difficulty. It seems to be otherwise ordained, and with Heaven's
> grace I accept my lot, and will apply what little remains of me
> to reach the promised land.[11]

Stratford's whole career had been based on promoting the peace and
progress of the Ottoman Empire in order to create a balance of power
between the Ottoman and Russian empires, to block the territorial
expansion of the latter, and thus to secure Britain's imperial route to
India. War between the Ottomans and the Russians was the last
thing Stratford desired. As Temperley summarised in 1936:

> The fact is, what he really wanted Turkey to do was to execute
> internal reforms, and he feared that the effect of war would

destroy both these and Turkey together. On the whole, I think, he fought for peace and might have achieved it, if left to himself.[12]

2

By January 1856 fighting in the Crimean War had come to an end. In Britain this brought celebration and relief of tension but also fanned the flames of blame. The fall of Kars on 23 November 1855 was yet another British calamity of the war, and Stratford was now widely portrayed as its sole cause. On 16 January 1856, *The Times* blamed him for the fall of Kars by invoking the popular notion that he was ruled by his temper, had adopted Turkish methods, was a dictator at Constantinople and a failure at communication:

> It may be said, then, that it is the misfortune of Lord Stratford to live in a state of dissention with almost every man with whom he is brought into contact ... He lives in an atmosphere of antipathies, and, accustomed during so many years to intercourse with Turkish officials and to the deference of Levantine society, he is impatient of any demur to what he conceives his authority. The disregard of his advice, or even the differing from his opinion, is enough to kindle a dislike which may last for years.[13]

Stratford commented on the campaign against him in a private dispatch he composed to Clarendon on 30 January 1856:

> The 'wondrous tale' is now taken up by the Times .... Let the public know all .... I may have made blunders, I may have my short comings. Nothing more likely. Who is not without them? But I have no fear of my Countrymen when they have the means of judging fairly before them.[14]

The campaign continued unabated and on 15 March 1856 in a piece titled, 'The Unacknowledged Ambassador', *Punch* sarcastically declared: 'We are astounded at the ingratitude shown by both

Houses of Parliament to our Ambassador at Constantinople. Will no noble Lord or honourable gentleman propose a vote of thanks to Lord Stratford de Redcliffe for the fall of Kars?'[15]

'Lord Stratford is very much depressed about the affair of Kars,' as Emilia Hornby, wife of Edmund, the British embassy official, wrote home from Constantinople on 28 March 1856, 'all the blame seems to be put on his shoulders, as all the disasters of the war were upon Lord Raglan's. Poor Raglan broke his heart (they all say here), and, after he was dead, the papers made him a hero. . .'[16] As Stratford was, so to speak, still available for blame, he was portrayed as the standing villain in contrast to the fallen hero of Raglan – and also to the rising hero of Florence Nightingale.[17]

At the end of April 1856, the House of Commons debated a motion which did not name Stratford but implied his significant responsibility for the fall of Kars by declaring it to have been 'in great measure owing to the want of foresight and energy on the part of Her Majesty's Administration.' The motion was managed by James Whiteside, a Conservative MP, who spoke forcefully and at length in accusation of Stratford. Palmerston, now prime minister, replied with a strong defense of Stratford. On 1 May 1856 the motion was voted down with Ayes 176 and Noes 303.[18]

On the day of the vote *The Times* reprinted without comment a fierce attack against Stratford which had appeared in a Manchester newspaper. It ran as follows:

> We have proconsuls, by another name, as irresponsible, tyrannical, arrogant, and vain as ever made the power of the Caesars a curse to the world. The British bashaw at Constantinople is a personage altogether unique .... he is an independent potentate, with his own court of independent officials, his own maxims and policy, over which his reputed masters at home can only exercise the shadow of control .... he does just what he pleases, consulting his own whims and obstinate prejudices like an absolute monarch. He is evidently too strong for the Government. He regards them as much more bound to obey his instructions than he is to obey theirs .... His

long residence in Turkey has turned him into a model Turk . . . .
we seriously question whether any Turkish official ever
displayed more contempt for the authority of his superiors, or
more insolence towards his superiors, than has been evinced
by Lord Stratford de Redcliffe, or whether the Turkish
Government ever betrayed a greater amount of pusillanimity in
dealing with a powerful vassal than the British Government has
shown in dealing with its haughty representative.[19]

A few days after the 'British bashaw' article, a spoof in *Punch* on 10
May 1856 referred to Stratford as 'Our Own Pasha at Constantinople'
and suggested that, 'There is no man so thoroughly Turkish, and
therefore so fit to deal with the Turks, as Lord Stratford.'[20]

CONCLUSION

'THE ELEMENTS OF NEW PARTITIONS'

1

Several months before the end of hostilities in the Crimean War, Charles Canning, the son of George and cousin of Stratford, took the oath of office as governor general of India, on 1 August 1855 at India House in London. At the dinner which followed the ceremony, Lord Palmerston, now prime minister, spoke proudly of:

> the significant fact that, whereas of old all civilisation came from India, through Egypt, now we, who were then barbarians, were carrying back civilisation and enlightenment to the parent source ...[1]

It was a telling expression of the historical, political and moral justification which many of the British attributed to their empire.

After overseeing Sultan Abdülmecit's investment as a supernumerary Knight of the Garter and then departing Constantinople for the last time in late October 1858, Stratford Canning finally realised his elusive dream of settling at home. During a long and pleasant retirement he was active in the House of Lords and served as a national authority on international affairs. In December 1869 he himself became a Knight of the Garter. Stratford maintained his faculties until to the end and died on 14 August 1880 at the age of 93. He was, according to one obituary, 'A marvelous character, with a career full of experiences.'[2]

Stratford Canning's career and even his life were almost coterminous with Britain's role in the so-called Eastern Question. He lived long enough to see his country's takeover of Cyprus and domination of the eastern Mediterranean Sea, in 1878. But death denied or spared him knowing the method by which the British finally secured their route to India via the Ottoman Empire: the occupation of Egypt in 1882, providing direct access to the Red Sea and the Indian Ocean.

2

Stratford Canning's diplomacy with the Ottoman Empire was realistic, resourceful, tenacious and at times even daring in its case-by-case and day-to-day application; and it was valuable for promoting stable relations between the Powers in the region of Europe's perennially most volatile international flashpoint. In assessing Canning, it is useful to recall that in the spring of 1812 Sultan Mahmud II found him the sole 'reliable' diplomat at Constantinople.[3]

3

The meaning of the 'Eastern Question' was considered by Albert Sorel – whom George Trevelyan considered 'the modern Thucydides'[4] – in his masterpiece of diplomatic history, *La Question d'Orient au XVIIIe Siècle. Les Origines de la Triple Alliance*. He found that the *Question d'Orient* or Eastern Question was 'in reality, a European question' because it was based on European relations and tendencies. He explained that when the European Powers carried out their partitions of Poland in the 1770s, their excuse for carving up a European country was to eliminate an irritation between them so that they, the Powers, would be stronger in their mission of restoring

European rule at Constantinople. Sorel wrote that Russia 'was condemning herself in Poland to the most gory of contradictions: to restore Byzantine civilization in Turkey, she was forced to enslave, in the middle of Europe, European civilization.'

British conduct in the next phase of the Eastern Question was also marked by contradiction: she supported the constructive reform of the Ottoman Empire, but, whether one finds this support to have been either a success or a failure or some of both, there is no doubting that Britain made this move only in order to secure her route to and her occupation of India. Britain worked to strengthen the sovereignty of one country in order to eliminate the sovereignty of another.

Sorel published *La Question d'Orient au XVIIIe Siècle* in 1878, just as the 19th-century phase of the Eastern Question was reaching its conclusion, with the British occupation of Egypt in 1882; and still 35 years before the outbreak of the Great War and its resulting World War II and Cold War, with its political partition of all of Europe and much of the whole planet. But in his history Sorel was already able to predict that the aggressive tendency demonstrated in the Eastern Question would eventually result in the European Powers' turning against each other:

After 1795 there was no more Poland to partition; it was the turn of Turkey and of Germany. It is possible, as of now, to foresee the moment when the alliance, having absorbed all around it, will turn against itself in preference to dissolving itself, and, suffering to the end the consequences of the causes which founded it, will find in its own bosom the elements of new partitions.[5]

NOTE ON THE TEXT

Nineteenth-century transliteration of Ottoman Turkish terms and names, when the language was still written in the Arabic script, demonstrates the challenge of communicating across cultures. The present-day Turkish transliteration of Ottoman words has been employed throughout this text. But in the quotation of different historical participants who enacted their own transliterations, variations have been inevitable. For instance, *Kaymakam*, the Ottoman title for a regional governor and still in use today as an official term in the Turkish Republic, is also spelled *Kaimakam, Caimakam* and *Caimacam* in historical passages that are quoted here. (*Kaîm-makâm, Qaim Maqam* and *Qaimmaqam* are found in other works.) Thus this word which is so mellifluous when spoken, offering both alliteration and assonance, is so confusing when encountered in its multiple written forms. The *Glossary of Ottoman Terms and Names* includes the various transliterations that appear throughout this work, plus definitions and commentary on usage.

Certain Ottoman terms and names were so well-known and widely-used that they entered European vocabularies: *firman* and *Topkapı Sarayı* becoming 'ferman' and 'Topkapi Saray' in English. These and other corruptions which became standardised in English have been employed throughout the text. But other spellings are also represented in the quotation of historical passages.

Earlier spelling and punctuation in English – such as 'shew' for our 'show' and 'publick' for our 'public', prolific use of the comma and capitalisation of abstract nouns – have been maintained in quotation.

GLOSSARY OF
DIPLOMATIC TERMS

Agrément or *Agréation*. Informal prior approval by a state for the accreditation to it of a designated diplomatic representative.

The Ancient Regulation of the Ottoman Empire. Reference to the Ottoman prohibition against passage of the Straits by foreign vessels. Long resisted by the Russian Empire but supported by certain other powers.

Archives, public and private. Public or governmental record – consisting of all dispatches and their enclosures, memoranda and other official diplomatic communication between a minister abroad and the home and host governments, as well as all internal administrative papers of an embassy such as formal communications between colleagues. Private record – collected and retained by an individual, consisting of documentation not included in the public record, such as drafts, informal communication with colleagues and private correspondence with acquaintances and any non-officials, plus printed memorabilia.

Articles. Formal sections of treaties. Both patent and separate or secret.

Attaché. Embassy official, a subject of the represented country who is either a low-ranking diplomat or a professional from another service who is attached to the mission with official status in order to exploit his expertise. Through the nineteenth century, almost always either a military advisor, a diplomatic amanuensis, an undercover secret-service operative, or a complete non-professional appointed on the grounds of pure nepotism.

Audience. Formal ceremony of a foreign minister's arrival and accreditation, and then of his departure and final leave. In each case, held first with the Grand Vizir in his offices (or, during his absence, with the *Kaymakam* in his) and then on a separate occasion with the Sultan in the *Arz Odasi*.

Capitulations, *Kapitülasyonlar*. From Latin *capita*, head, in reference to section headings – a formal concession (and specifically not a treaty) granted by the Ottoman Empire to a state in order to regulate the legal status of that state's subjects, both diplomatic personnel and merchants, resident in the Ottoman Empire. Usually included exemption from Ottoman religious law and taxation. All capitulations were abrogated by the Turkish Republic in the Treaty of Lausanne, 1923. (Not to be confused with military capitulation, as in surrender.)

Chancellery, Chancery. Department and buildings of an embassy devoted to maintaining the archive and other records including those relating to finances and administrative functions. Sometimes the location of consular, political and other sections.

Chargé d'affaires. Diplomatic agent classified in rank below an ambassador, envoy and minister.

The Concert of Europe. Highly theoretical concept that the European empires (minus the Ottoman Empire, at least until the Peace of Paris, 1858) administered a balance of power between themselves from the end of the Napoleonic Wars to World War I via a series of congresses which allowed them to settle diplomatic issues. Also referred to as the Congress System.

Congress, Conference. Congregation of plenipotentiaries intended either to negotiate peace after a major conflict, such as the Congress of Vienna (1814–15) for the Napoleonic Wars and the Congress of Paris (1856) for the Crimean War; or to address a perennial issue, such as the Conference in London (1827–32) concerning the Greek struggle for independence. Sometimes attended by not only plenipotentiaries but also major government ministers.

Consul. Embassy official below *chargé d'affaires*. Up to and through the nineteenth century, often a subject of a foreign power or even the host country, retained for local knowledge and connections.

Cypher. Code used to conceal parts or all of the text of a dispatch. Decyphered by means of a key. The effective final conclusion of a foreign minister's mission was his surrender of the embassy archive, cyphers and operational secrets to his successor.

Dispatches, Despatches. Medium of public or governmental regular correspondence between a chief of mission abroad and his home office, including enclosures. Numbered serially except when marked 'Private', 'Confidential' or 'Secret'. Occasionally written fully or partially in cypher. In exceptional cases, exhibited by a foreign minister directly to his counterpart in the government to which he is accredited as a demonstration of the instructions and intentions of his home government. Composed according to a specific literary style and compositional form, with substantial margins which allowed for reference to enclosures or later redaction by the author or for marking up by the addressee.

Enclosure. Supplemental material included with a dispatch, usually copies of relevant prior dispatches or of correspondence between colleagues or of memoranda exchanged with the host government, plus local maps and newspapers. Enclosures were referred to in the text of dispatches by means of lettered marginnotes, usually A, B, C, D, etc.

Envoy. Diplomatic agent classified in rank below an ambassador and above a minister and *chargé d'affaires*.

Extraordinary. Highest qualifying distinction of an ambassador, envoy or minister. Originally signified a non-resident temporary diplomatic mission, but in the nineteenth century much coveted and proliferated as an exalted status.

Giovani di Lingua. Student dragoman on apprenticeship, often a young relative of a full dragoman.

Good Offices. Various activities intended to produce negotiation and mediation between belligerents or parties at odds.

Guarantee. Provision of a treaty which pledges a state to specific diplomatic or military action, such as 'to guarantee the integrity' or sovereignty of another state from attack by belligerents.

Internuncio. Technical title of the ambassador of the Austrian Empire at Constantinople from 1678 to 1856.

Letter of Credence, Credentials. Instrument of authority of a diplomatic representative. Usually presented in formal ceremony by a chief of mission to the head of government or state to which he is accredited. Conferred by embassies upon non-governmental individuals such as merchants or interpreters, including foreign subjects and even those of the host government, for the official purpose of performing a diplomatic position such as consul or dragoman. See Audience and *Berat*.

The Levant Company, Turkey Company. British chartered company for commerce with the Levant. Founded in 1581 on the basis of a terminable licence which was renewed several times. Granted royal charter in 1605 as 'The Company of Merchants of England Trading to the Levant Seas'. Not a joint-stock company or a strict monopoly but rather a regulation of a trade. Its court or board, located in London, raised taxes among its members (which usually numbered about 800) and specifically denied this privilege to ambassadors. Until 1803 it held responsibility for appointment and removal (over which the Crown held virtual approval) and remuneration of ambassadors at Constantinople as well as of embassy secretaries, consuls, chaplains and dragomans. It funded embassy operations including upkeep of buildings, although sometimes with specific grants provided by the state. Disbanded in 1825.

Memorandum. Special and in-depth exposition exchanged between a host government and a foreign minister accredited to it, concerning a specific topic.

Minister. Diplomatic agent classified in rank below an ambassador and envoy and above a *chargé d'affaires*. Also a colloquial reference for a chief of mission. A foreign minister or minister abroad is one who has been sent on a mission in order to represent his government to another. This is distinct from the term Foreign Minister which is often applied to the home Minister or Secretary of State for Foreign Affairs.

Note. Official communication exchanged in written form between a host government and a diplomatic agent accredited to it, or his embassy colleague, often a dragoman. Delivered with or without signature as a matter of degree of formality.

Note Verbale. In effect, a note exchanged strictly in verbal form. Employed either to impart a less formal and less imperative sense than a note would; or to obviate the production of an accountable written record of the communication.

Oriental Secretary. Embassy official and subject of the represented country who has been trained as an interpreter and translator in the language and customs of the host country. This is opposed to a dragoman who is a native subject of the host country and natively knows its language and customs.

Ostensible. Open for examination, intended for free inspection, including sometimes even by other governments, in reference to diplomatic correspondence.

Plenipotentiary. Government representative invested with full powers either for the purpose of negotiating a specific treaty or for attending a conference or congress; or a formal designation of a diplomatic representative in supplement to ambassador, envoy or minister.

Patent. Open and published, such as articles of a treaty, as opposed to those separate or secret and undisclosed.

Précis. Working summary of a dispatch received from a diplomatic agent, prepared by a précis writer at a Foreign Office.

Quarantine. Waiting period required for the control of disease. Either for a landing of a ship or for ingress to and egress from an embassy during a public epidemic.

Queen's Messengers. The designation of the British diplomatic couriers, comprising an official government service.

Ratification. Final approval provided by a head of state for a treaty negotiated by plenipotentiaries.

Under Flying Seal. Diplomatic designation that a document such as a dispatch should be ostensible either to specifically designated colleagues or to any of them, during the course of its delivery to the addressee.

GLOSSARY OF OTTOMAN
TERMS AND NAMES

Ağa, Agha. Master or chief of an order such as the Janissaries.

The Archipelago. Reference to the Greek peninsula and islands.

Arz Odası. 'The Hall of Petitions'. Sultan's Throne Room, in the *Enderun,* the Third Courtyard of *Topkapı Sarayı,* immediately inside *Bâb-üs Sade,* The Gate of Felicity. Location of audiences with foreign diplomatic officials.

Bab-ı Ali. 'The Exalted Threshold'. Decorated entryway to the Ottoman seat of government. Source of the term 'The Sublime Porte'.

Bâb-ı Hümâyûn, 'The Imperial Gate'. First gate of *Topkapı Sarayı.*

Bâb-üs Selâm. 'The Gate of Peace'. Second or middle gate of *Topkapı Sarayı.* Entryway to *Divan meydanı.*

Bashaw. European corruption of *Paşa.*

Bairam, Bayram. Holiday.

Berat, Barat. Governmental deed. Concerning diplomatic relations, the Ottoman licence for embassies to provide Levantine Ottoman subjects with letters of credence in order to function as consuls or dragomans. This diplomatic status was much trafficked and abused for its coveted exemption from various aspects of Ottoman law and especially from the *Haraç.*

Beratlı, Beratli. The holder of a *berat.*

Bey, Beg. Originally designation of a regional leader or military commander. Evolved into a general title of respect.

Bin-başı, Bimbashi. 'Commander of a Thousand'. Military rank.

The Bosphorus. *Boğaz.* Ancient reference, taken from Aeschylus's play *The Suppliant Women,* to the strait of Constantinople. Connecting the Sea of Marmara and the Black Sea. (A separate, previous reference to the Bosphorus, from Aeschylus's play *Prometheus Bound,* refers to the Strait of Kerch, which connects the Black Sea and Sea of Azov, hence also known as the Bosphorus or Cimmerian Bosphorus.)

Büyükdere. 'The Great Valley'. In Greek *Kalos Agros,* 'The Beautiful Valley'. Usually refers to the valley's ancient village on the European shore of the upper Bosphorus, in sight of the *Symplegades* and of *Yuşa Tepe.* Neighbourhood preferred by diplomats for its beauty and relief from the complications of Pera.

Location of summer embassies and consulate *yalılar*. In the case of the Russians, also a convenient location for carrying out emergency withdrawal to home via the Black Sea. Famed for its conglomeration of seven or eight ancient and massive plane trees, together 47 yards in circumference, known as both *Kırk Ağaç* or Forty Trees and *Yedi Kardeş* or Seven Brothers, which was fabled for being site of encampment of army of Godfrey de Bouillon, one of the leaders of the First Crusade, when passing through Constantinople in winter 1096–97; and was cut down in the early twentieth century for road construction.

The Canal of Constantinople. Reference to the Bosphorus.

The Castles of the Dardanelles. Reference to the Ottoman fortresses located at the Dardanelles on both the European and Asian shores.

The Council. See *Divan*.

The Dardanelles. Reference to the strait that connects the Sea of Marmara and the Aegean Sea.

Derebey. 'Lord of the Valley'. Landed gentry with traditional hold over vast sways of territory. Challenging their grip on power was one of the main goals of the reforms of Sultan Mahmud II.

Divan. The Council. Reference to the Sultan's Imperial Council of ministers, conducted in a chamber on *Divan meydanı*.

Divan meydanı. 'Council Courtyard'. The Second Courtyard of *Topkapı Sarayı*, location of the ceremony of the payment of the Janissaries.

Dragoman. Earlier also Druggerman. European corruption of *tercüman*, translator. Levantine Ottoman subject in employ of an embassy as a translator and interpreter of Turkish language and local customs and politics.

Dragoman of the Porte. Dragoman in the employ of the Ottoman government for its communications with embassies. Often drawn from Phanariote families. The position of Chief Dragoman of the Porte was usually co-ordinated with or followed by an appointment as an Ottoman governor in the Principalities.

Elçi, Elchi, Eltchi, *Büyük Elçi*. Turkish term for minister or ambassador.

Efendi, Effendi. 'Master'. Turkish term of respect.

Ferman, *Firman*. Proclamation issued by the Sultan and carrying supreme authority.

Fetva, Fetwa. Legal judgment based on Sharia issued by a *Müftü*.

Frank. European resident of the Ottoman Empire who is not an Ottoman subject.

Galata. Levantine neighbourhood of Constantinople on the northern shore of the junction of the Golden Horn and the Bosphorus. From 1261 to 1453, a Genoese enclave ruled by its own *podesta* or governor and endowed with a system of military walls and towers. The earliest location in the city of residential embassies before they began to settle circa 1600 in the fields on the hills above and beyond *Galata*, originally known as the *Vines of Pera*.

The Golden Horn. *Haliç*. Largest natural harbour on the European coast of the Bosphorus, forming the northern shore of walled Constantinople.

The Grand Mufti. Reference to the chief *Müftü* of Constantinople.

The Grand Signor. Reference to the Sultan.

The Grand Vizir. Reference to the chief of the Vezirs. Head of the *Divan*.

Gülhane Decree. From 'Rosehouse', name of the park located before *Topkapı Sarayı* where the Decree was formally declared. Reference to the *Hatt-ı Şerif* of *Gülhane*, issued in 1839 and considered to be the founding document of the *Tanzimat*.

Haraç, Haratch. Poll tax on Ottoman Levantine subjects, exempting them from military service.

Harem. Separate women's quarters of either *Topkapı Sarayı* or a private estate.

Hatt-ı Şerif, Hatt-i Sherif, Hatti-scheriff. Imperial edit.

The Hellespont. Ancient reference to the strait which connects the Sea of Marmara and the Aegean Sea. Equivalent of the Dardanelles.

Imam, Imaum. Prayer leader.

Janissaries, Janizaries, *Yeniçeri*. 'The New Corps'. Elite infantry units and palace guards founded in thirteenth century. As keeper of the *ancien régime*, they resisted attempts at reform begun by Sultan Selim III in 1770s and eventually toppled him in 1807 and executed him and his successor the following year. Eliminated as an order in the *Vaka-i Hayriye* of June 1826.

Kethüda. 'Master of the House'. Prominent Ottoman official, at times on a par with Minister for Internal Affairs and the *de facto* deputy Grand Vizir.

Kaymakam, Kaimakam, Caimakam, Caimacam. Regional governor. The kaymakam of Constantinople would receive ambassadors as *ex officio* deputy Grand Vizir during the absence of the latter from the capital.

Kelimeteyn-i Şahadeteyn. Invocation chanted upon conversion to Islam.

Kol-ağası. Military rank, between *Bin-başı* and *Yüz-başı*.

Kiaya Bey. Equivalent to Minister of Home Affairs.

Levantine. Non-Muslim Ottoman subject of European heritage. Dragomans were drawn from Levantine families.

Mehkemé. Legal proceeding or tribunal.

Millet. Officially recognised religious community of the Ottoman Empire.

Müftü. Religious juror who is authorised to issue *Fetva*s.

Müezzin, Muzim. Crier who recites the call to prayer from the minaret.

Padishah. Reference to the Sultan.

Paşa. Title of provincial leader. Equivalent to 'Lord'.

Paşalık. Domain of a *Paşa*.

Pazar. Marketplace.

Pera. Originally known as *The Vines of Pera*. Present day *Beyoğlu*. Diplomatic quarter of Constantinople. Resident embassies first established there circa 1600. Through the nineteenth century, often noted by diplomats for its disease, vermin, congestion, noise- and air-pollution, fire, uprisings and intrigue.

Phanar, *Fener*. Neighborhood on the southern shore of the Golden Horn, the location of the Greek Ecumenical Patriarchate since 1586.

Phanariot, Phanariote. European reference to a native of Phanar, often used in description of one who is prominent in Ottoman commerce or government service.

Piaster, Piastre. Ottoman unit of currency.

The Principalities. European diplomatic reference to the Ottoman regions in the area of the mouth of the Danube River on the western shore of the Black Sea, long a region of contention between the Ottoman and Russian empires.

Raya, Rayah. Ottoman term equivalent to that of Levantine.

Reis Efendi. 'Head of Chancery'. Equivalent to Foreign Minister.

Scutari. European reference to the neighbourhood of *Üsküdar* on the Asian shore of the lower Bosphorus. Site of Chrysopolis, one of the original ancient Greek settlements on the strait, reportedly founded in the 660s BC. Location of the

Ottoman barracks which served as a British military hospital during the Crimean War, made most famous by Florence Nightingale.

The Seraglio. Reference to *Topkapı Sarayı*.

Seraskier. Commander-in-chief of a specific event.

Serdar-ı Ekrem. Supreme commander-in-chief.

The Seven Towers. Literal translation of and reference to *Yedi Kule*.

Shahin Shah. Reference to the Sultan.

Sharia. *Şeriyat*. Islamic law.

Sheikh-ul Islam. Supreme religious title accorded by Sultans to the *Müftü* of Constantinople.

Solaks, Soulaks. 'The Left-Handed'. Elite units of the Janissary corps.

The Straits. Collective term for the two Turkish or Thracian straits, the Bosphorus and the Dardanelles or Hellespont.

The Sublime Porte. The Porte. Reference for the imperial Ottoman government. Translation from the Ottoman *Bab-ı Ali*, the name for the processional entryway to the government offices. Usage is equivalent to that of 'the Court of St. James', 'the Kremlin'.

Süleymaniye. Imperial mosque at Constantinople, founded by Sultan Süleyman, designed by Mimar Sinan, constructed 1550–58.

Sunna. Body of custom and rulings based on the Qur'an.

The Sweet Waters of Asia. Reference to the only two full rivers that feed the Bosphorus from its Asian shore, as well as to the recreational area between them.

The Sweet Waters of Europe. Reference to the two rivers that are the source of the Golden Horn, as well as to the recreational area between them.

Symplegades. Ancient reference, from Greek mythology and depicted in *Jason and the Argonauts*, to the opening of the Bosphorus to the Black Sea.

Tanzimat. Reference to the Ottoman reform movement that was formerly launched by the *Gülhane* Decree in 1839.

Tekke. Religious educational institution.

Tercüman. Translator, the term 'dragoman' being a corruption of it.

Teskere, Tezkire. Official notification of various functions and statuses. Sometimes a reference to a residence permit for foreigners.

Therapia, *Tarabya*. Neighbourhood on the European shore of the Bosphorus, several kilometers south of *Büyükdere*, preferred by diplomats. Also the location of summer embassies and *yalı*s.

Topkapı. Topkapi. Top Kapousee. Neighbourhood in the western quarter of Constantinople along Theodosian Walls. Not to be confused with *Topkapı Sarayı*, which is located at the opposite end of the city.

Topkapı Sarayı, Topkapi Saray. Seat of Ottoman power, located at the very eastern end of the city. See *Arz Odası, Bâb-ı Hümâyûn, Bâb-üs Selâm, Divan, Divan meydanı, Harem*.

Tophane. Neighbourhood on the European shore of the lower Bosphorus, down the hill from Pera, surrounding a prominent port often employed by arriving and departing ambassadors. Location of an old Ottoman foundry.

Ulema. Collective term for Islamic jurists at Constantinople.

Vaka-i Hayriye. 'The Auspicious Event'. Elimination of the order of the Janissaries, proclaimed by Sultan Mahmut II after the Janissary uprising which began on 16 June 1826.

Vezir, Vizir. 'Counsellor'. A minister of the Sultan.

Yalı. Residence on the Bosphorus. Embassies usually rented and later owned their own such sites in order to have respite from the complications of *Pera* including disease, congestion, fire and uprisings.

Yedi Kule. Literally, Seven Towers. Ottoman fortress built around *Porta Aurea* or the Golden Gate of Byzantine emperors, located at the southern end of the Theodosian Walls of the fifth century AD. Employed as an elite prison for diplomatic representatives and sometimes their colleagues and even dragomans who were held hostage and *in communicado* by the Ottomans upon the outbreak of hostilities with their state. This practice fell into disuse after 1800 without ever being officially renounced by the Ottomans; thus the spectre of it hung heavily over diplomats at Constantinople through the 1820s. By the 1830s it seems to have been no longer feared.

Yüz-başı, Yuzbashi. 'Commander of a Hundred'. Military rank.

Zabitiye. Zaptieh. Revenue agents.

NOTES

Full citations of works are provided in the Bibliography.

Abbreviations

BL Add. MSS = The British Library United Kingdom
Additional Manuscripts Collection

TNA FO = The National Archives United Kingdom
Foreign Office Collection

TNA IR = Inland Revenue Collection

TNA SP = State Papers Collection

Acknowledgments

1. Leaf, *Troy. A Study in Homeric Geography*, p. 1: 'one of my chief aims is to illustrate the significance of impressions gained by personal contact with the scenes of history.'

Introduction 'The Stratford Legend'

1. Nicolson, *The Evolution of Diplomatic Method*, p. 2, employed the term 'diplomacy' in the sense of 'the art of negotiation'. Kennan, 'History and Diplomacy as Viewed by a Diplomatist', p. 170, defined 'the classic and central diplomatic function' as the 'duty of negotiating and mediating between governments with conflicting interests...' According to Davison, *Nineteenth Century Ottoman Diplomacy and Reforms*, p. 329, 'diplomacy in a narrow sense is the art of communication and negotiation between the governments of sovereign states. Diplomats are the practitioners of this art.'

2. Van Millingen, *Constantinople*, pp. 262–263: 'To live in Constantinople is to live in a very wide world . . . here is a mould in which to fashion a large life.' See above, p. 235, and below, pp. 310–311, note 32.

3. The historical nomenclature of the city is complex and various usages are legitimate. Referring to the nineteenth-century city as 'Istanbul' is desirable as an evocation of Ottoman civilisation. But 'Istanbul' was not employed in diplomatic communication either by the Ottoman government or any of the other European powers. 'Constantinople', and its Ottoman forms, 'Konstantiniya' and 'Konstantiniyye', were employed in all of the primary diplomatic documentation encountered during this study, including in the Ottoman. Furthermore, 'Konstantinya' and 'Konstantiniyye' were prominently employed in various aspects of Ottoman government through the nineteenth century and the former version even 'appears on the Imperial Ottoman coinage until the present [twentieth] century.' (Runciman, p. 207) 'Constantinople' is therefore employed throughout this text as the name of the city.

   The names of specific regions of the city were employed in diplomatic documentation, including 'Pera', 'Galata', 'Fener' or 'Phanar', 'Therapia' or 'Tarabya', 'Büyükdere' and 'Stamboul'. The latter term in diplomatic usage was a reference specifically to the area within the Byzantine walls. Otherwise it was sometimes a general European reference for the city as a whole.

4. These paintings are described in Chapter 3.

5. Stratford Canning to his mother, Bern, 16 November 1815, in Lane-Poole, *Life*, volume 1, p. 267. See above, p. 132.

6. Stratford Canning memoir, in Lane-Poole, *Life*, volume 1, p. 505. See above, p. 194.

7. *George F. Kennan on Russian Diplomacy*, p. 4. Stress from original. This is the published text of a lecture delivered by George F. Kennan at the Kennan Institute for Advanced Russian Studies, Washington, D. C. on 2 April 1985.

8. Gibbon, p. 508.

9. *Times*, 16 April 1844, p. 5. See above, p. 224.

10. Figes, p. 55.

11. Layard, p. 426. On the collaboration between Canning and Layard in the excavation and export from Nineveh, see Malley, 'The Layard Enterprise: Victorian Archaeology and Informal Imperialism in Mesopotamia' (2011).

12. The term 'Eastern Question' or *Question d'Orient* has always been circumscriptive, referring strictly to the western perspective that the situation of the Ottoman Empire was the source of diplomatic instability between the European powers.

   A more realistic perspective and approach was suggested by Philip Guedalla in 1927: 'The history of the Eastern Question . . . may be studied from either of two angles. It is customary in Europe to follow the European side of the duel. . . But it is sometimes worth while to examine the problem of Turkey from the

angle of Turkey.... . Some such foundation is urgently needed, if the
Englishman who thinks about the Eastern question is to understand what the
Turk thinks about the Western question.' (Guedalla, pp. 115–116)

The same method and formulation were elaborated by Roderick Davison
in 1978: 'The Eastern Question is usually considered from the western view
point – what great powers would have influence in the territories of the
Ottoman Empire? This view is not enough. For the Turk it was a Western
Question. Its essence was, I think, this – how can the integrity and
independence of the Ottoman Empire be upheld? How can foreign intervention
be prevented?' (Davison, 'Ottoman Diplomacy at the Congress of Paris (1856)
and the Question of Reforms', p. 169)

Albert Sorel declared in 1878 that the Eastern Question was 'in reality, a
European question' because it resulted from the Powers' partitions of Poland
in the 1770s and from their subsequent politics concerning whether the
Ottoman Empire would be partitioned and whether Germany would remain
partitioned. (Sorel, pp. 301, 308) See above, pp. 256–257.

13. TNA FO 78/133, 49. See above, p. 142.
14. [Stratford Canning], Stratford de Redcliffe, *The Eastern Question*, pp. 80–81.
     From his essay, 'Turkey. Part I,' originally published in *Nineteenth Century:
     A Monthly Review*, volume 1, number 4 (June 1877), p. 717.
15. Taylor, *Struggle for Mastery in Europe*, pp. 10, 53, note 4. See above, p. 242.
16. This distinction between imperiousness and bellicosity is from Harold
     Temperley, *England and the Near East*, p. 509: he observed of Stratford Canning
     that while 'his actions were not bellicose', he was at the same time an 'imperious
     man'. Temperley explained that 'a rough strong man is not necessarily a
     bellicose one.'
17. Temperley, 'Stratford de Redcliffe and the Origins of the Crimean War. PART I',
     p. 601. Canning rose to his new title, Viscount Stratford de Redcliffe, in 1852.
     See above, p. 239.
18. Temperley, *England and the Near East*, p. 314.
19. 'British Embassies, Ambassadors, and Their Salaries.' *Monthly Magazine, or,
     British Register,* new series, volume 9, number 49 (January 1830), pp. 13, 14,
     15: 'The present system sends out an incumbrance of the Foreign Office, who
     knows no more of foreign life than he could learn from flirtation in the green-
     room of the Opera; or some dandy Peer who hangs heavy on the minister's
     hands, and who, if he but speak the worst French that ever issued from the lips
     of man, and can fold a letter, looks on himself as qualified for the conduct of
     affairs.... The idler of rank abroad has seldom more than two resources for
     getting rid of the burthen of time – gaming and intrigue.... The whole
     tribe of this coxcumbry must be swept away like chaff. The Lord Fredericks and
     Lord Alphonsos – the whole *élite* of that incomparable caste of younger
     brotherhood, should be cashiered.'

20. *Manchester Times and Gazette,* 6 June 1835, p. 2. The terms "prints and fustians" refer to clothes made of heavy woven cloth and were considered working-class wear.

21. *Punch, Or the London Charivari,* 24 April 1858, p. 171. The other definitions were:

'PASSPORT. A contrivance to prevent ports from being passed.'

'CONSUL. An officer expressly forbid to offer consolation to British subjects in trouble.'

'CHANCERY (of a LEGATION). That part of the office into which when once papers get, nothing ever comes of them.'

'PROTOCOL. From the Greek πρωτος, first, and κόλλος, glue. The most superficial cement by which nations can be held together.'

A few months later appeared 'Work for the Toothpickers', *Freeman's Journal and Daily Commercial Advertiser,* 23 November 1858, p. 2, which included: 'The diplomatic body, with a few trifling exceptions, have nothing to do except smoke cigars, pick their teeth, and dress for dinner. They are paid liberally for the charms of the *far niente,* and represent the majority of the empire at the least possible expenditure of labour and time. Hence the foreign embassy is a special object of ambition to the aristocracy.' [*Dolce Far Niente* – How sweet it is to do nothing.]

22. *North Wales Chronicle,* 9 January 1858, p. 6. Identified as 'From the *Observer*'.

23. A. P. Stanley, 'Preface' to [Stratford Canning], *The Eastern Question,* p. xiv: 'the dark shadow of the Turkish Empire cast its own shade of unpopularity over the statesman [Stratford Canning] who had been so deeply identified in the public mind with the arduous task of supporting its existence; and the long retirement from public life ... threw into the background those services to his country ...'

24. *Glasgow Herald,* 16 August 1880, p. 4.

25. *Times,* 16 August 1880, p. 9.

26. *Pall Mall Gazette,* 11 September 1880, p. 7. Stratford's pension had ended with his death. *The Illustrated London News,* 9 September 1876 , p. 235, reported that Stratford's pension at that time amounted to £1786 per annum.

27. See Chapters Seven and Eleven concerning Stratford's mission to St. Petersburg in 1824 and the Russians' rejection of him as ambassador to their court in 1832.

28. Sir Henry Bartle Edward Frere (1815–84) became British High Commissioner of Southern Africa in 1877. In January 1879 he ordered the invasion of Zululand, which led to the Anglo-Zulu War. For this he was ignominiously recalled home by government in 1880. The main part of Frere's career was spent as a powerful British secretary and governor in India, 1834–67. Bartle Frere happened to be the nephew of John Hookham Frere (1769–1846), the close friend and political ally of George Canning and along with him one of the founders of the *Anti-Jacobin.*

29. *Reynolds's Newspaper,* 19 September 1880, p. 4.

30. *Hansard's Parliamentary Debates,* Third Series, volume 324, columns 219–220, debate for 23 March 1888.

31. TNA IR 59/108, 'Stratford de Redcliffe last will and testament', dated and signed 15 September 1875, plus probate documents from after Stratford's death. These records show his final assets at £17,986.7.7 and debts at £17,924.4.5. The *Illustrated London News,* 16 October 1880, p. 387, reported his assets at death to be 'under £18,000'. The entry for Stratford Canning in the *Oxford Dictionary of National Biography* (2004) also reported, 'Wealth at death under £18,000' (Chamberlain, p. 932).

32. Cambon, p. 37. Translation from French is mine. Harold Nicolson, *Diplomacy,* p. 57, found Cambon to be 'one of the most intelligent and high-minded of professional diplomatists.'

33. Schmitt, '"With How Little Wisdom"', pp. 310–311.

34. Taylor, 'The Rise and Fall of Diplomatic History', pp. 86–86. During the last phase of World War II, in March 1945, Herbert Butterfield, 'Tendencies in Historical Study in England', p. 217, suggested that, 'In times of upheaval and conflict, the pressure of great events is bound to put much strain upon the study and writing of history.'

35. Sermon of A. P. Stanley, Dean of Westminster, 22 August 1880. Quoted in Lane-Poole, *Life,* volume 2, p. 466.

36. Stratford Canning memoir, in Lane-Poole, *Life,* volume 1, p. 19. See above, p. 79.

37. Mehitabel Canning to Stratford Canning, [England], 1809, in Lane-Poole, *Life,* volume 1, p. 119. See above, p. 79.

38. Stratford Canning memoir, in Lane-Poole, *Life,* volume 1, pp. 192–193.

39. Layard, pp. 374–375, 431.

40. Lear, p. 71.

41. Edmund Hornby, pp. 70–71. An observation concerning Stratford Canning by Emilia Hornby, wife of Edmund, is provided above, p. 253.

42. Private letter of Edmund Calvert to Count [Alexandre Bartholomeo Stephane] Pisani, Rhodes, 26 October 1881. Manuscript in collection of Giles and Priscilla Hunt. Quoted with permission.

43. Temperley, 'Stratford de Redcliffe and the Origins of the Crimean War. PART II', p. 297, quoting Clarendon's personal archive, British Library. The insertion of '[Stratford]', '[ectionate]' (into 'aff[ectionate]ly') and '[George]' are by Temperley.

44. *Examiner,* 2 January 1858, p. 2, employed 'eye of the lynx' to refer to Stratford's watch over diplomatic affairs. And Cyrus Hamlin, an American missionary who came to Constantinople during the Crimean War and in 1863 founded there Robert College, the first American university abroad, noted that Stratford's 'wonderful eye seemed to search into the character' of those with whom he spoke. (Hamlin, 'The Political Duel', p. 453)

45. 'Stratford Canning, Viscount Stratford de Redcliffe' by George Richmond, chalk, 1853, Primary Collection, NPG 1513, National Portrait Gallery UK.

46. 'Stratford Canning, Viscount Stratford de Redcliffe' by George Frederic Watts, oil on panel, 1856–57, Primary Collection, NPG 684, National Portrait Gallery UK.

47. National Portrait Gallery UK, Room 23, caption of portrait listed in previous note, examined on various occasions since 2006 and lastly on 13 October 2012. The Gallery's caption of 'Sir Richard Francis Burton', by Frederic Leighton, Baron Leighton, oil on canvas, 1872–85, Primary Collection, NPG 1070, describes Burton as being '... profoundly attracted to the East, as to all things strange and exotic...'

48. Findley, p. 581.

49. *Times*, 4 April 1896, p. 8.

50. Nicolson, *Diplomacy*, p. 227.

51. *Times*, 4 April 1896, p. 8. The 'biographer' referred to here is Stanley Lane-Poole.

52. *Times,* 16 August 1880, p. 9.

53. Bright, p. 383.

54. See Chapter 7 on the Stratford's meetings at Petersburg in 1825, and Chapter 11 on the Russians' rejection of him as ambassador to their court in 1832.

55. Charlotte Canning journal entry, dated Windsor, August 28, 1843. Quoted in Surtees, p. 86. Charles Canning (1812–62) was the son of George Canning. In late 1855 Charles and Charlotte went to India where he served as last Governor General and First Viceroy and oversaw the British repression of the Great Indian Rebellion of 1857–59. Their fate in India is superbly recounted in Michael Maclagan, *'Clemency' Canning. Charles John, 1st Earl Canning. Governor-General and Viceroy of India 1856–1862* (1962). Charlotte Canning's watercolours of India and plus her fascinating epistolary and journal reports on the life of the country are marvelously presented in Charles Allen, *A Glimpse of the Burning Plain* (1986).

56. For Erdem, see Chapters Nine and Fourteen; Ismail, Chapters Five and Six; Subaşı, Chapters Eleven and Thirteen.

57. *Times*, 4 October 1888, p. 13.

58. *Athenaeum*, 18 June 1887, p. 801. This review, which appeared the year before the biography was published, referred to the first volume of the work upon its delivery to the publisher and must have been based on an advance examination of the text. The review noted that the second volume was also forthcoming and that the whole text 'is expected to appear in November'.

59. *Edinburgh Review,* volume 169, number 345 (January 1889), p. 203.

60. Davison, *Reform in the Ottoman Empire*, p. 446.

61. Puryear, p. 457.

62. Seton-Watson, p. 474.

63. Lane-Poole, *Life,* volume 1, pp. xiii-xiv.

64. Ibid., volume 1, p. 100.

65. Ibid., volume 1, p. 399, and volume 2, p. 266.
66. Ibid., volume 2, p. 58. Stress from original.
67. Ibid., volume 1, p. 81.
68. Ibid., volume 2, p. 58
69. Ibid., volume 2, p. 121.
70. Ibid., volume 2, p. 253.
71. Ibid., volume 2, p. 350.
72. Ibid., volume 2, p. 421.
73. Temperley, 'Stratford de Redcliffe and the Origins of the Crimean War. PART I,' p. 604.
74. Ismail, p. 176. See above, p. 107.
75. Edmund Hornby, p. 72.
76. Lane-Poole, *Life,* volume 2, p. 446.
77. Kinglake's work covered the history of the Crimean War up to the death of Lord Raglan. The work was originally commissioned by Lord Raglan's family.
78. *Times*, 24 May 1884, p. 10.
79. Kinglake, volume 1, chapter VIII, pp. 113–114: '... if the Ambassador was unrelenting, and even harsh in the exercise of his dominion over the Turks, he was faithful to guard them against enemies from abroad. He chastened them himself, but he was dangerous to any other man who came seeking to hurt his children.'

   Kinglake, volume 1, chapter XI, p. 148: 'The Turks had returned to their old allegiance. They could take their rest, for they knew that Lord Stratford watched. Him they feared, him they trusted, him they obeyed.'

   Kinglake, volume 1, chapter XX, p. 384: '... Lord Stratford had power over the minds of Turkish Statesmen; and he exerted it with so great a force, that, although it was now impossible for them to obey him without having to face a religious insurrection, they obeyed him nevertheless. The fury of the armed divines, insisting upon the massacre of worldlings, was less terrible to them than the anger of the Eltchi. To his will they bent.'
80. *The Encyclopedia Britannica*, eleventh edition (1911), volume 25, s.v. 'Stratford de Redcliffe, Stratford Canning', p. 998. It is an exaggeration to say that Stratford was 'always mentioned as the "great Elchi"' throughout Kinglake's work. But the term was indeed invented and applied several times in this work. Kinglake also employed a shortened form, 'the Eltchi', including in the last passage quoted in the previous note.
81. Lane-Poole, *Life*, volume 2, pp. 54–55.
82. Lane-Poole employed 'the Great Elchi' 30 times and 'the Elchi' 98 times throughout the biography.
83. The noun 'Elchee' – with variants 'elchi', 'eltchi', and defined as 'an ambassador' – was included in the predecessor of *The Oxford English Dictionary* and has been maintained in all its unabridged editions, including in the present online version. (*A New English Dictionary on Historical Principles* (1897), volume 3, part 2, s.v. 'Elchee, noun'; *The Oxford English Dictionary*. [First edition],

(1933, reprinted 1961), volume 3, s.v. 'Elchee, noun'; *The Oxford English Dictionary*. Second edition (1989), volume 5, s.v. 'Elchee, noun'; *The Oxford English Dictionary Online* (June 2012), s.v. 'Elchee, noun'. All of these entries cite Kinglake's usage of 'the great Eltchi' in his history.)

84. The term was even employed as the title of a book: Leo Gerald Byrne, *The Great Ambassador. A Study of the Diplomatic Career of the Right Honourable Stratford Canning...* (1964). The first page of the Introduction of this book, page v, includes: 'To the Turks he was Buyuk Elchi – the Great Ambassador.' According to Semmel, page 185, Byrne's book 'is little more than a summary, and not an entirely accurate one, of Lane Poole's *Life.*'

85. Fletcher and Ishchenko, pp. 12–13.

86. Chamberlain, p. 928.

87. Salmon and Spencer, p. 577. The text of Salmon and Spencer includes '[ambassador]'.

88. Figes, p. 60.

89. Farewell address of the American missionaries at Constantinople, titled, 'To the Right Honourable Viscount Lord Stratford de Redcliffe, Peer of England, Ambassador Extraordinary,' 12 October 1858, TNA FO 352/49. The address was published, with minor changes in punctuation, in *The Missionary Herald, Containing the Proceedings of the American Missionary Board of Commissioners for Foreign Missions*, volume 55, issue 1 (January 1859), pp. 23–25. In his response, dated 13 October 1858, TNA 78/1378, enclosed in dispatch number 8 to the Earl of Malmesbury, Stratford noted: 'I would not, on my side conceal that, while acting as an instrument for good under the authority of a truly religious Sovereign and the guidance of an Ever Merciful Providence, I have merged all partial considerations, suggested by difference of country or of church discipline in the paramount objects of furthering the general progress of Protestantism and promoting its ultimate success.' A copy of this was published, also with minor changes in punctuation and mistakenly dated 12 October 1858, in the same issue of *The Missionary Herald*, pp. 25–26.

Chapter 1   Apprenticeship in Diplomacy

1. Stratford Canning to Richard Wellesley, off Tenedos, 19 October 1808, in Lane-Poole, *Life*, volume 1, p. 43. This is Richard Wellesley (1787–1831), Stratford's friend from Eton and oldest son of Richard Colley Wellesley (1760–1842), the 1st Marquess Wellesley, oldest brother of the Duke of Wellington, Governor-General of Bengal (1798–1805) and Secretary of State for Foreign Affairs (1809–12).

2. Temperley, *England and the Near East*, p. 46.

3. Another possible British method at this time of attempting to keep the Ottomans out of the French camp, was reported by an obscure source. On 24 July 1808 Dutch newspapers were quoted in Vienna as follows: 'According

to a private letter from Constantinople, an English agent had arrived in that capital, in hopes that he would be able to bribe some members of the Divan, and seduce the Porte from her alliance with France; but he was discovered and sent away.' ('From the Dutch papers. Vienna, July 24', *Morning Chronicle*, 23 August 1808, p. 2. The *Morning Chronicle* was a Whig broadsheet.)

4. TNA FO 78/55, George Canning instructions to Paget, 16 May 1807.

5. TNA FO 78/56, Paget dispatches of 30 July and 22 October 1807. Paget arrived at the Dardanelles on 28 July and departed by 22 October 1807.

6. Paget, p. 331.

7. Arbuthnot, p. 4.

8. George Canning learnt of the Treaty as early as 16 July 1807 from a secret informant at the scene. (Rose, 'Canning and the Secret Intelligence from Tilsit', p. 65)

9. Adair, volume 1, p. 3. The reference to Paget's conduct read: '... Plenipotenitary Paget, without waiting for the arrival of a new negotiator, departed for Malta.' Translation from French is mine.

10. Ibid., author's preface, p. xix-xxi.

11. During the mission, Stratford Canning wrote to George Canning on 18 November 1808: 'The directions which you gave me upon leaving England to write you, I understood in a manner which most probably you never meant; yet under that impression I have thought it my duty to keep a constant eye upon every step which Mr. Adair has taken in the Execution of the Business intrusted to his management.' (TNA FO 352/1(3), 193)

12. Stratford Canning to George Canning, Bern, 27 August 1817: 'When you sent me with Mr. Merry to Copenhagen [1807] and subsequently with Adair to Constantinople [1808], a few weeks in the former instance, and as many months in the latter, were understood to be the utmost term of my absence from England ...' (Letter reprinted in Lane-Poole, *Life*, volume 1, p. 281)

13. Hinde, p. 18.

14. Leicester Stanhope, p. 535.

15. Byron, *Works of Lord Byron*, p. 531: 'Even this thy genius, Canning! may permit, /Who, bred a statesman, still wast born a wit, /And never, even in that dull House, couldst tame / To unleavened prose thine own poetic flame; Our last, our best, our only orator, / Even I can praise thee – Tories do no more: /Nay, not so much; – they hate thee, man, because / Thy Spirit less upholds them than it awes.'

16. Hunt, *Duel*, p. 134.

17. George Canning, *Letter-Journal*, pp. 206–207, 209, 288, 289.

18. Hunt, *Mehitabel Canning*, p. 135.

19. Stratford Canning memoir, in Lane-Poole, *Life*, volume 1, pp. 29–30.

20. *Report from the Select Committee on Diplomatic Service*, section 1658, page 156: proceedings of 13 May 1861, testimony of Stratford de Redcliffe.

21. *Glasgow Herald*, 16 August 1880, p. 4.

22. Back in 1791 Adair had made a fact-finding mission to Petersburg for Fox which had brought him under Tory suspicion of having sabotaged the foreign policy of Pitt.
23. Adair, volume 1, author's preface, p. vii.
24. Thomas, volume 1, pp. 225, 229. Buff and blue were the colours of the Whigs.
25. *Gentleman's Magazine and Historical Review*, volume 44, no. 4 (October 1855), p. 536.
26. *The Anti-Jacobin* (London), 25 June 1798, p. 62. 'BOBBA-DARA-ADUL-PHOOLA' is often quoted in the slightly modified form of 'BAWBA-DARA-ADUL-PHOOLA' because this is the form it took in the anthology, Canning, Ellis, Frere, *Poetry of the Anti-Jacobin* (London: J. Wright, 1799), poem XXXIII, p. 206. It also took this form in several later editions of the anthology.
27. Adair, volume 1, author's preface, pp. xx–xxi.
28. George Canning himself had been closely associated with Fox and the Whigs before he eventually joined the Tories as a disciple of Pitt in 1792. According to Giles Hunt, *Duel*, p. 25, George 'had been brought up as a fervent supporter of Fox and the Opposition Whigs' and 'had always hero-worshipped Fox'. On Adair's close association with Fox, see below, p. 295, note 23.
29. Adair, volume 1, pp. 2–5.
30. TNA FO 195/1, 27.
31. TNA FO 352/1(2), 169.
32. Stratford Canning to his sister, Bess, Sicily, 20 August 1808, in Lane-Poole, *Life*, volume 1, pp. 40–41.
33. TNA FO 352/1(2), 171–172.
34. Thomas Barthold, sometimes spelled Berthold in official documents, originally Tomaso Bartholde, was appointed a student dragoman at the British embassy at Constantinople in January 1774 (TNA SP 105/203). By July 1789 he became acting 'cancellier' of the embassy, in charge of administering all commercial and consular affairs (*Oracle Bell's New World*, 8 July 1789, p. 4). But by November 1792 he was dismissed from this post due to his 'libertinism + dissipation' and from having failed to keep his office in order (TNA SP 105/121, 384–386). He was retained in the embassy as fourth dragoman (the lowest dragoman rank) and eventually promoted to third. In February 1796 the British *chargé d'affaires* in Constantinople granted Barthold a six month leave of absence in order to accompany his own family to England. But he did not return to his post at the end of this leave. He was reported as missing by the Constantinople embassy to the Levant Company general court in London on 10 April 1798 (TNA SP 105/126, 164, TNA SP 105/122, 96–97). In September 1798 the Levant Company in London learnt that Barthold was in Ireland, 'he went there by the desire of the Ottoman Ambassador [in London] respecting a Ship carried in there; we have by the desire of one of our Members given him permission to stay two Months longer in that Country ...' (TNA SP 105/122, 106–108). On 28 December 1789 'As the Company have some reason to think that permitting him to stay a little longer will be agreeable to the [Ottoman] Ambassador, it has

extended his Liberty til the Month of March next [1799]...' (TNA SP 105/122, 114–115). Barthold however missed this deadline also and was thus fully dismissed by the Company on 24 May 1799 (TNA SP 105/122, 125).

35. Johnston, p. 110: David Morier, when also a member of the Paget mission, had a poor opinion of Barthold and wrote of him in a letter dated 1 June 1807: 'I have seen [him] sporting a pair of highly polished yellow breeches in High Street.'

36. Johnston, p. 116.

37. Stratford Canning memoir, in Lane-Poole, *Life*, volume 1, p. 86.

38. TNA FO 352/1(2), 172.

39. Ibid., 93–94.

40. Ibid., 174.

41. Ibid., 174–183.

Chapter 2   The Treaty of the Dardanelles

1. TNA FO 352/1(2), 176.

2. Johnston, p. 117.

3. M. S. Anderson, a completely reliable authority, stated in his *Eastern Question*, p. 44, that the British did indeed threaten 'to blockade Smyrna and the Dardanelles'. But Anderson did not indicate the source for this data.

4. TNA FO 352/1(2), 176–177.

5. Bartholomeo Pisani (d. 1826) was appointed as student dragoman of the British embassy at Constantinople in early 1773 when his uncle, Stephano Pisani, was second dragoman of the embassy. For details of the Pisani family, see Sturdza, pp. 587–589.

6. Juchereau de Saint-Denys, p. 63, note (1) referred to 'M. Berto Pisani, who, in serving with zeal and intelligence his government .... Having escaped by a miracle the fury of the Turks, he was conducted in the quality of a prisoner of war to Bursa, and from there to Kutyar [Kütahya?], where he remained until the reestablishment of peace between Great Britain and the Porte.' Translation from French is mine.

7. *Times*, 8 October 1787, p. 3.

8. TNA FO 352/1(2), 178–179.

9. Adair, volume 1, pp. 36–37.

10. TNA FO 352/1(2), 190.

11. Stratford Canning to Richard Wellesley, off Tenedos, 19 October 1808, in Lane-Poole, *Life*, volume 1, p. 42.

12. TNA FO 352/1(2), 183.

13. Adair, volume 1, pp. 36–37, 44–45.

14. TNA FO 352/1(2), 183–184.

15. TNA FO 352/1(3), 193.

16. Ibid., 195.

17. Throughout his career Stratford appropriated many bonuses, reimbursements and pensions for his dragomans, including for Bartholomeo Pisani and his widow; for those dragomans who had losses in the great fire of Pera of 2 August 1831 (see above, p. 198, and below, p. 304, note 51); and for those dragomans who remained at Constantinople after he was forced to close the British embassy and quit the city after the Battle of Navarino in October 1827, with his arranging for their legal protection by another embassy (see above, p. 177, and below, p. 300, notes 49-50). And concerning the chief dragoman of the British embassy in the 1840s, Frédéric Pisani (1781-1871, the nephew of Bartholomeo), whom Stratford knew since his first mission to Constantinople when Pisani was a 'Giovani di Lingua' or dragoman student apprentice at the British embassy (list of dragomans, 21 April 1810, TNA FO 78/70, 73), A. H. Layard recorded: 'Sir Stratford . . . had the highest esteem for him, and the most complete reliance upon his fidelity, and upon his tact and ability in negotiating with the Porte.' (Layard, pp. 453-454) For Layard's further observations on Frédéric Pisani's abilities, see below, p. 307, note 27.
18. Adair, volume 1, p. 84.
19. Ibid., p. 98.
20. TNA FO 352/1(2), 189.
21. Adair, volume 1, p. 112.
22. TNA FO 352/1(2), 189.
23. TNA FO 93/110/2.
24. TNA FO 93/110/1B, 4. The English translation of the full text of Article XI is as follows: 'As ships of war have at all times been prohibited from entering the canal of Constantinople, viz., in the straits of Dardanelles and of the Black Sea [the Bosphorus], and as this ancient regulation of the Ottoman Empire is in future to be observed by every Power in time of peace, the Court of Great Britain promises on its part to conform to this principle.'
25. The 'ancient regulation' of the Ottoman Empire would be recognised by the other Western powers in the Treaty of London of 13 July 1841. Hurewitz, volume 1, p. 81, editor's commentary.
26. Wood, *History of the Levant Company*, p. 50.
27. Headlam-Morley, p. 216, partially quoted in Wood, *History of the Levant Company*, p. 180, footnote 4.
28. TNA FO 93/110/1B, 3.
29. Lewis, p. 1171.
30. Groot, pp. 236-237.
31. Naff, 'The Ottoman Empire', passim. On later Ottoman attempts to reform berats, see Naff, 'Reform and the Conduct of Ottoman Diplomacy.'
32. TNA FO 93/110/2.
33. TNA FO 78/63, 89-90.
34. TNA FO 195/4, 12-13. George Canning further upbraided Adair for making the original and signed copies of the treaty only in Turkish and French and neglecting to do so in English. Adair then explained to Canning that the

Ottomans could not make treaties in English because they and their dragomans did not know English at all. (Adair, volume 1, pp. 229–230) Stratford later recorded in his mission log that '... the Ratifications of the publick Treaty, together with those of the four Secret Articles, were exchanged at Constantinople on the 27th of July, 1809'. Stratford added in the margin of the log, in his own hand and over his initials: 'The Separate + Secret [Fifth] Article was ratified; but ordered to be exchanged only under particular circumstances.' (TNA FO 352/1 (2), 190–191) The exchange of the secret and separate fifth article would remain the source of debate between the two countries but would never occur.

35. TNA FO 195/4, 10.
36. TNA FO 352/1(3), 197. Even before the conclusion of the peace Stratford had praised Adair to George, such as on 18 November 1808, TNA FO 352/1(3), 193: 'The unmeasured Confidence he [Adair] had on every occasion shewn towards me, enables me to bear witness to the zeal with which he has pursued the objects of his mission at hazard almost beyond the bounds of his Instructions, and to the open + honest manner in which he communicated to you the measures that he had adopted + the motives by which he had been influenced. His letters to you from Gibraltar, Palermo, + Malta contain so full an account of all that has occurred relative to this Mission, that not a word remained for me to add on the subject. His Dispatches of to day appear to me equally full + circumstantial...'
37. TNA FO 352/1(2), 190.
38. Johnston, p. 118.
39. Stratford Canning memoir, in Lane-Poole, *Life*, volume 1, pp. 46–47.
40. TNA FO 352/1(2), 190, from Stratford's log of the mission: '... we at length passed the Castles of the Dardanelles on the 25th of January. On the following day we anchored off the Seraglio Point, + on the 27th landed in Pera.'

Chapter 3   Stranded at Constantinople

1. Edward Lear letter to his sister, Ann, 12 August 1848, Therapia, Constantinople, in Noakes, p. 84.
2. Stratford Canning to Richard Wellesley, Constantinople, 9 November 1809, in Lane-Poole, *Life*, volume 1, p. 70.
3. Newton, 'Stratford Canning's Pictures', pp. 81–83. Several of the pictures are reproduced in large colour prints in Newton, *Images of the Ottoman Empire.*
4. This is likely the sole work in the collection for which a probable first-hand account exists, from the travel journal of a young British architect, C. R. Cockerell, who arrived in Constantinople in June 1810. 'Mr. Canning, of whose kindness on all occasions I cannot speak too highly,' as Cockerell recorded, 'has obliged me exceedingly in lending me a large collection of fairly faithful drawings of interiors of mosques, some of them never drawn before, as well as other curious buildings here, made by a Greek of this place.' Cockerell detailed

his acquaintance with 'the Greek who did the mosques for Canning. We have paid each other several visits, and became fairly intimate by dint of dragomen, mutual admiration, and what was a superb present from me, a little Indian ink and two English pencils.' But unfortunately Cockerell never recorded the artist's name. One of the artist's portraits (Victoria and Albert Museum designation D.124–1895) is likely a depiction of Stratford's audience with the Kaymakam (marking Stratford's ascent to chief of mission of the British Embassy), which Cockerell himself attended: 'On July the 30th [1810] Canning had his audience of the Caimakam, who is substitute for the Grand Vizir while the latter is away with the army [fighting the Russians in the Danubian Principalities] .... The ceremony of audience was very short. The Caimakam appeared amidst cries of "Marshalla! Marshalla!" Then Canning and he sat face to face and delivered their speeches.' (Cockerell, pp. 14, 18, 21–22)

5. The theory of these three figures' representing Stratford and his Armenian interpreter or guide and Janissary guard, was made together by Charles Newton and myself as we viewed the original paintings at the Prints and Drawings Reading Room of the Victoria and Albert Museum on 10 August 2011. Cited with permission.

6. Newton, 'Stratford Canning's Pictures of Turkey', pp. 77, 81.

7. Stratford Canning's 'Account of the Three Last Insurrections at Constantinople, and the Present State of the Turkish Empire', dated 25 March 1809, TNA FO 78/63, 182–196.

8. McNeill, p. xv: 'People change their ways mainly because of some kind of stranger has brought a new thing to their attention. The new thing may be frightening; it may be delightful; but whatever it is, it has the power to convince key persons in the community of the need to do things differently. If this is true, then contacts between strangers with different cultures become the main drive wheel of history, because such contacts start or keep important changes going. The central theme of human history, after all, is change – how people did new things in new ways, meeting new situations as best they could.'

9. TNA FO 352/1(3), 204. Quoted in Lane-Poole, *Life*, volume 1, p. 51.

10. Bury, pp. 5, 6, 7, 30: 'The idea of human Progress then is a theory which involves a synthesis of the past and a prophecy of the future .... It may surprise many to be told that the notion of Progress, which now seems so easy to apprehend, is of comparatively recent origin .... You may conceive civilisation as having gradually advanced in the past, but you have not got the idea of Progress until you go on to conceive that it is destined to advance indefinitely in the future .... The progressive period, which is conveniently called the Renaissance, lasted from the fourteenth into the seventeenth century. The great results, significant for our purpose, which the human mind achieved at this stage of its development were two. Self-confidence was restored to human reason, and life on this planet was recognised as possessing a value independent of any hopes or fears connected with a life beyond the grave.'

11. TNA FO 78/63, 211.

12. Adair, volume 1, p. 179.

13. Ibid., p. 194.
14. TNA FO 352/1(3), 204. Quoted in Lane-Poole, *Life*, volume 1, p. 51.
15. TNA FO 78/65, 1.
16. Stratford Canning to his sister, Bess, Constantinople, 12 June 1809, in Lane-Poole, *Life*, volume 1, p. 72.
17. Hunt, *Mehitabel Canning*, p. 222.
18. *Times*, August 16, 1880, p. 9.
19. Stratford Canning memoir, in Lane-Poole, *Life*, volume 1, p. 65.
20. Stratford Canning to Richard Wellesley, Constantinople, 9 November 1809, in Lane-Poole, *Life*, volume 1, p. 70.
21. Stratford Canning memoir, Lane-Poole, *Life*, volume 1, p. 69.
22. David Morier to Stratford Canning, Persia, 5 December 1809, in Lane-Poole, *Life*, volume 1, p. 74.
23. TNA FO 352/1(3), 213.
24. Joseph Planta to Stratford Canning, Gloucester Lodge, Brompton, 2 October 1809, in Lane-Poole, *Life*, volume 1, p. 76. Stress from original.
25. George Canning to Stratford Canning, [London], 9 October 1809, in Lane-Poole, *Life*, volume 1, p. 79.
26. Stratford Canning to his sister, Constantinople, 12 January 1810, in Lane-Poole, *Life*, volume 1, p. 80.
27. Stratford Canning to George Canning, Constantinople, 8 January 1810, in Lane-Poole, *Life*, volume 1, p. 78.
28. Adair's departure from Constantinople had been delayed due to the French defeat of the Austrians at Wagram on 5-6 July 1809, and the two powers then concluding an armistice. This prevented the posting of a British ambassador at Vienna, which was Adair's assignment.
29. TNA FO 78/68, 67.
30. Clarke, pp. 481-482.
31. Wellesley, volume 2, pp. 310-311, 312.
32. Nicolson, *Congress of Vienna*, p. 59.
33. Muir, p. 285.
34. A British newspaper confirmed the Sultan's generosity, *Caledonian Mercury*, 2 July 1810, p. 2: 'The Grand Seignor has ordered a considerable sum of money to be distributed among the Christians who suffered by the late fire at Pera.'
35. TNA FO 78/68, 217-218.
36. TNA FO 78/70, 66-68.
37. 'Foreign intelligence. From the German papers.' *Caledonian Mercury*, 11 August 1810, p. 2.
38. Stratford Canning to Richard Wellesley, Constantinople, 31 May 1810, in Lane-Poole, *Life*, volume 1, p. 111.
39. *Times*, 7 July 1952, p. 2: 'An Eton v. Harrow Discovery. Score Book of 1805. From a Correspondent.' In the first innings, Byron scored 7 and Canning scored 12. See also *Athenaeum*, 27 October 1888, p. 555.
40. Hobhouse journal entry for 24 May 1810, BL Add. MSS 56529.

41. Byron, '*In My Hot Youth*', p. 251.
42. Hobhouse journal entry for 19 May 1810, BL Add. MSS 56529.
43. Ibid., 15 and 16 May 1810, BL Add. MSS 56529.
44. Ibid., 20 May 1810, BL Add. MSS 56529.
45. Ibid., 10 June 1810, BL Add. MSS 56529.
46. Ibid., 6 July 1810, BL Add. MSS 56529.
47. Stratford Canning memoir, in Lane-Poole, *Life*, volume 1, p. 86.
48. Hobhouse journal entry for 28 May 1810, BL Add. MSS 56529.
49. [Stratford Canning], *Shadows of the Past*, p. 160.
50. Hobhouse journal entry for 28 May 1810, BL Add. MSS 56529.
51. Ibid., 31 May 1810, BL Add. MSS 56529.
52. Ibid., 1 June 1810, BL Add. MSS 56529.
53. TNA FO 78/68, 336.
54. Byron, '*In My Hot Youth*', p. 256, text of letter, plus editor's note number 1. *Deuteronomy*, chapter 5, verse 21, King James version, reads: 'Neither shalt thou desire thy neighbour's wife, neither shalt thou covet thy neighbour's house, his field, or his manservant, or his maidservant, his ox, or his ass, or any thing that is thy neighbour's.'
55. Byron, '*Famous in My Time*', p. 23.
56. Stratford Canning memoir, in Lane-Poole, *Life*, volume 1, p. 86.
57. Hobhouse journal entry for 10 July 1810, BL Add. MSS 56529.
58. Chamier, pp. 60–61.
59. Stratford Canning to Richard Wellesley, Constantinople, 7 July 1810, in Lane-Poole, *Life*, volume 1, p. 87.
60. Adair, volume 2, p. 87; and TNA FO 352/1(7), 341.
61. Hobhouse journal entry for 14 July 1810. BL Add. MSS 56529.
62. Stratford Canning to Robert Adair, Constantinople, 13 July 1810, in Lane-Poole, *Life*, volume 1, pp. 88–89.
63. Robert Adair to Stratford Canning, 15 July 1810, in Lane-Poole, *Life*, volume 1, pp. 89–90.
64. Stratford Canning memoir, in Lane-Poole, *Life*, volume 1, p. 52.

Chapter 4   Chief of Mission

1. The Ottomans and Russians fought wars in 1710–11, 1735–39, 1768–74, 1787–92, 1806–12, 1828–9, 1853–5, 1877–8, and 1914–17.
2. Stratford Canning memoir, in Lane-Poole, *Life*, volume 1, p. 153.
3. The Ottoman and Russian governments had both allowed the Neapolitan ministers to maintain their embassies even though their government had effectively expired upon being incorporated into Napoleon's empire.
4. Anderson, 'Great Britain and the Russo-Turkish War of 1768–74', p. 40.
5. TNA FO 78/70, 129.

6. The Reis Efendi told Pisani that Stratford's analyses contained some information that he did not yet have. Pisani reported to Stratford that the Reis Efendi seemed in general very well informed of European affairs. TNA FO 352/1(7), 409–410.

7. Neale, pp. 205–206.

8. TNA FO 352/1(7), 341.

9. Johnston, pp. 147, 148.

10. David Morier to Stratford Canning, Persia, 7 November 1809, in Lane-Poole, *Life*, volume 1, p. 73.

11. Johnston, p. 147.

12. Ibid.

13. Galt, p. 281.

14. Stratford Canning to Richard Wellesley, Constantinople, 9 November 1809, in Lane-Poole, *Life*, volume 1, p. 71.

15. Johnston, p. 138. Almost 40 years later, in 1849, another British visitor, Herbert Byng Hall, one of the Queen's royal messengers, described Pera as a 'mass of folly, extravagance and vanity! ... I know of no public thoroughfare on earth where a display of spurious wealth – if I may so term it – is more revolting to every sense of pleasure than that to be met with in the crowded streets of Pera ...' (Hall, pp. 99, 100)

16. Johnston, pp. 148–149.

17. Clarke, pp. 483–484.

18. Stratford Canning memoir, in Lane-Poole, *Life*, volume 1, p. 47.

19. Johnston, p. 119.

20. Mehitabel Canning to Stratford Canning, [England], 1809, in Lane-Poole, *Life*, volume 1, p. 119.

21. Stratford Canning memoir, in Lane-Poole, *Life*, volume 1, p. 19.

22. TNA FO 352/1(7), 344.

23. Ibid., 345.

24. TNA FO 78/70, 182.

25. TNA FO 352/1(7), 346–347.

26. Ibid., 349,

27. TNA FO 352/1(7), 353.

28. Ibid., 354.

29. TNA FO 78/70, 254.

30. Ibid., 260.

31. Ibid., 206.

32. Ibid., 217.

33. Stratford Canning memoir, in Lane-Poole, *Life*, volume 1, p. 91.

34. William Wellesley-Pole (1763–1845). Long-time Tory Member in the House of Commons. Held various Admiralty and government positions.

35. Muir, pp. 123–124, 397. Muir notes that 'Moll Rafles' was 'a well-known courtesan, at this time Wellesley's mistress.'

36. Jackson, volume 1, p. 216.

37. Middleton, p. 106. Concerning Wellesley's tenure as Secretary of State for Foreign Affairs, Allan Cunningham, p. 69, concluded that there was 'no excuse whatsoever for his complete failure to exploit Constantinople as the one formal point of diplomatic entry into Europe still at his disposal.'

38. L. S. Benjamin's notes in Wellesley, volume 2, p. 69.

39. Guedalla, 'Lord Wellesley', pp. 214–215.

40. Butler, p. 363.

41. TNA FO 78/70, 56. Wellesley was perhaps reminded about the mission in Constantinople by the return of Adair to Britain exactly one week earlier, on 16 November 1810 (TNA FO 78/65, 371). Stratford replied to this first communication of Wellesley on 6 March 1810 that he had in fact already made the acquaintance of the suspected imposter and was quite sure that he was in fact legitimate. But Stratford assured Wellesley that he would follow his instructions to be on guard with the suspect (TNA FO 78/73, 90–91).

42. TNA FO 78/70, 58–60.

43. Ibid., 181.

44. The Chief Dragoman of the Porte, Demetrious Mourousi, the older brother of Panagios, was attending the Grand Vizir at the theatre of war on the Danube. The Mourousi (Morusy, Moruzzi) family, Phanariot Greeks of Constantinople, had served the Ottoman government as dragomans for decades.

45. TNA FO 78/73, 123–124.

46. TNA FO 78/74, 77–79.

47. Wellesley sent Stratford at least 12 dispatches, between 23 November 1810 and 14 December 1811, none of them relating to the diplomatic issues of the mission in Constantinople. Evidence for nine of these are contained in TNA FO 78/73. They related to the following issues, in the chronological order in which they were composed: an imposter; diplomatic gifts; unsuitability of Giovanni Reggio to act as British consul at Canea; death of Vincent Linker of the 6th battalion and 60th British Regiment on 9 October 1807; announcement that Stratford was to be replaced in Constantinople by the diplomatist and previous ambassador there, Robert Liston; the death of Sidky Efendi, the Ottoman *chargé d'affaires* in London; the confirmation of the receipt of dispatches; instructions to distribute enclosed political pamphlets translated in both French and German; the impending visit to Constantinople of Baron Geramb, 'a Hungarian of high birth'. The existence of three other dispatches is indicated by secondary evidence: one directing Stratford to combat insurance fraud involving British shipping; one announcing the death of Princess Amelia; and the other instructing him to be on the search for manuscripts of classical works that were thought by Lord Sligo to be contained within Topkapi Saray. The sole dispatch that would have held any real meaning for Stratford, concerning his replacement by Liston, was sent from London on 21 March 1811 and arrived in Constantinople about four months later. It must have raised Stratford's hopes that he would soon be relieved of his post, but Liston did not arrive until the end of June 1812.

48. Kennan, 'History and Diplomacy as Viewed by a Diplomatist', p. 172.
49. Mikhailovskii-Danilovskii, pp. 62–63: The Russians attacked with 17,300 soldiers by land and 2,600 by ship on the Danube, suffering 8,515 casualties including 4 generals and 363 officers.
50. Bell, pp. 495–496.
51. TNA FO 352/1(7), 356.
52. Ibid. Stress from original.
53. TNA FO 78/73, 24.
54. TNA FO 78/70, 43.
55. When Wellesley was approached by Lord Burghersh about procuring a diplomatic position in Austria for his 27-year-old son, Wellesley replied 'there is no opening there, but Constantinople is vacant'. The younger Burghersh passed on the offer even though a family friend advised that the mission would be 'a pleasant trip' and provide 'a sight of the Levant'. (Jackson, volume 1, p. 217)
56. TNA FO 78/73, 7.
57. Robert Adair to Stratford Canning, [England], July 1811, in Lane-Poole, *Life*, volume 1, p. 177.
58. Stratford Canning to his sister, Bess, Constantinople, 3 September 1811, in Lane-Poole, *Life*, volume 1, p. 178.
59. Hamel, p. 97.
60. Stanhope and Meryon, volume 1, p. 59.
61. Hamel, p. 100.
62. Lane-Poole, *Life*, volume 1, pp. 115–116.
63. Hamel, pp. 116–117. Also in Wellesley, volume 2, pp. 56–59.
64. Lane-Poole, *Life*, volume 1, p. 119.
65. The original copy of this letter reposes at British Library Add. Manuscript 37310, 77–80. Lady Hester labelled it as 'Private'.
66. Lady Stanhope to Stratford Canning, Damascus, 3 October 1812, in Lane-Poole, *Life*, volume 1, p. 120.
67. TNA FO 78/78, 33.
68. Hamel, p. 114.
69. Van Millingen, *Constantinople*, pp. 262–263. See below, pp. 310–311, note 32.

Chapter 5   Piracy on the Aegean, War on the Danube

1. TNA FO 78/74, 143–144. Stratford's letter was marked by the Foreign Office as received on this date.
2. Wellesley submitted his resignation on 12 January 1812 and this became effective on 18 February of the same year.
3. Stratford Canning diary on negotiations with Ottoman Foreign Office, in Lane-Poole, *Life*, volume 1, pp. 94–95.
4. TNA FO 78/73, 246, 247.

5. Stratford Canning diary on negotiations with Ottoman Foreign Office, in Lane-Poole, *Life*, volume 1, p. 95.
6. Stratford Canning diary on negotiations with Ottoman Foreign Office, in Lane-Poole, *Life*, volume 1, p. 96.
7. TNA FO 352/3, 173.
8. TNA FO 78/74, 235.
9. Ibid., 220.
10. Ibid., 248–249, 251–252.
11. Ibid., 296–298; and TNA FO 352/3, 44–45.
12. TNA FO 78/74, 92.
13. TNA FO 352/3, 46–47. Stress from original.
14. Stratford Canning diary on negotiations with Ottoman Foreign Office, in Lane-Poole, *Life*, volume 1, p. 99.
15. TNA FO 78/74, 293.
16. Stratford Canning memoir, in Lane-Poole, *Life*, volume 1, p. 100.
17. TNA FO 352/3, 48. Stress from original.
18. Ibid., 178–179.
19. Lane-Poole, *Life*, volume 1, p. 101.
20. TNA FO 78/77, 5.
21. TNA FO 78/79, 36–39.
22. Joseph Planta to Stratford Canning, [London], [1811], in Lane-Poole, *Life*, volume 1, p. 106.
23. Stratford Canning memoir, in Lane-Poole, *Life*, volume 1, pp. 109, 110.
24. Ismail, pp. 164–165. The *de facto* armistice of 15 October 1811 was officially signed on 8 December 1811.
25. Stratford Canning memoir, in Lane-Poole, *Life*, volume 1, p. 144.
26. Ismail, pp. 170–171.
27. Ibid., p. 171.
28. Stratford Canning memorandum to Galib Efendi, 12 July 1811, in Lane-Poole, *Life*, volume 1, p. 154.
29. TNA FO 352/3, 153. Stress from original.
30. TNA FO 78/77, 21–22.
31. TNA FO 78/77, 54.
32. Stratford Canning memoir, in Lane-Poole, *Life*, volume 1, p. 162.
33. Stratford Canning dispatch #6 to Wellesley, 21 February 1812, in Lane-Poole, *Life*, volume 1, p. 162.
34. Ismail, p. 173.
35. Stratford Canning memoir, in Lane-Poole, *Life*, volume 1, p. 163.
36. Ismail, p. 176. The insertion of '[Canning]' into the quotation is by Ismail.
37. Stratford Canning to Richard Wellesley, Constantinople, 7 January 1812 in Lane-Poole, *Life*, volume 1, pp. 178–179.
38. Stratford Canning to Mehitabel Canning, Constantinople, 7 January 1812, in Lane-Poole, *Life*, volume 1, pp. 180–182.

39. Stratford Canning to Mehitabel Canning, Constantinople, March 18 1812, in Lane-Poole, *Life*, volume 1, p. 182.
40. TNA FO 78/77, 94.
41. Ibid., 141.
42. Ibid., 160.
43. Ibid., 188.
44. Wellesley, volume 1, p. 289.
45. Middleton, p. 317.
46. Ibid., p. 311. Also according to Middleton, p. 106: Castlereagh's term of ten years, 1812–22, was 'the longest consecutive service of any British foreign secretary.'
47. TNA FO 78/79, 104–105. Liston would arrive at the Dardanelles on 12 June 1812 and then at Constantinople on 28 June 1812.
48. TNA FO 78/77, 140.
49. Stratford Canning memoir, in Lane-Poole, *Life*, volume 1, p. 166.
50. Ibid., p. 169.
51. TNA FO 78/77, 284–285.
52. Ibid., 282.
53. TNA FO 352/2A(1), 215. The Reis Efendi's order did go out but it arrived too late as the next day Gordon got through the Ottoman headquarters on the Danube and made it through to the Russians.
54. TNA FO 352/2A(1), 220. Stress from original.
55. Ibid., 222–223.
56. Ibid., 216–217.
57. Stratford Canning written instructions to Chief Dragoman Bartholomeo Pisani, 19 May 1812, in Lane-Poole, *Life*, volume 1, p. 172.
58. TNA FO 352/2A(1), 228.
59. Ismail, pp. 178–180.
60. TNA FO 78/79, 88–89.
61. Napoleon I, p. 198, item 286. Translation is mine from: *'Le fond de la grande question est toujours là: Qui aura Constantinople?'*
62. Las Cases, p. 101.

Chapter 6   The Treaty of Bucharest

1. TNA FO 78/77, 226.
2. The treaty was composed only in French. The original French text, with a Russian translation, including the two secret articles, is provided in *Vneshniaia politika*, pp. 407–412. This is the sole publication of the two secret articles. The French text of the patent 16 articles of the treaty (minus the two secret articles) is provided in *British and Foreign State Papers*, pp. 908–914. A table of contents in English for all 16 patent articles, plus English translations of the texts of articles III, IV and VIII, are provided in Hertslet, pp. 2030–2032.

3. Article IV established the European boundary along the Pruth River from Moldavia to its confluence with the Danube, and then along the Danube eastward to the Black Sea. Ottoman fortresses along the rivers were to be dismantled and 'No Fortifications or Buildings shall henceforth be erected thereon; they shall remain deserted . . .' Translation from French is mine.

4. TNA FO 78/77, 226.

5. Ismail, pp. 181–182.

6. TNA FO 78/77, 226–227.

7. TNA FO 352/3, 149.

8. Ibid., 148.

9. Ismail, pp. 184–185.

10. The impasse over the second secret article was continued well after Stratford's departure from Constantinople. It was resolved on 15 July 1812, in no relation to his actions and primarily due to the ingenuity and bravery of several Ottoman officials. The complicated story has been masterfully researched and related by F. Ismail, pp. 183, 187. The two secret articles were never ratified but the tenuous peace between the Ottomans and Russians held.

11. Robert Liston to Stratford Canning, Constantinople, 28 August 1812, in Lane-Poole, *Life*, volume 1, p. 185: Liston had been informed by his military advisor, Robert Gordon, that the Russian army on the Danube had consisted of 'above fifty thousand effective men'.

12. Mowat, p. 257.

13. Mowat, p. 281, quotes a Russian study, *Shornik imperatorskago russkago istoricheskago obshchestva*, volume 31, [1881], that 'The unexpected signing of this treaty excited in the highest degree the indignation of Napoleon.' But the source on which the Russian study based this claim is not provided by Mowat.

14. Ismail, p. 188.

15. TNA FO 78/77, 303.

16. Ibid., 320–321.

17. Ibid., 302.

18. Ibid., 331.

19. TNA FO 78/79, 106. Liston also recommended Morier 'as a person who might be employed with much advantage to His Majesty's service.' Liston's praise must have had effect because Castlereagh later employed Morier as his own assistant at the Congress of Vienna. Morier enjoyed a pleasant career in the Foreign Office, serving in various posts, including minister plenipotentiary at Bern, Switzerland from 1832 to 1847, after which he retired. The friendship of David Morier and Stratford Canning lasted from August 1808 until Morier's death in July 1877.

20. Lane-Poole, *Life*, volume 1, pp. 182–184, including Stratford Canning memoir.

21. *Ipswich Journal*, 5 December 1812, p. 12; and Lane-Poole, *Life*, volume 1, pp. 26–27.

22. Stratford Canning memoir, in Lane-Poole, *Life*, volume 1, p. 211. *Foreign Office List of 1856*, p. 65, confirms that Stratford 'was offered but declined a Russian Order in 1814', on instruction from the British Foreign Office. In January 1842, while visiting Greece on the way to his new posting at Constantinople, Stratford was offered Greek Order of the Saviour but the British Foreign Office instructed him to decline it.

23. Stratford Canning memoir, in Lane-Poole, *Life*, volume 1, p. 251.

24. Ibid., 193. Many years later Stratford did consent to meet with Wellesley. *Quarterly Review*, volume 149, number 298 (April 1880), p. 401, provided Stratford's polite reminiscence, in advanced age, of his encounter with Wellesley when called upon by him: 'I went in consequence to Fulham, where Lord Wellesley was then residing. I found him in his garden, and walked about with him for a good hour teeming with interest, derived from his character and intellectual qualities. Our conversation was chiefly political, and in the whole course of it, at one time figured the commanding statesman, at another the accomplished orator, to say nothing of wit, scholarship, and the recollections of bygone events.'

25. Wilson, p. 124.

26. TNA FO 78/78, 156–157.

27. TNA FO 78/79, 180–181.

28. Ibid., 190–191. Stress from original.

29. Ibid., 198. Stress from original.

30. Ibid., 201.

31. Ibid., 212. Stress from original.

32. Wilson, p. 395. Stress from original.

33. Robert Liston to Stratford Canning, Constantinople, 28 August 1812, in Lane-Poole, *Life*, volume 1, p. 185.

34. Lane-Poole, *Life*, volume 1, p. 175.

35. David Morier letter to Henry Addington, 1869, in Lane-Poole, *Life*, volume 1, p. 176.

36. TNA FO 352/2A(1), 209.

37. Ismail, p. 185.

38. *Morning Chronicle*, 3 August 1812, p. 3.

39. Johnston, p. 151.

Chapter 7   Return to Constantinople

1. Stratford Canning memoir, in Lane-Poole, *Life*, volume 1, pp. 185, 266.

2. *Foreign Office List for 1856*, pp. 12, 65: Stratford was appointed to the Bern post on 28 June 1814 and to the Washington post on 18 July 1820.

3. Stratford Canning to his mother, Bern, 16 November 1815, in Lane-Poole, *Life*, volume 1, p. 267.

4. Hunt, *Mehitabel Canning*, pp. 301–302.

5. Stratford Canning to his sister, Bess, 18 December 1817, in Lane-Poole, *Life*, volume 1, pp. 275–276.
6. Stratford to George Canning, Switzerland, 27 August 1817, in Lane-Poole, *Life*, volume 1, p. 280. Stratford's first letter at this time to George, requesting help in getting out of diplomacy and established in London, was dated 7 July 1817.
7. Stratford Canning to Joseph Planta, Switzerland, 30 September 1817, in Lane-Poole, *Life*, volume 1, p. 278.
8. George Canning to Stratford, 7 October 1818, in Lane-Poole, *Life*, volume 1, p. 282.
9. See above, p. 60.
10. Lane-Poole, *Life*, volume 1, pp. 283–85, 297–298, 335; and *Foreign Office List for 1853*, pp. 12, 43.
11. Stratford Canning to Gally Knight, [London], 24 January 1820, in Lane-Poole, *Life*, volume 1, p. 288.
12. Stratford Canning to his mother, Washington, D. C., 8 October 1820, in Lane-Poole, *Life*, volume 1, p. 299.
13. *The Encyclopedia Britannica*, eleventh edition (1911), volume 25, s.v. 'Stratford de Redcliffe, Stratford Canning', p. 997.
14. Stratford Canning to his sister, April 1821, quoted in Hunt, *Mehitabel Canning*, p. 312.
15. Stratford Canning to his mother, Washington, D. C., 4 November 1821, in Lane-Poole, *Life*, volume 1, p. 325.
16. George Canning letter of 29 July 1824, in George Canning, *George Canning and His Friends,* volume 2, p. 267.
17. Crawley, *Question of Greek Independence*, pp. 30–31. Here are found the details of the Greek provisional government's disagreement with the Russian Memoir.
18. Crawley, *Question of Greek Independence*, p. 32.
19. TNA FO 352/9C, 317. Stress from original.
20. TNA FO 352/9A, 90–91, 104, 113.
21. Stratford Canning memoir, in Lane-Poole, *Life*, volume 1, p. 349.
22. TNA FO 65/147, 88.
23. Stratford Canning memoir, in Lane-Poole, *Life*, volume 1, p. 349.
24. Stratford Canning to his mother, 8 February 1825, in Lane-Poole, *Life*, volume 1, p. 355.
25. Stratford Canning memoir, in Lane-Poole, *Life*, volume 1, p. 357.
26. This unfortunate education is detailed in Kliuchevskii, lecture LXXXIII, pp. 187–190.
27. TNA FO 65/147, 103.
28. Stratford's dispatches concerning his meetings with Nesselrode repose at TNA FO 65/147.
29. On the Russians' rejection of Stratford as ambassador to their court in 1832, see Chapter 11. On the recycling of this story during the Crimean War, see Chapter 15.
30. TNA FO 352/10B(7), 579. Stress from original.

31. Stratford Canning to his mother, 2 July 1825, in Lane-Poole, *Life*, volume 1, p. 384.
32. Crawley, 'Anglo-Russian Relations 1815–40', p. 53.
33. Crawley, *Question of Greek Independence*, p. 49.
34. George Canning to Stratford, 9 January 1826, in Lane-Poole, *Life*, volume 1, p. 395.
35. TNA FO 78/133, 49.
36. Ibid., 86–87.
37. Crawley, 'A Forgotten Prophecy', p. 213.
38. Stratford Canning to George, Washington, 29 September 1821, in Lane-Poole, *Life*, volume 1, p. 307. Stratford's usage of 'bag and baggage' here in reference to the Ottomans was later famously employed in the same function by Gladstone in his pamphlet, *Bulgarian Horrors and the Question of the East* (London: John Murray, 1876), p. 31: 'Let the Turks now carry away their abuses in the only possible manner, namely by carrying off themselves. Their Zaptiehs and their Mudirs, their Bimbashis and the Yuzbashis, their Kaimakams and their Pashas, one and all, bag and baggage, shall, I hope, clear out from the province they have desolated and profaned.' Gladstone dedicated the pamphlet to 'Viscount Stratford de Redcliffe, with the admiration which all accord to him, and the esteem which has grown with a friendship of more than forty years.'
39. Stratford Canning to Joseph Planta, 30 July and 1 October 1821, [Washington], in Lane-Poole, *Life*, volume 1, p. 346.
40. [Stratford Canning], *Eastern Question*, p. 160.
41. TNA FO 78/79, 276–286. Stress from original.
42. *Foreign Office List for 1856*, pp. 12, 65.
43. Stratford Canning memoir, in Lane-Poole, *Life*, volume 1, p. 391.
44. TNA FO 78/141, 60.
45. Ibid., 20–21.
46. TNA FO 352/13A, 32. Reprinted in Lane-Poole, *Life*, volume 1, pp. 432–433.
47. Stratford Canning to George, 4 June 1826, in Lane-Poole, *Life*, volume 1, p. 409.
48. Stratford Canning memoir, in Lane-Poole, *Life*, volume 1, p. 416.

Chapter 8   The Destruction of the Janissaries

1. Layard, p. 419.
2. Stratford Canning memoir, in Lane-Poole, *Life*, volume 1, pp. 417–418.
3. See above, pp. 53–55.
4. [Stratford Canning], *Eastern Question*, pp. 161–162.
5. Stratford Canning memoir, in Lane-Poole, *Life*, volume 1, pp. 419–420.
6. Bartholomeo Pisani report to Stratford Canning, Pera, 16 June 1826, in Lane-Poole, *Life*, volume 1, p. 420.
7. TNA FO 78/143, 56–65.

8. Ibid., 67–68. Stress from original.

9. Ibid., 132–137.

10. Ibid., 171–172.

11. TNA FO 352/13A, 48–51. Partially quoted in Lane-Poole, *Life*, volume 1, p. 433, but not including Stratford's words of concern for his wife.

12. TNA FO 352/13A, 62–65.

13. TNA FO 78/144, 74–75.

14. Extracted from weekly reports of Richard Wood, August–September 1826, [Pera], in Lane-Poole, *Life*, volume 1, pp. 434–435.

15. Stratford Canning to his mother, Therapia, 21 October 1826, in Lane-Poole, *Life*, volume 1, pp. 435–437.

16. TNA FO 352/17A(3), 199–204. Stress from original. Planta's letter is the sole extant piece of evidence about the premature birth and death of the child. All other letters referring to it were likely either expunged by Stratford from his personal archive before he provided it to Lane-Poole; or they were among those many documents which Stratford provided to Lane-Poole and were subsequently lost.

17. TNA FO 352/17A(3), 207, 209–210.

18. Stratford Canning to his mother, [Constantinople], 5 April 1827, in Lane-Poole, *Life*, volume 1, p. 440.

19. TNA FO 352/17A(3), 219. Partially quoted in Lane-Poole, *Life*, volume 1, p. 447.

20. TNA FO 352/17A(3), 224–225.

21. [George Canning], *Illness and DEATH*, p. 8. In the final terrible days of his illness, George Canning was taken from his home to the nearby residence of the Duke of Devonshire, Chiswick House. Canning died in the bedroom on 8 August 1827.

22. [George Canning], *Illness and DEATH*, p. 8.

23. Charles James Fox (1749–1806), the Whig leader who served short terms as foreign secretary in 1782, 1783 and in 1806, was a family friend of the Cannings. He had died in the bedroom of the home of the Duke of Devonshire, Chiswick House, on 13 September 1806. Fox was the political patron of Robert Adair in the Whig party and launched his career as a diplomat. (See above, p. 30.) As another close associate of Fox, the English poet, Samuel Rogers, recorded in his *Recollections*, p. 97: 'How fondly the surviving friends of Fox cherished his memory! Many years after his death, I was at a fête given by the Duke of Devonshire at Chiswick House. Sir Robert Adair and I wandered about the apartments. "In which room did Fox expire?" asked Adair. I replied, "In this very room." Immediately Adair burst into tears with a vehemence of grief such as I hardly ever saw exhibited by a man.' Perhaps Adair's tears were also prescient: his next master as foreign secretary, George Canning, died in the same room on 8 August 1827.

24. *Times*, 9 August 1827, p. 2. Liverpool retired as prime minister in April 1827 after falling seriously ill, and he died on 4 December 1828. Perceval was assassinated as prime minister on 11 May 1812.

25. Mrs. Barnett wrote to Stratford from London on 10 August 1827, TNA FO 352/17A(2), 160A: 'It was determined, I hear, on Wednesday night [8 August] to send off a Messenger to you immediately. Why that determination was altered, I know not. Ill tidings fly swiftly, but I dread your being kept in suspence by the real truth by all kinds of contradictory reports.'

26. Stratford to Dudley, 5 September 1827: 'An express dispatched from Paris or the 17th Ultimo arrived this morning or late last night at the French Ambassador's with a confirmation of the afflicting intelligence of Mr. Canning's death.' TNA FO 78/156, 90. A copy is also found at TNA PRO 30/29/15/15, 29.

27. Stratford Canning memoir, in Lane-Poole, *Life*, volume 1, p. 452.

28. TNA FO 352/17A(3), 232. As Joseph Planta wrote to Stratford on 7 August 1827, TNA FO 352/17A(3), 228, he thought right up to the final days that George 'had no other ill than Lassitude + fatigue, from which the rest and quiet which he was to obtain in the Country would relieve him . . .'

29. TNA FO 352/17A(2), 167–170.

30. TNA FO 352/17A(3), 250–252. Stress from original.

Chapter 9   The Battle of Navarino

1. TNA FO 78/157, 157–158, 160. Stratford also reported in this dispatch that he first received word that there had been conflict at Navarino on 28 October 1827.

2. Woodhouse, p. 18.

3. Ibid., p. 21.

4. The full texts of the Treaty of London and its subsequent instructions to the commanders of the allied fleets in the Levant are printed in Codrington, *Piracy in the Levant*, volume 1, pp. 504–512.

5. Edward Codrington (1770–1851) was in command of HMS *Orion* in Admiral Nelson's fleet off of Cadiz at the Battle of Trafalgar, 21 October 1805. In December 1826 Codrington was appointed commander-in-chief in the Mediterranean. (Laughton, p. 385)

6. Crawley, *Greek Independence*, pp. 76–77.

7. The British Vice-Admiral, Codrington, also wrote to his Admiralty for instruction but this was a futile and probably a *pro forma* gesture as a reply required many weeks. Instructions were sent out by the British Foreign Minister Dudley to Codrington on 15 October 1827 and arrived weeks later, well after the battle at Navarino.

8. The full text of the joint protocol is printed in Woodhouse, pp. 60–62.

9. TNA FO 352/19C(8), 59, 61. Codrington's dispatch to Stratford of 8 September 1827 is marked, 'Off Hydra'. His next extant dispatch to Stratford here contained, of 16 September 1827, is marked, 'Off Navarin'.

10. TNA FO 352/17B(7), 161. Stratford's included the following qualification: 'My request, essential as its object is, must of course be subordinate to the demands of the public service.'

11. Stratford Canning memoir, in Lane-Poole, *Life*, volume 1, p. 450.

12. According to *Naval Chronicle*, volume 18 (1807), p. 469: 'The port Navarin is the most spacious in the Morea ... It is closed to the south by the isle of Sphacteria, celebrated by Thucycides for the massacre of the Lacedemonians, who had taken refuge there after their defeat by the Athenians in a naval action ...'

13. It has never been clearly demonstrated who fired the first shot and why. An excellent account of the issue is provided in Woodhouse.

14. Woodhouse, pp. 140–141.

15. *John Bull* (London), 19 November 1827, p. 364

16. *Times*, 14 November 1827, p. 2

17. TNA FO 352/19C(1), 10.

18. TNA FO 352/17B(7), 88.

19. TNA FO 352/17B(7), 93–94.

20. Stratford Canning to George, 30 May and 12 June 1827, in Lane-Poole, *Life*, volume 1, p. 446. Stratford wrote similarly to Planta on 11 June 1827, in Lane-Poole, *Life*, volume 1, p. 447: 'I conceive that if we must either proceed at once to [military] measures + give them a fair trial, or relinquish our own mediation ... or recall the ambassador, and put the Embassy on the lowest scale consistent with a tolerable maintenance of bare friendly relations with the Porte.'

21. According to C. G. Pitcairn Jones, the editor of the Navarino volume in the Navy Records Society series, published in 1934, Codrington ' ... left Malta for the Levant in order to make a personal investigation of the whole piracy question'. (Pitcairn Jones, Introduction, in Codrington, *Piracy in the Levant*, p. xxviii) This was in reference to attacks against British ships in the region. But according to Laughton in the *Oxford Dictionary of National Biography*, Codrington departed Malta with his ships because ' ... he was induced by the great proliferation of piracy and the urgent appeals of Stratford Canning, the ambassador at Constantinople, to attempt to reduce the horrors of the war of Greek independence.' (Laughton, p. 385)

22. TNA FO 352/17B(7), 99.

23. Codrington, *Memoir*, volume 1, p. 397, editor's note.

24. Stratford to Codrington, 27 July 1827, TNA FO 352/17B(7), 102: 'As matters have turned out, I am not sorry that your arrival in the Archipelago has been delayed. That crisis in the affairs of Greece which has been so long expected, + so long unexpectedly retarded, is now to all appearance most rapidly approaching, and I conceive your presence on the scene to be in no small degree important. I am as yet, however, without any decisive Instructions from H. M.'s

Government . . . I am of the opinion that two and perhaps even *three* weeks may elapse before I receive them . . . .' Stress from original.

25. Codrington, *Memoir*, volume 1, pp. 417–418.

26. TNA FO 352/17B(7), 135–136. Stress from original. This is partially quoted by Woodhouse, p. 53.

27. TNA FO 352/17B(7), 153–156. This is partially quoted by Lane-Poole, *Life*, volume 1, p. 449.

28. Crawley, *Greek Independence*, p. 84.

29. Temperley, *The Foreign Policy of Canning 1822–1827*, p. 404.

30. According to Crawley, 'Anglo-Russian Relations 1815–40', p. 53, 'Navarino was the unexpected but probably inevitable result of the instructions given to the Admirals [by their home governments] and of the advice of Stratford Canning from Constantinople . . .'

　　C. G. Pitcairn Jones, in his notes to Codrington, *Piracy in the Levant*, p. 1, note 1, found that while Stratford 'deplored' the Battle of Navarino, he was 'himself largely responsible for it' due to especially his 1 September 1827 directive to Codrington. Pitcairn Jones also affirmed that Stratford's 1 September directive 'was sufficiently clear to save Codrington from the charge of having exceeded his instructions'.

31. A few months after Navarino, in December 1827 Dudley sent Codrington ten 'Queries' about the battle for him to answer in writing. Codrington provided specific answers for each question but also attached an addendum in which, according to Woodhouse, ' . . . he went on to explain the uncertainty he had been in about the justification in using force in the last resort, until he had received the letters of Stratford Canning, particularly those of 19 August and 1 September, which left him in no further doubt.' (Woodhouse, p. 160. The source here is a published booklet, financed by Codrington, *Queries and Answers* [no date], which consisted of Dudley's ten queries and Codrington's answers including the added commentary. Woodhouse examined the booklet and Dudley's ten queries are reprinted in his *Navarino*. But no extant copy of Codrington's booklet has been located.)

32. Stratford Canning memoir, in Lane-Poole, *Life*, volume 1, pp. 449, 453: 'In truth I should have avoided the expression of 'cannon-shot,' and used, though writing privately, the more diplomatic phrase of coercion or forcible measures, had I received the slightest intimation of Sir Edward's fiery and enterprizing spirit.'

　　Stratford also attempted in the same section of his memoir to argue away the significance of his directives but his generalising argument was quite effete: 'One thing is certain that, whatever justification the admirals might derive from local circumstances, neither the letter nor the spirit of their instructions could be cited to warrant their hazardous but effective decision.'

　　The second excerpt from the memoir is followed in Lane-Poole's work by a somewhat ambiguous sentence in brackets which reads, '[The recommendation of cannon-shot applied only to the stoppage of warlike supplies]'. The use of brackets apparently denotes commentary added by Lane-Poole but it could also be original to Stratford's memoir, intended to denote an explanatory interjection.

33. Rose, 'Navarino', p. 15.

34. Callières, p. 45. Translation from French is mine.

35. TNA FO 78/155, 376. A few weeks later, on 16 September 1827, TNA FO 78/156, 260, Stratford also reported to Dudley that, '... four hundred Greek ears were exhibited at the Gate of the Seraglio.' The ears were identified by an inscription also nailed to the gate. Bartholomeo Pisani several years earlier reported to Lord Strangford on 6 May 1821 (British Library Add. Manuscripts 36301), that he encountered several thousand pairs of Greek ears and noses nailed to the entrance of Topkapi Saray.

36. Stratford Canning memoir, in Lane-Poole, *Life*, volume 1, p. 452.

37. TNA FO 352/17B(7), 199.

38. Stratford Canning memoir, in Lane-Poole, *Life*, volume 1, p. 453.

39. The embargo was officially lifted in the first week in January 1828.

40. TNA FO 78/157, 164, 169–171. Stratford also reported that he was concerned about the security of 'the Franks residing at Pera; but no indications of violence have hitherto appeared amongst the populace; and the Government is well aware that its own interest much more than our's is concerned in the preservation of good order.' Woodhouse, p. 146, noted that Stratford and his French and Russian colleagues, '... thought it only decent to present their regrets to the Porte on 2 November [the day after they received confirmation of the battle of Navarino]. But after that no one was quite sure how they should react.'

41. As the later chaplain of the British embassy at Constantinople, Robert Walsh, wrote in his sketch of 'The Prison of the Seven Towers': 'It was generally supposed ... the Sultan would think himself justified in imprisoning the ambassadors of all the powers leagued against him at Navarino, in retaliation for that wanton and unprovoked attack...' (Walsh, p. 22) Stratford would attribute the fact that the local population did not rise up against the embassies in retribution for 'an event which in earlier times might have roused them to acts of sanguinary vengeance' as being due to its weariness from the destruction of the Janissaries the previous year. (Stratford Canning memoir, in Lane-Poole, *Life*, volume 1, p. 454.)

42. TNA FO 78/157, 195–198.

43. TNA FO 78/158, 112–114, 120.

44. Stratford Canning memoir, in Lane-Poole, *Life*, volume 1, p. 455.

45. TNA FO 78/158, 124–125.

46. Stratford Canning memoir, in Lane-Poole, *Life*, volume 1, p. 455–456.

47. TNA FO 78/158, 131, 133.

48. Ibid., 181–182. *Times*, 24 December 1827, p. 2, quoting *Gazette de France* (Paris), dateline 'Bucharest, Dec. 1 [1827]': 'M. de Ribeaupierre has made every preparation; he has requested the Consul of the Netherlands to protect the Russian subjects during his absence. A circular has in consequence been sent to

all the Consuls. Mr. Stratford Canning has also recommended his countrymen to the Minister of the Netherlands, and M. Guilleminot has recommended his to the Plenipotentiary of Spain.'

49. TNA FO 352/16B, 699. Stratford had informed the dragomans already by 12 November 1827 that he was allowing them to choose either to come away with him or to stay behind.

50. TNA FO 78/158, 198. The prepayment of salary was for the rest of the month of December 1827.

51. TNA FO 352/16B, 701–702.

52. TNA FO 352/16B, 703. These pecuniary directives to Calavro Imberto were made by Stratford on his next-to-last day in town before departure, on 7 December 1827.

53. TNA FO 78/165, 28.

54. Stratford's dispatch to Dudley, marked 'Private', on 5 December 1827, TNA FO 352/18(4), 570–571. Stratford also reported that, 'The Russian Envoy is at Buyukdere, with his Vessels at his door, and I hardly expect to see him again.'

55. TNA FO 352/20A(2), 106.

56. *Bell's Life in London and Sporting Chronicle*, 6 January 1828, p. 2. It was further reported here that, '. . . On the whole, only seven Englishmen, of the mercantile class, remained in Constantinople on the 8th [December 1827].'

57. *Times*, 14 December 1827, p. 2. The Lloyd's agent also recorded data on European ships at ready in the harbour of Smyrna: 'The French have two frigates and three or four small vessels in port under Admiral de Rigny. The [British warships] *Cambrian, Dryad, Raleigh, Gannet,* and *Chamelion,* are now here. The *Parthian* sailed last night, and the *Rose,* after watering at Voli, will proceed to Malta.' Stress from original.

58. *Times*, 4 December 1827, p. 2.

59. TNA FO 352/17B(7), 225.

60. TNA FO 352/16B(8), 731.

61. TNA FO 78/158, 204. An unrelenting north wind prevented Ribeaupierre and his embassy from departing by ship via the Black Sea to Russia. Eventually, on 16 December 1827, they sailed down the straits to the Dardanelles where they were met by the Russian frigate *Constantine.* The Russian consulate in Constantinople was (and still is) located at Büyükdere on the northern Bosphorus near the junction with the Black Sea. This provided a strategic escape route to Russian ports. However a south wind was required for this action whereas a north wind usually blows here, as Ribeaupierre experienced.

62. 'Messrs. Guilleminot and Stratford Canning had quitted the Port at two o'clock in the afternoon, and at five they were out of sight.' The *Morning Chronicle,* 7 January 1828, p. 2, quoting the *Gazette de France,* dateline 'Constantinople, Dec. 9', quoting the *Augsburg Gazette,* 'in a letter, dated 8th December, in the evening'.

63. Stratford Canning memoir, in Lane-Poole, *Life,* volume 1, pp. 456–457.

64. TNA FO 352/17B(7), 229.

65. *Morning Chronicle*, 26 January 1828, p. 2, quoting *Gazette de France*, January 24, 1828, dateline 'Constantinople, Dec. 31 [1827]'. See note 61 above for details of the departure of the Russian ambassador, Ribeaupierre, from Constantinople on 16 December 1827.
66. TNA FO 352/16B, 106.
67. Stratford's letter to the British merchants of Smyrna, dated 'On board His Majesty's frigate *Dryad*, in the Bay of Vourla, Dec. 19, 1827'. Reprinted in *Times*, 28 January 1828, p. 2, quoting *Gazette de France* (Paris), dateline 'Smyrna, Dec. 22.'
68. Slade, volume 1, p. 285.
69. TNA FO 352/20A(2), 101–103. A copy is found at TNA FO 78/158, 27–29.
70. *Times*, 22 February 1828, p. 3. Also printed here was another letter from Constantinople, dated January 11 [1828], which read: '. . . For several days past arrests have been carried into execution against the Armenian bankers, and other respectable persons of that nation. It was given out at first, that these arrests were produced by a religious quarrel among the sects; but yesterday an order was issued that all Armenians belonging to Angora [native to Ankara], with their families, are to quit the capital for that place within 12 days. It is thought that these will amount to 8,000 individuals, and a general apprehension prevails that some further extensive proscriptions are in contemplation.'
71. Grigorii Aleksandrovich Stroganov (1770–1857), Grand Chamberlain of the Russian Court, Count of the Russian Empire (1826), Russian ambassador to Sweden, Spain and Ottoman Empire. On 30 July 1821 Stroganov broke diplomatic relations and departed Constantinople during the diplomatic crisis which resulted from the Ottoman government's execution of the Ecumenical Patriarch Grigorios V on Easter Sunday, April 1821.
72. *Morning Chronicle*, 21 January 1828, p. 2, quoting 'German Papers', dateline 'Constantinople, Dec. 17'.
73. Chesney, p. 36.
74. Stratford Canning memoir, in Lane-Poole, *Life*, volume 1, p. 459.
75. Aksan, p. 343.
76. Chesney, pp. 39–40, 68–69, 73 and Slade, volume 1, pp. 294, 297. Chesney quotes the declaration of war made by Nesselrode on 25 April 1827, and Slade quotes the declaration made the next day by Tsar Nicholas.
77. Erdem, '"Do not think of the Greeks as agricultural labourers"', p. 76.
78. Chesney, pp. 193–196.
79. Slade, p. 383.

Chapter 10   'Last Act of the Greek Drama'

1. *Morning Chronicle*, 27 February 1828, p. 4. At Ancona Stratford was required to pass a six-day quarantine.
2. Stratford Canning memoir, in Lane-Poole, *Life*, volume 1, p. 458.

3. *Morning Chronicle*, 27 February 1828, p. 4.
4. Stratford Canning memoir, in Lane-Poole, *Life*, volume 1, pp. 458–459.
5. Crawley, *Question of Greek Independence*, pp. 93, 108.
6. Aberdeen was appointed Secretary of State for Foreign Affairs on 2 June 1828 and would serve until 21 November 1830. He would later serve in the same position from 2 September 1841 until July 1846. (Middleton, p. 282)
7. TNA FO 78/164, 27.
8. Charles MacFarlane, a British visitor to the Ottoman capital, wrote in his *Constantinople in 1828*, p. 278: 'Wherever I went in Constantinople, in Pera, Galata or Scutari, the Turks were all anxious to know whether the English and French ambassadors were not about returning; they . . . avowedly considered the presence of those two representatives as a palladium; and when it was made known, at the end of May [1828], that the Porte had written letters to the Elchis, inviting them back to Stamboul, there was great satisfaction expressed.'
9. TNA FO 78/165, 240; and Lane-Poole, *Life*, volume 1, p. 466.
10. TNA FO 78/165, 354.
11. Stratford Canning to Eliza, 5 September 1828, in Lane-Poole, *Life*, volume 1, p. 469.
12. Stratford Canning to Eliza, 15 December 1828, in Lane-Poole, *Life*, volume 1, p. 476.
13. Stratford Canning to Joseph Planta, 17 January 1829, in Lane-Poole, *Life*, volume 1, p. 487.
14. TNA FO 78/164, 28. Aberdeen's instructions to Stratford were dated 2 July 1828.
15. BL Add. MSS 43090, 65.
16. Stratford Canning to an unnamed friend, [early April 1829], in Lane-Poole, *Life*, volume 1, p. 489. Stress from original.
17. Stratford Canning to Joseph Planta, Naples, 27 April 1829, in Lane-Poole, *Life*, volume 1, pp. 490–491.
18. Crawley, *Question of Greek Independence*, p. 144.
19. Middleton, p. 282.
20. Ibid., p. 302.
21. TNA FO 352/22(2), 8–9. Stress from original. Michael Warr, himself a professional diplomat, was explicit in his judgment that, '. . . Lord Aberdeen was at this stage a thoroughly bad Foreign Secretary. He was a tortured man, introspective and nervous. He hated war, and seemed to have no feelings for the Greeks and their history, though he was a Greek scholar.' (Warr, p. 67) Crawley found that Aberdeen's 'policy was vacillating and unreliable.' (Crawley, 'Anglo-Russian Relations 1815–40', p. 53)
22. Gordon, pp. 85–86.
23. Iremonger, pp. 114–115.
24. Stratford submitted a long memorandum to Palmerston on 19 December 1832, TNA FO 78/211, 333–362, in which he emphatically called for the British government to provide immediate military support to the Ottoman Empire in

support against the invasion of Ibrahim Paşa. This is reprinted in full in Crawley, *Question of Greek Independence*, pp. 237–245. The report included: '.... To Great Britain the fate of this Empire [Ottoman] can never be indifferent. It would affect the interests of her Trade and East-Indian Possessions, even if it were unconnected with the maintenance of her relative Power in Europe....' The report detailed that if Ibrahim were to take over the Ottoman government or if he were establish his own state out of Ottoman provinces, this could only lead to a the strengthening of the conservative forces and depletion of national resources, and possibly to continuous civil war or foreign invasion, any combination of which would seriously destabilise the region.

25. *The Encyclopedia Britannica*, eleventh edition (1911), volume 25, s.v. 'Stratford de Redcliffe, Stratford Canning', p. 997.

26. Stratford Canning memoir, in Lane-Poole, *Life*, volume 2, p. 8.

27. Ibid., p. 2. Stratford sat for Old Sarum together with his father-in-law, James Alexander, who had himself sat for it from 1812 to 1832 and since 1826 with his own brother, Josias Du Pre Alexander. According to Farrell, p. 208: 'Old Sarum, which had experienced very few contests (the last in 1751), had been an extreme example of a rotten borough for almost its entire representative history. It was duly disfranchised by the Reform Act in 1832...' And according to Salmon and Spencer, p. 574: 'In the House he [Stratford] followed an independent line similar to that mapped by his cousin [George Canning], and he appeared in Lord Palmerston's list of liberals in June 1828, though he was curiously absent from another contemporary reckoning of the Canningnite rump.'

28. Stratford Canning memoir, in Lane-Poole, *Life*, volume 2, p. 2.

29. Salmon and Spencer, p. 575.

30. Ibid., p. 576.

31. Stratford Canning memoir, in Lane-Poole, *Life*, volume 2, pp. 9–10. Stratford also noted here that during the campaign (if it could be called that) for the Stockbridge seat, he visited 'a shoemaker or cobbler, whose vote, however saleable, was to be solicited. The man was at dinner with his family. On seeing us, he exclaimed, without rising from his seat, "I know what you are come for, and do you see this knife, I advise you to clear out, that is all." I replied that we were much obliged to him for his hint, and wished him a pleasant afternoon.'

32. See above, p. 302, note 6.

33. Stratford Canning memoir, in Lane-Poole, *Life*, volume 1, pp. 493–494.

34. Joseph Planta letter to Stratford, Constantinople, 21 September 1832, in Lane-Poole, *Life*, volume 2, p. 17: 'I entirely agree in what you say of the happiness of being out of the way of politics. They have become wicked and discouraging things...'

35. TNA FO 352/25B (4), 3.

36. TNA FO 78/209, 159.

37. Stratford Canning memoir, in Lane-Poole, *Life*, volume 1, p. 505.

38. TNA FO 352/25B (4), 15.

39. TNA FO 352/25A (1), 108–11. Stress from original.
40. TNA FO 78/209, 246, 255.
41. TNA FO 352/25B (4), 14–15.
42. *Foreign Office List for 1856*, pp. 29, 54, details Samuel MacGuffog as still serving as physician at the British Embassy at Constantinople and also notes: 'was appointed Physician to the British Factory at Constantinople by the Levant Company in 1816; on the surrender of the Levant Company's charter, in 1825, was appointed Physician to the British Embassy.' In one written instruction to MacGuffog, dated 30 March 1832, in Lane-Poole, *Life*, volume 1, p. 570, Stratford addressed him as 'illustrious Plenipo.!'
43. The next year, in 1833, Stratford's successor at Constantinople, John Ponsonby, discovered MacGuffog's 'humbler channel through which to convey in an unheeded manner certain facts to his [the Sultan's] ear – Abdey Bey, the Sultan's Jester'. (Ponsonby dispatch to Lord Palmerston, dated Therapia, Constantinople, 19 December 1833. TNA FO 78/225, 152.)
44. Stratford Canning memoir, in Lane-Poole, *Life*, volume 1, pp. 510–511; and TNA FO 78/211, 18.
45. TNA FO 352/25A (1), 429. And quoted in Lane-Poole, *Life*, volume 1, p. 511.
46. TNA FO 78/211, 279–280. In Stratford's letter to Palmerston of 9 August 1832, quoted in Lane-Poole, *Life*, volume 1, p. 513, Stratford wrote that the gift of the Sultan's portrait represented an investiture 'with his Grand Order'. Palmerston apparently allowed Stratford to keep this special token of the Sultan's appreciation, in contrast to the policy of the British Foreign Office. See correspondence between Stratford, Palmerston and Backhouse in August and October 1832, TNA FO 78/211 and TNA FO 352/25B (2).
47. Stratford Canning memoir, in Lane-Poole, *Life*, volume 1, p. 518.
48. Gally Knight to Stratford Canning, 18 September 1832, in Lane-Poole, *Life*, volume 1, pp. 517–518.
49. TNA 352/24A, 296. And quoted in Lane-Poole, *Life*, volume 1, p. 517.
50. TNA FO 78/211, 315.
51. TNA FO 97/406, 78–91. Stratford wrote in part; ' . I feel confident that that Your Lordship will give their [dragomans'] case that kind and equitable consideration to which the extent of their misfortune and the nature of their public services so strongly entitles them.'
52. *Illustrated London News,* 3 November 1888, p. 528.
53. Woodhouse, p. 177.
54. *Times*, 7 April 1931, p. 9: 'Canning's Statue in Athens. From our Correspondent. ATHENS, April 6. M. Venizelos, the Prime Minister, this morning unveiled the statue of George Canning which has been presented to Greece by Mr. and Mrs. Charles Boot, of Sheffield and London. The statue is the work of Chantrey, and was ordered by the first Duke of Sutherland.'
55. *Foreign Office List for 1856*, p. 65.
56. Masson, p. 1.

57. *The Navarino Centenary and Greek War of Independence Commemorative Exhibition...Catalogue*, passim. The exhibition consisted of over 30 items representing Byron (including locks from his hair and a snuff-box used by him), four items representing Codrington, two items representing de Rigny, one item representing George Canning (a small bust), and zero items representing Stratford Canning.

58. At the first monastery, in Stratford's account of the visit, 'As we passed under the gateway, the monks turned aside, muttering "It is forbidden." After this salve to their conscience, they threw their scruples to the winds and came forward most courteously to do honour to their "forbidden" guests. We were regaled with coffee in the abbot's own sanctum, and admired the glorious view from his window.' The last monastery which the Cannings visited that day, Agios Pavlos, marked their departure with bellringing that lasted so long 'the sound reached our ears while still up in the mountains'. (Stratford Canning memoir, in Lane-Poole, *Life*, volume 2, pp. 217–218)

The event was reported by *The Lady's Newspaper* (London), 7 December 1850, p. 307: 'Lady Canning has caused the monks of the Holy Mountain to break their vows. The brotherhood allow no female to enter their boundary. Sir Stratford, however, was accompanied to the Mount by his Lady and daughters.'

Chapter 11   The Case of Avakim

1. Satow, p. 125, stated that the rejection was officially made 'on the ostensible ground that the appointment was made without previous notice having been given, since it was only ten days after it had been officially gazetted that Palmerston mentioned it to the Russian ambassador in London.'

2. Walker, 'Rejection of Stratford Canning', p. 62, suggested that the rejection was due in part to the fact that, 'Testimony at the Decembrist trials pointed to [Stratford] Canning having promised money to a Polish secret society, in alliance with Russian revolutionaries....' Walker described this testimony as 'vague and unsatisfactory' and most likely without basis in fact. But he also suggested that the testimony may have turned the Russians against Stratford. Lane-Poole, *Life*, volume 2, p. 18, noted: 'It was said that Madame Lieven, the wife of the Russian ambassador in London, had taken some offence, and had revenged herself by intriguing against Sir Stratford's reception at Petersburg.'

3. On the strained exchanges between Stratford and Nesselrode at Petersburg in 1825, see above, pp. 139–140.

4. Dispatch marked 'private' from Bligh to Palmerston, Petersburg, 17 November 1832, TNA FO 65/201. In his response to Bligh, also marked 'private', 14 December 1832, TNA FO 65/201, Palmerston noted his opinion of the Russian rejection of Stratford: 'The truth is the whole thing is a mere remnant of the apostalical and holy-alliance abomination of the name of [George] Canning; and the assertions as to Stratford Canning's bad temper, and

irritability, and impracticality, are conventional fabrications of political dislike.' Palmerston also referred here to Stratford as 'a man of high honour and unblemished character'.

5. Hamlin, 'Political Duel', p. 451.

6. Lane-Poole, *Life*, volume 2, pp. 23, 30, 35, 36. In 1835 Aberdeen, Secretary of State for War and the Colonies, offered Stratford the position of governor general of Canada, but Stratford also declined this in order to take up the seat for Lynn in the House of Commons. He officially held this seat until 5 February 1842 (Salmon and Spencer, p. 571) but effectively gave it up in November 1841 when he departed London for Constantinople to begin a new mission there as ambassador.

7. *Saturday Review of Politics, Literature, Science and Art*, 15 December 1888, p. 713.

8. Lane-Poole, *Life*, volume 2, p. 49.

9. Middleton, p. 282: Aberdeen's second term as foreign secretary lasted from 2 September 1841 to July 1846.

10. Stratford Canning memoir, in Lane-Poole, *Life*, volume 2, p. 50.

11. See above, p. 199.

12. See above, pp. 302–303, note 24, for Stratford's long memorandum of 19 December 1832 to Palmerston on this topic.

13. Vereté, 'Palmerston and the Levant Crisis, 1832', rejects the notion that before 1833 Palmerston may have wavered as to whether to support the Ottoman government of Mehmet Ali. Vereté suggests that Palmerston was consistently in support of the Ottomans and in agreement with Stratford's position concerning support for Ottoman reform. But Vereté provides no theory as to why Palmerston did not heed Stratford's advice to provide military support to the Ottoman Empire against Mehmet Ali in 1832.

14. Stratford Canning memoir, in Lane-Poole, *Life*, volume 2, p. 90.

15. *Correspondence*, pp. 1–3. The execution in fact took place on Tuesday, 22 August 1843.

16. *Times*, 11 April 1844, p. 7.

17. Subaşı, p. 5.

18. Ibid., pp. 6–7.

19. Ibid., p. 8.

20. *Times*, 10 July 1830, p. 3: 'Shocking Occurrence at Smyrna. (From the *Smyrna Gazette* of the 30th of May.)'

21. *Correspondence*, p. 2: Stratford dispatch #1 to Aberdeen of 23 August 1843, mentioning that articles 61 and 71 of the British capitulations related to the fate of property of Englishmen who converted. Stratford also noted here that an extradition treaty between the Russians and Ottomans relating to 'refugees and malefactors' was expressly applied to individuals who had converted to the religion of the other country, (though these were later exempted from such extradition by an article of the Treaty of *Küçük-Kaynarca* in 1774).

22. TNA FO 352/1 (3), 415.

23. Stratford dispatch to Dudley, marked 'Separate', 12 June 1827, TNA FO 78/155, 50–51.
24. *Times*, 31 December 1838, p. 5.
25. 'Heart and Soul'. BBC World Service programme, 'Apostasy – Could I Stop Being a Muslim?' Originally broadcast 5 November 2008.
26. Sturdza, p. 589.
27. Layard, pp. 453–454. Layard wrote further of Frédéric Pisani: 'He was gifted with the most imperturbable patience and long-suffering, and was never moved by the outbursts of anger [of Stratford] to which he was frequently exposed, and which broke harmlessly upon him – an additional recommendation to his chief.' Concerning Stratford's 'highest esteem' for Frédéric Pisani (also according to Layard) and their long association, see above, p. 281, note 17.
28. TNA FO 78/521.
29. Ibid. Stratford's note is a post-script dated 1 September 1843 attached to his dispatch of 27 August 1843.
30. *Correspondence*, p. 2.
31. Ibid., pp. 3–4. The original was composed in French and the translation into English is from *Correspondence*.
32. Stratford Canning memoir, in Lane-Poole, *Life*, volume 2, p. 91. An obvious typo in the quotation marks here has been corrected.
33. TNA FO 78/521.
34. *Correspondence*, pp. 11–12.
35. Ibid., p. 9.
36. Ibid., pp. 13–14. The original was composed in French and the translation into English is from *Correspondence*.
37. Stratford dispatch to Aberdeen of 17 November 1843, in *Correspondence*, p. 15.

Chapter 12   Disputation on Qur'anic Theology

1. *Correspondence*, p. 16: Post-script of Stratford's dispatch of 1 December 1843 to Aberdeen.
2. *Correspondence*, p. 17.
3. Ibid., p. 18.
4. Ibid., pp. 19–20.
5. Stratford dispatch to Aberdeen of 10 February 1843. *Correspondence*, pp. 24–25.
6. See above, p. 214.
7. Ibid.
8. *Times*, 15 April 1844, p. 4.
9. Stratford Canning memoir, in Lane-Poole, *Life*, volume 2, p. 92.
10. Schauffler, p. 182.
11. Stratford Canning memoir, in Lane-Poole, *Life*, volume 2, p. 92.
12. TNA FO 78/554. Stress from original. Charles Alison's report on his examination of the Qur'an for passages concerning punishment for apostasy

from Islam was included as an enclosure to Stratford's dispatch to Aberdeen of 17 February 1843.

13. Peters and de Vries, p. 14.

14. Lane-Poole, *Life*, volume 2, p. 93, footnote 1.

15. Ibid., p. 94. Lane-Poole also explicitly pointed out, in opposition to the second argument of Stratford and Charles Alison, that if a law or punishment were based in the Traditions as opposed to in the Qur'an, this did not at all reduce their legitimacy: 'The Muslim makes no distinction between the various sources of his law: whether based on a clear statement in the Koran, or on a private remark of Mohammed, or on the deductions and explanations of commentators and doctors, it is all one to him – the ordinance of God himself. In the lips of a Turk, "the law of the Koran" means the law whether traced distinctly to the Koran or not: it is equally holy and irrevocable.'

16. Stratford's dispatch to Aberdeen, 6 March 1844. *Correspondence*, pp. 33–34.

17. In response to Stratford's rejection of the Ottoman draft statement, Aberdeen wrote on 6 April 1844 that it was the opinion of government that Stratford had '…acted rightly in refusing to receive it…' *Correspondence*, p. 35.

18. Ibid., p. 34.

19. Ibid., p. 37.

20. Stratford dispatch #49 to Aberdeen, 23 March 1844, in Lane-Poole, *Life*, volume 2, p. 98. Temperley, *England and the Near East*, p. 227: 'The Sultan repeated the same assurances to the ambassador of France and to the patriarch of the Greek Orthodox Church.'

21. Stratford Canning memoir, in Lane-Poole, *Life*, volume 2, p. 96.

22. *Times*, 16 April 1844, p. 5. The correspondent noted his source for reporting on the Sultan's hand-shake with Stratford: 'My authority is from one of the Turks present on the occasion.'

23. TNA FO 352/33B, copy of Sultan's declaration of recognition of Protestant *millet*.

24. Hamlin, 'Turkey Fifty Years Ago', p. 18. Before the reform, Protestants were administratively ruled by the Armenian Patriarchate, and Bulgarians by the Greek Patriarchate. It was the recognition of the Protestant *millet* which subsequently led, according to Hamlin, to the recognition of the Bulgarian *millet* and challenged the authoritarianism of the Patriarchates. After the reforms, 'The bishops have less fear of the Patriarch,' as Hamlin wrote, 'the priests less fear of his bishop, and the people less fear of the priest.'

25. This is discussed in Chapter 15.

26. Temperley, 'British Policy Towards Parliamentary Rule and Constitutionalism in Turkey (1830–1914)', p. 159.

27. Davison, 'Turkish Attitudes Concerning Christian-Muslim Equality', p. 846.

Chapter 13   Advocate of Ottoman Progress

1. *Times*, 16 April 1844, p. 5.
2. *Times*, 15 April 1844, p. 4.
3. *Times*, 24 April 1844, pp. 8–9.
4. *Times*, 26 April 1844, p. 4.
5. TNA FO 78/552, Aberdeen dispatch #9 to Stratford, dated 20 January 1844.
6. TNA FO 78/552, Aberdeen dispatch #10 to Stratford, dated 20 January 1844. Also quoted in Temperley, *England and the Near East*, pp. 227–228.
7. TNA FO 78/558, Stratford dispatch #112 to Aberdeen, dated 1 June 1844. Also quoted in Lane-Poole, *Life*, volume 2, p. 99.
8. Stratford Canning dispatch #27 to Aberdeen, 10 February 1844, TNA FO 78/554.
9. Stratford Canning dispatch #35 to Aberdeen, 29 February 1844, TNA FO 78/554.
10. Stratford Canning dispatch #49 to Aberdeen, 23 March 1844, in Lane-Poole, *Life*, volume 2, pp. 97–98.
11. Stratford Canning dispatch #89 to Aberdeen, 17 May 1844, TNA FO 78/557.
12. In Stratford's instructions to F. Pisani of 8 March 1844, enclosed in his dispatch #56 to Aberdeen, 23 March 1844, TNA FO 78/555, he wrote that over the last few days he had received several reports of new cases 'insulting to Christianity ... and tending to persecute its followers'. He instructed Pisani to communicate them in person to Rifaat Paşa: '... A flagrant case of this description has just come to my knowledge. An Armenian boy, only eight years old, was received into a Turkish Harem, detained there against the wishes of his father, and finally, notwithstanding his tender undiscriminating age, circumcised as a Turk. This boy's father is named Paraz Aghlon Agob, and it was in the House of Shakir Bey Arnaout Oghlon of AkSeray, that the act of injustice and compulsion took place .... A Greek girl of tender age has been decoyed into a Harem near Broussa, and on pretence of her wishing to embrace Islamism, withheld cruelly from her relations. A similar attempt was lately made near Ghio. By a letter from Adrianople, I learn that two boys of that City, ten and twelve years old respectively, another of eleven at the Forty Churches, a boy at Chermen, and yet another boy of eleven at Adrianople, have been in like manner made Turks .... You will press these remarks upon the attention of the Minister for Foreign Affairs, and you will urge in forcible terms the justice and expediency of restoring the children to their Christian parents without loss of time, and of taking measures to prevent such intolerable abuses in the future....' In the dispatch Stratford reported to Aberdeen that in response to his appeal, '... Rifaat Pasha has promised to obtain the restitution of two of the children in question to their distracted parents; but owing to some unexplained cause of complaint His Excellency's promises remain without effect...'

13. Extract of letter by The Reverend W. O. Allan, Pera, 7 June 1845, to J. G. Wood, Esq. *Home and Foreign Missions Record for the Free Church of Scotland*, August 1845, p. 187.
14. Malcolm-Smith, p. 163.
15. Lane-Poole, *Life*, volume 2, p. 455, quoting *Lives of the Lords Strangford*.
16. *Glasgow Herald*, 16 August 1880, p. 4.
17. Tracy, p. 351.
18. Hamlin, 'The Political Duel', p. 454.
19. Brewer, p. 362.
20. *Times*, 13 February 1954, p. 7.
21. Hobsbawm, pp. 117, 158.
22. Subaşı, p. 1.
23. Schmitt, 'Diplomatic Preliminaries', p. 46.
24. Malcolm-Smith, p. 168.
25. Temperley, 'British Policy Towards Parliamentary Rule and Constitutionalism in Turkey (1830–1914)', pp. 156–157.
26. Warr, pp. 86, 88.
27. Subaşı, pp. 17, 18.
28. *Times*, 17 August 1880, p. 7.
29. See above, p. 93.
30. Stratford Canning to his mother, 8 February 1825, in Lane-Poole, *Life*, volume 1, p. 356.
31. *Hansard's Parliamentary Debates*, Third Series, volume 149, column 1781, debate for 27 April 1858.
32. Alexander Van Millingen, *Constantinople*, pp. 262–263:

> To live in Constantinople is to live in a very wide world. The city, it is true, is not a seat of lofty intellectual thought. Upon none of its hills have the muses come to dwell. It is not a centre of literary activity; it is not a home of Art.... And yet, it is certain that to live in Constantinople is to live in a wide world. It is not for any lack of incentive that a resident here fails 'to think imperially' or to feel on an imperial scale. When a man possessed by the genius of the place* quits the city to reside elsewhere, the horizon of his life contracts and dwindles, as when a man descends from the wide views of a mountain peak to the life pent within the walls of a valley. For nowhere else is the mind not only confronted, but, if one may express it thus, assailed by so many varied subjects demanding consideration, or the heart appealed to by so many interests for its sympathy.
>
> The very geography of the place offers a wide outlook. As a part of his everyday experience, a resident of Constantinople lives within site of Europe and Asia. Every day of his life, he sees the waterway that runs between the two great continents thronged with vessels of every nation, hurrying to and fro to bring the ends of the earth together. ** Then, how much human power had been enthroned here – the dominion of Byzantium for one thousand years; the rule of Constantine and his

successors for eleven centuries; the sway of the Ottoman Sultans through four hundred and fifty years. If what we see has aught to do with what we are, here is a mould in which to fashion a large life....

*'the genius of the place': A possible invocation of Gibbon's reference to Constantinople in his *Decline and Fall*, Volume the Sixth, Chapter LXVIII, p. 508: 'the genius of the place will ever triumph over the accidents of time and fortune.'

**'the ends of the earth': A possible invocation of the inner inscription (still extant today) in the bema mosaic of the Byzantine Church of Hagia Eirene, Istanbul: 'Hear us, O God our Saviour; the hope of all the ends of the earth and of them who are afar off upon the sea.' Translated and identified as 'an extract from Psalm lxv. verses 5, 6 (the lxiv. in the Septuagint version)' in Van Millingen, *Byzantine Churches*, p. 95.

Chapter 14   'Heaven Help Me!'

1. Stratford dispatch to Palmerston, Constantinople, 12 June 1852, in Lane-Poole, *Life*, volume 2, p. 215.
2. Stratford Canning to Earl of Malmesbury, unnumbered dispatch, Trieste, 28 June 1852. TNA FO 78/892.
3. Correspondence between Stratford and Stanley, 8 March 1851, 2 April 1851, 5 March 1852, 27 March 1852, in Lane-Poole, *Life*, volume 2, pp. 220–224.
4. Temperley, *England and the Near East*, p. 303.
5. Ibid., p. 305.
6. Temperley, 'Stratford de Redcliffe and the Origins of the Crimean War, PART I', p. 606.
7. Maxwell, p. 12.
8. See above, pp. 226, 234.
9. Gordon, pp. 270–271, quoted in Lane-Poole, 'The Attack on Lord Stratford de Redcliffe', p. 320.
10. Maxwell, p. 29.
11. Queen Victoria to the Earl of Aberdeen, Windsor Castle, 5 November 1853, printed in Victoria, Queen of Great Britain, *The Letters of Queen Victoria*, p. 560: the Queen 'wishes to make some observations on the subject of Lord Stratford's last private letters communicated to her yesterday by Lord Clarendon. They exhibit clearly on his part a *desire* for war, and to drag us all in it ....'
12. Wolff, p. 182.
13. Temperley, *England and the Near East*, pp. 313–314.
14. Taylor, *Struggle for Mastery in Europe*, p. 53, note 4.
15. Stratford to his wife, Paris, early March 1853; Dresden, 20 March 1853; and Constantinople, 5 April 1853, in Lane-Poole, *Life*, volume 2, pp. 236, 240, 246.

16. Stratford's efforts on behalf of the hospitals, plus those of his wife who came out to Constantinople with her three daughters in September 1854, are covered in detail by Lane-Poole, *Life*, volume 2, pp. 374–388.
17. Lane-Poole, *Life*, volume 2, p. 352.
18. *Report from the Select Committee on Diplomatic Service*, p. 163, section 1724.
19. Erdem, 'Wherever Slavery Exists', p. 57.
20. Sturdza, p. 589.
21. Erdem, 'Wherever Slavery Exists', p. 60, note 16.
22. Ibid., pp. 61, 66.
23. Ibid., pp. 63–64.

Chapter 15   'Our Own Pasha At Constantinople'

1. *Times*, 7 April 1855, p. 5.
2. On the Russians' rejection of Stratford in 1832 and its roots in his mission to Petersburg in 1825, see Chapters 7 and 11.
3. Temperley, 'The Alleged Violations of the Straits Convention by Stratford de Redcliffe', p. 657.
4. Taylor, *The Struggle for Mastery in Europe*, p. 53, note 4.
5. Temperley, 'Stratford de Redcliffe and the Origins of the Crimean War, PART I', pp. 611–612.
6. Temperley, 'The Alleged Violations of the Straits Convention by Stratford de Redcliffe', pp. 670–671.
7. Temperley, 'Stratford de Redcliffe and the Origins of the Crimean War, PART I', p. 617.
8. Ibid., pp. 620–621.
9. Ibid., PART II, pp. 271–273.
10. Ibid., pp. 281–282.
11. Stratford to his wife, Constantinople, 23 January 1854, in Lane-Poole, *Life*, volume 2, p. 341.
12. Temperley, *England and the Near East*, p. 509.
13. *Times*, 16 January 1856, p. 8.
14. TNA FO 352/49 (6).
15. *Punch, Or the London Charivari*, 15 March 1856, p. 108.
16. Emilia Hornby, p. 257.
17. The popular image of Florence Nightingale was almost directly opposite that of Stratford Canning during the Crimean War: the lady, the caring nurse not involved in politics and new to Constantinople, as opposed to the old male, the professional diplomat and political figure long at Constantinople and supposedly all-powerful there.
18. *Hansard's Parliamentary Debates*, Third Series, volume 141, columns 1594–1688 and 1803–1906, debates for 28 April–1 May 1856 and vote of 1 May 1856.

19. *Times*, 1 May 1856, p. 9, reprinting without commentary an editorial from the *Manchester Examiner.* The term 'bashaw' had earlier been applied to Stratford in James Graham's letter to Clarendon of 9 May 1853 (see above, p. 241). One thus wonders whether its appearance also here in press in May 1856 was a complete coincidence.
20. *Punch, Or the London Charivari*, 10 May 1856, p. 188. Here one is reminded of Clarendon's letter to Lord Cowley of 10 November 1853 (see above, p. 242), in which Stratford was declared to be *'bent on war'* and 'just as wild as the Turks themselves'.

Conclusion 'The Elements of New Partitions'

1. Kaye, p. 380. The dinner was held in the banqueting hall of the London Tavern.
2. *Hull Packet and East Riding Times*, 20 August 1880, p. 4.
3. See above, p. 107.
4. Trevelyan, p. 76.
5. Sorel, pp. 301, 308, 309.

BIBLIOGRAPHY OF SOURCES CITED

Unpublished Primary Sources Cited

(1) The National Archives United Kingdom [former Public Record Office] (TNA)

(1A) Records of Foreign Office (FO)
    FO 65   (Russian Empire)
    FO 78   (Ottoman Empire)
    FO 93   (Protocols of Treaties)
    FO 97   (General Correspondence)
    FO 195   (Embassy and Consulates, Ottoman Empire)
    FO 352   (Stratford Canning Papers)
    FO 781   (Constantinople, Ottoman Empire)

(1B) Records of Boards of Stamps, Taxes, Excise, Stamps and Taxes, and Inland Revenue (IR)
IR 59 (Selected Death Duty Accounts)

(1C) Records of State Paper Office, including Papers of Secretaries of State (SP)
SP 105 (Archives of British Legations)

(2) The British Library United Kingdom (BL)
Department of Manuscripts, Additional Manuscripts Collection (Add. MSS.)
Add. MSS. 36301 (Bartholomeo Pisani)
Add. MSS. 37310 (Richard Colley Wellesley)
Add. MSS. 43090 (Lord Aberdeen)
Add. MSS. 56529 (John Cam Hobhouse)

(3) National Portrait Gallery, United Kingdom, Room 23

(3A) Caption of portrait, 'Stratford Canning, Viscount Stratford de Redcliffe' by George Frederic Watts, oil on panel, 1856–57, Primary Collection, NPG 684. Last examined on 13 October 2012.

(3B) Caption of portrait, 'Sir Richard Francis Burton', by Frederic Leighton, Baron Leighton, oil on canvas, 1872–85, Primary Collection, NPG 1070. Last examined on 13 October 2012.

(4) Private letter of Edmund Calvert to Count [Alexandre Bartholomeo Stephane] Pisani, Rhodes, 26 October 1881. Manuscript in collection of Giles and Priscilla Hunt.

Periodical Primary Sources Cited

Anti-Jacobin (London): 1798, 1799
Athenaeum (London): 1855, 1887
Bell's Life in London and Sporting Chronicle (London): 1828, 1847
Caledonian Mercury (Edinburgh): 1810, 1856
Contemporary Review (London): 1879
Edinburgh Review (Edinburgh): 1889
English Historical Review (Oxford): 1889
Examiner (London): 1858
Freeman's Journal and Daily Commercial Advertiser (Dublin): 1858
Gentleman's Magazine and Historical Review (London): 1855
Glasgow Herald (Glasgow): 1880
Home and Foreign Missionary Record for the Free Church of Scotland (Edinburgh): 1845
Hull Packet and East Riding Times (Hull): 1880
Illustrated London News (London): 1855, 1856, 1876, 1880, 1888
Ipswich Journal (Ipswich): 1812
John Bull (London): 1827, 1829
Lady's Newspaper (London): 1850
Leeds Mercury (Leeds): 1856
Manchester Examiner (Manchester): 1856
Manchester Times and Gazette (Manchester): 1835
Monthly Magazine, or, British Register (London): 1830
Morning Chronicle (London): 1808, 1812, 1828
Naval Chronicle (London): 1807
North Wales Chronicle (Bangor): 1858
Oracle Bell's New World (London): 1789
Pall Mall Gazette (London): 1880
Punch, Or the London Charivari (London): 1856, 1858
Quarterly Review (London): 1880
Reynolds's Newspaper (London): 1880
Saturday Review of Politics, Literature, Science and Art (London): 1888
Times (London): 1787, 1812, 1827, 1828, 1830, 1842, 1844, 1856, 1861, 1876, 1880, 1888, 1896, 1927, 1931, 1952, 1954

Published Primary Sources Cited

Adair, Robert. *The Negotiations for the Peace of the Dardanelles in 1808–09; with Dispatches and Official Documents.* Volumes 1 and 2. London: Longman, Brown, Green and Longmans, 1845.

Arbuthnot, Charles. *The Correspondence of Charles Arbuthnot.* A. Aspinall, ed. Camden Third Series, volume 65. London: Royal Historical Society, 1941.

Brewer, Josiah. *A Residence at Constantinople, in the Year 1827. With Notes to the Present Time.* New Haven: Durrie & Peck, 1830.

'The British Ambassador and the American Missionaries. Address of the Missionaries. Reply of the Ambassador.' [June 1852]. *The Missionary Herald, Containing the Proceedings of the American Missionary Board of Commissioners for Foreign Missions,* volume 48, issue 9 (September 1852): 267–270.

British and Foreign State Papers. 1825–1826. Vol. XIII. Compiled by the Librarian and Keeper of the Papers, Foreign Office. London: James Ridgway and Sons, 1848.

Byron, George Gordon, Baron. '*Famous in My Time.*' *Byron's Letters and Journals. Volume II. 1810–1812.* L. Marchand, ed. London: John Murray, 1973.

——. '*In My Hot Youth.*' *Byron's Letters and Journals. Volume I. 1798–1810.* L. Marchand, ed. London: John Murray, 1973.

——. *The Works of Lord Byron. Complete in One Volume.* London: John Murray, 1842.

Canning, George. *An Account of the Illness and DEATH of the Right Honourable Mr. Canning.* (Chiswick, London, 1827). Bulletin pasted into album of obituary notices. British Library, general reference collection, shelfmark 1878.d.12.(8.).

——. *George Canning and His Friends, Containing Hitherto Unpublished Letters, Jeux d'Esprit, etc.* Volume 2. J. Bagot, ed. London: John Murray, 1909.

——. *The Letter-Journal of George Canning: 1793–1795.* P. Jupp, ed. Camden Fourth Series, volume 41. London: Royal Historical Society, 1991.

——, G. Ellis, J. H. Frere et al. *The Poetry of the Anti-Jacobin.* London: J. Wright, 1799.

[Canning, Stratford], Stratford de Redcliffe. *The Eastern Question. By the Late Viscount Stratford de Redcliffe. K.G., G.C.B. Being A Selection from His Writings During the Last Five Years of His Life.* London: John Murray, 1881.

——. 'His Lordship's Reply' [13 October 1858]. *The Missionary Herald, Containing the Proceedings of the American Missionary Board of Commissioners for Foreign Missions,* volume 55, issue 1 (January 1859): 25–26. [See 'Farewell Address of the Missionaries at Constantinople to Lord Stratford de Redcliffe', 12 October 1858]

——. *Shadows of the Past. In Verse.* London: Macmillan and Co., 1866.

——. [Memoir. Unpublished manuscript, completed in 1874, subsequently lost. All references to the Memoir are from the sole extant source for it, Lane-Poole, *Life.*]

Chamier, Frederick. *Life of a Sailor.* London: Richard Bentley, 1850.

Chesney, Colonel [Francis Rawdon]. *The Russo-Turkish Campaign of 1828 and 1829, with a View of the Present State of Affairs in the East.* New York: Redfield, 1854.

Clarke, Edward Daniel. *Travels in Various Countries of Europe, Asia and Africa. Part the Second. Greece, Egypt and the Holy Land. Section the Third.* Chapter XV, 'Constantinople'. London: T. Cadell and W. Davies, 1816: 480–524.

Cockerell, C. R. [Charles Robert] *Travels in Southern Europe and the Levant, 1810–1817. The Journal of C.R. Cockerell.* S. P. Cockerell, ed. London, New York, Bombay: Longmans, Green and Co., 1903.

Codrington, Edward. *Memoir of the Life of Admiral Sir Edward Codrington. With Selections from His Public and Private Correspondence. Edited by His Daughter Lady Bourchier.* Volume 1. London: Longmans, Green, and Co., 1873.

————. *Piracy in the Levant 1827–8. Selected from the Papers of Admiral Sir Edward Codrington K. C. B.* Lieutenant-Commander C. G. Pitcairn Jones R. N., ed. and intro. Publications of the Naval Records Society. Volume 72. London: Naval Records Society, 1934.

Correspondence Relating to Execution in Turkey for Apostasy from Islamism. Presented by Her Majesty's Command to the House of Commons, in Pursuance of their Address of the 3rd of May, 1844. State Papers, volume 51. London: T. R. Harrison, 1844.

'Farewell Address of the Missionaries at Constantinople to Lord Stratford de Redcliffe' [12 October 1858]. *The Missionary Herald, Containing the Proceedings of the American Missionary Board of Commissioners for Foreign Missions*, volume 55, issue 1 (January 1859): 23–25. [See Stratford Canning, 'His Lordship's Reply', 13 October 1858.]

Foreign Office List for 1856. Seventh Publication. London: Harrison, 1856.

Galt, John. *Voyages and Travels, in the Years 1809, 1810, and 1811: Containing Statistical, Commerical and Miscellaneous Observations on Gibraltar, Sardinia, Sicily, Malta, Serigo and Turkey.* London: T. Cadell and W. Davies, Strand, 1812.

Gladstone, W. E. [William Ewart]. *Bulgarian Horrors and the Question of the East.* London: John Murray, 1876.

Hall, Herbert Byng. *The Queen's Messenger or Travels on the High-ways and Bye-ways of Europe.* London: John Maxwell and Company, 1865.

Hamlin, Cyrus. 'The Political Duel between Nicholas, the Czar of Russia, and Lord Stratford de Redcliffe, the Great English Ambassador.' *Proceedings of the American Antiquarian Society*, New Series, volume 9 (October 1893–October 1894): 451–460.

————. 'Turkey Fifty Years Ago.' *The Missionary Herald, Containing the Proceedings of the American Board of Commissioners for Foreign Missions*, volume 85, number 1 (January 1889): 16–19.

Hansard's Parliamentary Debates Third Series, volume 141. London: Cornelius Buck, 1856.

————. Third Series, volume 149. London: Cornelius Buck, 1858.

————. Third Series, volume 324. London: Cornelius Buck & Son, 1888.

Hornby, Edmund. *Sir Edmund Hornby, an Autobiography.* D. L. Murray, intro. London: Constable & Co Ltd, 1929.

Hornby, Emilia Bithynia. *Constantinople During the Crimean War.* London: Richard Bentley, 1863.

Hunt, Giles, ed. and notes. *Mehitabel Canning: A Redoubtable Woman. Family Letters.* Hertfordshire: Rooster Books Limited, 2001.

Hurewitz, J. C., ed. *Diplomacy in the Near and Middle East: A Documentary Record 1535–1914.* Volume 1. Princeton: D. Van Nostrand Co., 1956.

Jackson, George. *The Bath Archives. A Further Selection from the Diaries and Letters of Sir George Jackson, K.C.H., From 1809 to 1816.* Volume 1. Lady Jackson, ed. London: Richard Bentley and Son, 1873.

Juchereau de Saint-Denys, Antoine de. *Révolutions de Constantinople en 1807 et 1808, Précédées d'Observations Générales sur l'État Actuel de l'Empire Ottoman.* Volume 2. Paris: A La Librairie de Brissot Thivars, 1819.

Las Cases, [Emmanuel Auguste Dieudonné], Compte de. *Journal of the Private Life and Conversations of the Emperor Napoleon at Saint Helena.* Volume 2, Part 3. London: Henry Colburn and Co., 1823.

Layard, Austen Henry. *Early Adventures in Persia, Suscana, and Babylonia.* Volume 2. London: J. Murray, 1887.

Lear, Edward. *The Letters of Edward Lear: to Chichester Fortesque, Lord Carlingford and Frances, Countess Waldengrave.* Lady Strachey, ed. London: T. Fisher Unwin, 1907.

MacFarlane, Charles. *Constantinople in 1828. A Residence of Sixteen Months in the Turkish Capital and Provinces, with an Account of the Present State of the Naval and Military Power, and of the Resources of the Ottoman Empire.* London: Saunders & Otley, 1829.

Masson, Edward. 'Remarks on Mr Baillie Cochrane's Pamphlet on Greece', [Masson's letter to Stratford Canning, 16 March 1847].' *Hume Tracts.* London: University College, 1847. http://www.jstor.org/stable/60207459?seq=1 (accessed on 29 January 2012).

Maxwell, Herbert. *The Life and Letters of George William Frederick Fourth Earl of Clarendon K. G., G. C. B.* Volume 2. London: Edward Arnold, 1913.

Napoleon, I. *Lettres Inédites de Napoléon Ier (an VIII – 1815), publiées par Léon Lecestre....* Volume 1, second edition. Paris: E. Plon, Nourrit et Cie, Imprimeurs-Éditeurs, 1897.

The Navarino Centenary and Greek War of Independence Commemorative Exhibition to be held at the Greek Legation, 21 October – 11 November 1927. Catalogue. London: St. Clemen's Press, Ltd., 1927.

Paget, Arthur. *The Paget Papers: Diplomatic and Other Correspondence of the Right Hon, Sir Arthur Paget, G. C. B. 1794–1807.* Volume 2. A. B. Paget, ed. London: William Herneman, 1896.

Report from the Select Committee on Diplomatic Service: Together with the Proceedings of the Committee, Minutes of Evidence, Appendix, and Index. [House of Commons]. London: Her Majesty's Stationary Office, 1861.

Rogers, Samuel. *Recollections of the Table-Talk of Samuel Rogers to Which is Added Porsoniana.* London: Edward Moxon, 1856.

Schauffler, William G. *Autobiography of William G. Schauffler. For Forty-Nine Years a Missionary in the Orient.* Edited by His Sons. E. A. Park, intro. New York: Anson D. F. Randolph & Company, 1887.

Skene, James Henry. *With Lord Stratford in the Crimean War.* London: Richard Bentley and Son, 1883.

Slade, Adolphus. *Records of Travels in Turkey, Greece, &c. And of a Cruise in the Black Sea, with the Capitan Pasha, in the Years 1829, 1830, and 1831.* Volume 1. London: Saunders and Otley, 1833.

Stanhope, Hester Lucy and Charles Lewis Meryon. *Travels of Lady Hester Forming the Completion of Her Memoirs, Narrated by Her Physician.* Volume 1. London, 1846.

Stanhope, Leicester. *Greece in 1823 and 1824; Being a Series of Letters, and Other Documents, on the Greek Revolution, Written During a Visit to that Country. A New Edition...To Which Are Added, Reminiscences of Lord Byron.* London: Sherwood, Gilbert and Piper, 1825.

Stratford de Redcliffe. See Canning, Stratford.

Thomas [Keppel], George, Earl of Albemarle, *Fifty Years of My Life*. Volume 1. London: Macmillan and Co., 1876.

Tracy, C. C. 'Turkish Missions Report' [June 1891]. *Medical Missions at Home and Abroad*. Medical Missionary Association (London), New Series, volume 3, (August 1891).

Victoria, Queen of Great Britain. *The Letters of Queen Victoria. A Selection of Her Majesty's Correspondence Between the Years 1837 and 1861....* Arthur Christopher Benson, Viscount Esher, eds. Volume 2. London: John Murray, 1907.

Vneshniaia politika Rossii XIX i nachala XX veka. Dokumenty ministerstva inostrannykh del. Seriia pervaia 1801–1815. Tom shestoi 1811–1812. [Foreign Policy of Russia of the XIX and Early XX Century. Documents of the Ministry of Foreign Affairs. First Series 1801–1805. Sixth volume 1811–1812.] A. L. Harochniukin, ed. Moscow: Gosudarstvennoe izdatel'svo politicheskoi literatury, 1962.

Walsh, Robert. *Constantinople and the Scenery of the Seven Churches of Asia Minor Illustrated*. First Series. London and Paris: Fisher, Son, & Co., 1839.

Wellesley, Richard Colley. *The Wellesley Papers. The Life and Correspondence of Richard Colley Wellesley, Marquess Wellesley, 1760–1842....* Volumes 1 and 2. L. S. Benjamin, ed. and intro. London: Herbert Jenkins, 1914.

Wilson, Robert. *Private Diary of Travels, Personal Services, and Public Events...* Rev. H. Randolph, ed. Volume 1. London: John Murray, 1861.

Wolff, Henry Drummond. *Rambling Recollections*. London: Macmillan and Co., 1908.

Secondary Sources Cited

Aksan, Virginia H. *Ottoman Wars 1700–1870: An Empire Besieged*. Harlow: Longman/Pearson, 2007.

Allen, Charles. *A Glimpse of the Burning Plain. Leaves from the Indian Journals of Charlotte Canning*. London: Michael Joseph, 1986.

Anderson, M. S. *The Eastern Question: A Study in International Relations*. London, Melbourne, Toronto: Macmillan; New York: St. Martin's Press, 1966.

———. 'Great Britain and the Russo-Turkish War of 1768–74.' *English Historical Review*, volume 69, number 270 (January 1954): 39–58

Bell, James. *A System of Geography, Popular and Scientific, or Physical, Political, and Statistical Account of the World and its Various Divisions*. Volume 2. Glasgow: Archibald Fullarton and Co., 1832.

Benyon, John. 'Frere, Sir (Henry) Bartle Edward, first baronet (1815–1884).' *Oxford Dictionary of National Biography*. Volume 20. Oxford: Oxford University Press, 2004: 984–987.

Bright, J. Franck. 'Review of Lane-Poole, *Life of the Right Honourable Stratford Canning, Viscount Stratford de Redcliffe* (1888), in *The English Historical Review*, volume 4, number 14 (April 1889): 382–388.

Bury, J. B. *The Idea of Progress. An Inquiry into its Origin and Growth*. New York: The Macmillan Company, 1932.

Butler, Iris. *The Eldest Brother. The Marquess Wellesley, the Duke of Wellington's Eldest Brother*. London, Sydney, Auckland, Toronto: Hodder and Stoughton, 1973.

Butterfield, Herbert. 'Tendencies in Historical Study in England.' *Irish Historical Studies*, volume 4, number 15 (March 1945): 209–223.

Byrne, Leo Gerald. *The Great Ambassador. A Study of the Diplomatic Career of the Right Honourable Stratford Canning, K. G., G. C. B., Viscount Stratford de Redcliffe, and the Epoch during Which He Served as the British Ambassador to the Sublime Porte of the Ottoman Sultan*. Columbus, Ohio: Ohio State University Press, 1964.

Callières, François, *De La Manière de Négocier Avec Les Souverains. De L'Utilité des Négociations, du Choix des Ambassadeurs & Des Envoyez, & des Qualitez Nécessaires Pour Réüssir Dans Ces Emplois*. Amsterdam, 1716.

Cambon, Jules. *Le Diplomate*. Paris: Hachette, 1926.

Chamberlain, Muriel E. 'Canning, Stratford, Viscount Stratford de Redcliffe (1786–1880).' *Oxford Dictionary of National Biography*. Volume 9. Oxford: Oxford University Press, 2004: 924–932.

Crawley, C. W. 'Anglo-Russian Relations 1815–40.' *Cambridge Historical Journal*, volume 3, number 1 (1929): 47–73.

———. 'A Forgotten Prophecy (Greece 1820–1821).' *Cambridge Historical Journal*, volume 1, number 2 (1924): 209–213.

———. *The Question of Greek Independence: A Study of British Policy in the Near East*, 1821–1833. Cambridge: Cambridge University Press, 1930.

Cunningham, Allan. *Collected Essays. Volume One. Anglo-Ottoman Encounters in the Age of Revolution*. Edward Ingram, preface and ed. London: Frank Cass, 1993.

Davison, Roderick. *Reform in the Ottoman Empire 1856–1876*. Princeton: Princeton University Press, 1963.

———. *Nineteenth Century Ottoman Diplomacy and Reforms*. Istanbul: Isis Press, 1999.

———. 'Turkish Attitudes Concerning Christian-Muslim Equality in the Nineteenth Century.' *American Historical Review*, volume 59, number 4 (July 1954): 844–864.

The Encyclopedia Britannica, Eleventh edition, volume 25, s.v. 'Stratford de Redcliffe, Stratford Canning'. Cambridge, England: at the University Press; New York, NY, 1911: 997–998.

Erdem, Y. Hakan. "Do not think of the Greeks as agricultural labourers": Ottoman responses to the Greek War of Independence.' *Citizenship and the Nation-State in Greece and Turkey*. Social and Historical Studies on Greece and Turkey Series. F. Birtek, T. Dragonas, eds. London and New York: Routledge, 2005.

———. "'Wherever Slavery Exists, the Whole Society Suffers": the White Slave Trade Controversy during the Crimean War', in *The Crimean War 1853–1856. Colonial Skirmish or Rehearsal for World War? Empires, Nations and Individuals*, J. W. Borejsza, ed. Warsaw: Wydawnictwo Neriton, Instytut Historii PAN, 2011: 53–78.

Farrell, Stephen. 'Old Sarum,' *The History of Parliament: The House of Commons, 1820–1832*. Volume 3. D. R. Fisher, ed. Cambridge: Cambridge University Press for The History of Parliament Trust, 2009: 206–209.

Figes, Orlando. *The Crimean War: A History*. New York: Metropolitan Books. Henry Holt and Company, 2010. Published simultaneously in London by Penguin Books as *Crimea*.

Findley, Carter V. 'Sir James W. Redhouse (1811–1892). The Making of a Perfect Orientalist?' *Journal of the American Oriental Society*, volume 99, number 4 (October–December 1979): 573–600.

Fletcher, Ian and Natalia Ishchenko. *The Crimean War. A Clash of Empires.* Staplehurst: Spellmount, 2004.

Gibbon, Edward. *The History of the Decline and Fall of the Roman Empire.* Volume the Sixth. London: A. Strahan and T. Cadell, In the Strand, 1791.

Gordon, Arthur [Lord Stanmore]. *The Earl of Aberdeen.* London: Sampson Low, Marston & Company, 1893.

Groot, Alexander H de. 'Protection and Nationality. The Decline of the Dragomans,' in *Istanbul et Les Langues Orientales. Actes du Collque Organisé par l'IFÉA et l'INALCO....* Frederic Hitzel, ed. Paris: L'Harmattan, 1997.

Guedalla, Philip. 'Lord Wellesley', in his *Collected Essays. Volume II. Men of Affairs.* London: Hodder and Stoughton, 1927.

———. 'Some Turks', in his *Collected Essays. Volume III. Men of War.* London: Hodder and Stoughton, 1927.

Hamel, Frank. *Lady Hester Stanhope: A New Light on Her Life and Love Affairs.* London: Cassell & Co., 1913.

Headlam-Morley, James. 'The Black Sea, the Bosphorus and the Dardanelles', in his *Studies in Diplomatic History.* London: Methuen & Co., 1930.

'Heart and Soul'. BBC World Service programme, 'Apostasy - Could I Stop Being a Muslim?' Produced by Innes Bowen and presented by Shiraz Maher. Originally broadcast 5 November 2008.

Hertslet, Edward. *The Map of Europe by Treaty: Showing the Various Political and Territorial Changes Which Have Taken Place Since the General Peace of 1814.* Volume 3. London: HMSO, 1875.

Hinde, Wendy. *George Canning.* London: Collins, 1973.

Hobsbawm, Eric. *Globalisation, Democracy and Terrorism.* London: Little, Brown, 2007.

Hunt, Giles. *The Duel: Castlereagh, Canning and Deadly Cabinet Rivalry.* London, New York: I.B.Tauris, 2008.

Iremonger, Lucille. *Lord Aberdeen. A Biography of the Fourth Earl of Aberdeen, K.G., K.T., Prime Minister 1852–1855.* London: Collins, 1978.

Ismail, F. 'The Making of the Treaty of Bucharest, 1811–1812.' *Middle Eastern Studies*, volume 15, number 2 (May 1979): 164–192.

Johnson, Chalmers. *The Sorrows of Empire. Militarism, Secrecy, and the End of the Republic.* New York: Henry Holt, 2004.

Johnston, Henry McKenzie. *Ottoman and Persian Odysseys: James Morier, Creator of Haji Baba of Isphahan, and His Brothers.* London, New York: I.B.Tauris, 1998.

Kaye, John William. *A History of the Sepoy War in India, 1857–1858.* Volume 1. London: W. H. Allen & Co., 1864.

Kennan, George F. *George F. Kennan on Russian Diplomacy in the 19th Century and the Origins of World War I: A Special Report.* Washington, D. C.: Kennan Institute for Advanced Russian Studies. Woodrow Wilson International Center for Scholars, 1986.

———. 'History and Diplomacy as Viewed by a Diplomatist.' *The Review of Politics*, volume 18, number 2 (April 1956): 170–177.

Kinglake, Alexander William. *The Invasion of the Crimea: Its Origin, and an Account of its Progress Down to the Death of Lord Raglan.* Volume 1. William Blackwood and Sons: Edinburgh and London, 1863.

Kliuchevskii, Vasilii Osipovich. *Sochineniia v deviati tomakh. Chast' piataia. Kurs russkoi istorii.* [Essays in nine volumes. Part Five. A Course in Russian history.] Moscow: Mysl', 1989.

Lane-Poole, Stanley. 'The Attack on Lord Stratford de Redcliffe.' *National Review* (London), volume 24, number 141 (November 1894): 316–333.

———. *The Life of the Right Honourable Stratford Canning, Viscount Stratford de Redcliffe.* Volumes 1 and 2. London: Longmans, Green, and Co., 1888.

Laughton, J. K. 'Codrington, Sir Edward (1770–1851)', rev. Roger Morriss. *Oxford Dictionary of National Biography*, volume 12. Oxford: Oxford University Press, 2004: 385–386.

Leaf, Walter. *Troy. A Study in Homeric Geography.* London: Macmillan and Co., Limited, 1912.

Lewis, Bernard. *The Encyclopedia of Islam.* New edition, volume 1, s.v. 'Beratlı.' Leiden: E. J. Brill; London, Luzac & Co., 1960: 1171.

Lloyd, E. M. 'Somerset, FitzRoy James Henry, first Baron Raglan (1788–1855), rev. John Sweetman.' *Oxford Dictionary of National Biography.* Vol. 51. Oxford: Oxford University Press, 2004: 582–588.

Maclagan, Michael. *'Clemency' Canning. Charles John, 1st Earl Canning. Governor-General and Viceroy of India 1856–1862.* London: Macmillan & Co Ltd; New York: St. Martin's Press, 1962.

Malcolm-Smith, E. F. [Elizabeth Frances]. *The Life of Stratford Canning, Lord Stratford de Redcliffe.* London: Ernest Benn, 1933.

Malley, Shawn. 'The Layard Enterprise: Victorian Archaeology and Informal Imperialism in Mesopotamia', in Z. Babrani, Z. Celik, E. Eldhem, eds., *Scramble for the Past: A Story of Archaeology in the Ottoman Empire, 1753–1914.* Istanbul: SALT, 2011: 99–123.

McNeill, William H. *A History of the Human Community: Prehistory to the Present.* Upper Saddle River, NJ: Prentice Hall, 1997.

Middleton, Charles Ronald. *The Administration of British Foreign Policy 1782–1846.* Durham: Duke University Press, 1977.

Mikhailovskii-Danilovskii, [Aleksandr Ivanovich]. *Opisanie turetskoi voiny v tsarstvovanie Imperatora Aleksandra, s 1806-go do 1812-go goda...* Chast' vtoraia. [Description of the Turkish War during the Tsardom of Emperor Alexander, from 1806 to 1812... Part Two.] Petersburg, 1843.

Mowat, R. B. *The Diplomacy of Napoleon.* London: E. Arnold and Co., 1924.

Muir, Rory. *Britain and the Defeat of Napoleon, 1807–1815.* New Haven and London: Yale University Press, 1996.

Naff, Thomas. 'The Ottoman Empire and the European State System.' in H. Bull and A. Waston, eds. *The Expansion of International Society.* Oxford: Clarendon Press, 1984.

———. 'Reform and the Conduct of Ottoman Diplomacy in the Reign of Selim III, 1789–1807.' *Journal of the American Oriental Society*, volume 83, number 3 (August-September 1963): 295–315.

Neale, J. E. 'The Diplomatic Envoy.' *History, the Quarterly Journal of the Historical Association* (London), new series, volume 13, issue 51 (October 1928): 204–218.

A New English Dictionary on Historical Principles; Founded Mainly on the Materials Collected by The Philological Society. Volume 3, part 2, s.v. 'Elchee, noun'. Oxford: at the Clarendon Press, 1897.

Newton, Charles. *Images of the Ottoman Empire*. T. Stanley, intro. London: V & A Publications, 2007.

———. 'Stratford Canning's Pictures of Turkey.' *The V & A Album*. The Victoria and Albert Museum (London), volume 3 (1984): 76–83.

Nicolson, Harold. *The Congress of Vienna: A Study in Allied Unity: 1812–1822*. New York: Harcourt, Brace and Company, 1946.

———. *Diplomacy*. London: Thornton Butterworth Ltd., 1939.

———. *The Evolution of Diplomatic Method...Being the Chichele Lectures delivered at the University of Oxford in November 1953*. London: Constable & Co. Ltd., 1954.

Noakes, Vivien. *Edward Lear: the Life of a Wanderer*. London: Collins, 1968.

The Oxford English Dictionary, [First edition], volume 3, s.v. 'Elchee, noun'. Oxford: at The Clarendon Press, 1933, reprinted 1961.

The Oxford English Dictionary, Second edition, volume 5, s.v. 'Elchee, noun'. Oxford: at The Clarendon Press, 1989.

The Oxford English Dictionary Online. s.v. 'Elchee, noun'. Oxford: Oxford University Press, June 2012. http://www.oed.com.proxy.uchicago.edu/view/Entry/60173 (accessed on 5 September 2012).

Peters, Rudolph and Gert J. J. de Vries. 'Apostasy in Islam.' *Die Welt des Islams* (Bochum), new series, volume 17, issue 1/4 (1976–1977): 1–25.

Puryear, Vernon John. *England, Russia and the Straits Question, 1844–1856*. Berkeley: University of California, 1931.

Rose, J. Holland. 'Canning and the Secret Intelligence from Tilsit (July 16–23, 1807).' *Transactions of the Royal Historical Society*, fourth series, volume 20: (1906): 61–77.

———. 'Navarino. A Decisive Conflict. The Liberation of Greece.' *Times* (London), 19 October 1927, pp. 15–16.

Runciman, Steven. 'Constantinople-Istanbul.' *Revue des Études Sud-Est Européenes* (Bucharest), volume 7, number 1 (1969): 205–208.

Salmon, Philip and Howard Spencer. 'Canning, Stratford (1786–1880)'. *The History of Parliament: The House of Commons, 1820–1832*, D. R. Fisher, ed., volume 4. Cambridge: Cambridge University Press for The History of Parliament Trust, 2009: 571–578.

Satow, Ernest. *A Guide to Diplomatic Practice*. Third Edition. London, New York, Toronto: Longmans, Green and Co., 1932.

Schmitt, Bernadotte E. 'The Diplomatic Preliminaries of the Crimean War.' *American Historical Review*, volume 25, number 1 (October 1919): 36–67.

———. '"With How Little Wisdom."' *American Historical Review*, volume 66, number 2 (January 1961): 299–322.

Semmel, Bernard. Review of Byrne, *The Great Ambassador. A Study of the Diplomatic Career of the Right Honourable Stratford Canning (1964)*, in *American Historical Review*, volume 71, number 1 (October 1965): 185–186.

Seton-Watson, R. W. [Robert William]. Review of Malcolm-Smith, *Life of Stratford Canning, Lord Stratford de Redcliffe (1933)*, in *Slavonic and East European Review*, volume 12, number 35 (January 1934): 474–476.

Sorel, Albert. *La Question d'Orient au XVIIIᵉ Siècle. Les Origines de la Triple Alliance*. Paris: E. Plon et Cⁱᵉ, Imprimeurs-Èditeurs, 1878.

Sturdza, Mikhail-Dimitri. *Dictionaire Historique et Généalogique des Grandes Familes de Gréce, d'Albanie at de Constantinople*. Paris: Mikhail-Dimitri Sturdza, 1983.

Subaşı, Turgut. 'The Apostasy Question in the Context of Anglo-Ottoman Relations.' *Middle Eastern Studies*, volume 38, number 2 (April 2002): 1–34.

Surtees, Virginia. *Charlotte Canning, Lady-in-Waiting to Queen Victoria and Wife of the First Viceroy of India 1817–1861*. London: John Murray, 1975.

Taylor, A. J. P. 'The Rise and Fall of Diplomatic History', in his *Englishmen and Others*. London: Hamish Hamilton, 1956.

———. *The Struggle for Mastery in Europe, 1814–1918*. London: Oxford University Press, 1971.

Temperley, Harold. 'The Alleged Violations of the Straits Convention by Stratford de Redcliffe between June and September, 1853.' *English Historical Review*, volume 49, number 196 (October 1934): 657–671.

———. 'British Policy Towards Parliamentary Rule and Constitutionalism in Turkey (1930–1914).' *Cambridge Historical Review*, volume 4, number 2 (1933): 156–191.

———. *England and the Near East. The Crimea*. London: Longmans, Green, and Co., 1936.

———. 'The Foreign Policy of Canning 1820–1827.' *The Cambridge History of Foreign Policy 1783–1919*. A. W. Ward and G. P. Gooch, eds., volume 2. Cambridge: Cambridge University Press 1923.

———. *The Foreign Policy of Canning 1822–1827: England, The Neo-Holy Alliance, and the New World*. London: G. Bell and Sons, Ltd, 1925.

———. 'The Last Phase of Stratford de Redcliffe, 1855–8.' *English Historical Review*, volume 47, number 186 (April 1932): 216–259.

———. 'Stratford de Redcliffe and the Origins of the Crimean War. PART I.' *English Historical Review*, volume 48, number 192 (October 1933): 601–621.

———. 'Stratford de Redcliffe and the Origins of the Crimean War. PART II.' *English Historical Review*, volume 48, number 194 (April 1934): 265–298.

Trevelyan, George. *An Autobiography & Other Essays*. London, New York, Toronto: Longmans, Greeen and Co., 1949.

Van Millingen, Alexander. *Byzantine Churches in Constantinople. Their History and Architecture*. London: Macmillan and Co., Limited, 1912.

———. *Constantinople. Painted by Warwick Goble. Described by Alexander Van Millingen*. London: Adam & Charles Black, 1906.

Vereté, M. 'Palmerston and the Levant Crisis, 1832.' *Journal of Modern History*, volume 24, number 2 (June 1952): 143–151.

Walker, Franklin A. 'The Rejection of Stratford Canning by Nicholas I.' *Bulletin of the Institute of Historical Research* (The University of London), volume XL (1967): 50–64.

Warr, Michael. *A Biography of Stratford Canning: Mainly His Career in Turkey*. Oxford: Alden Press, 1989.

Wood, Alfred C. *A History of the Levant Company*. Oxford: Oxford University Press, 1935.

Woodhouse, C. M. *The Battle of Navarino*. London: Hodder and Stoughton, 1965.

INDEX

.

www.ingramcontent.com/pod-product-compliance
Lightning Source LLC
Chambersburg PA
CBHW071834270326
41929CB00013B/1988